Joseph Weber
Mark Wutka

D0471870

BEA WebLogic Workshop

KICK START

SAMS

201 West 103rd Street, Indianapolis, Indiana 46290

BEA WebLogic Workshop

Copyright © 2003 by Sams Publishing

All rights reserved. No part of this book shall be reproduced, stored in a retrieval system, or transmitted by any means, electronic, mechanical, photocopying, recording, or otherwise, without written permission from the publisher. No patent liability is assumed with respect to the use of the information contained herein. Although every precaution has been taken in the preparation of this book, the publisher and author assume no responsibility for errors or omissions. Nor is any liability assumed for damages resulting from the use of the information contained herein.

International Standard Book Number: 0-67232-417-2

Library of Congress Catalog Card Number: 2002107160

Printed in the United States of America

First Printing: September 2002

05   04   03   02   4   3   2   1

Trademarks

All terms mentioned in this book that are known to be trademarks or service marks have been appropriately capitalized. Sams Publishing cannot attest to the accuracy of this information. Use of a term in this book should not be regarded as affecting the validity of any trademark or service mark.

Warning and Disclaimer

Every effort has been made to make this book as complete and as accurate as possible, but no warranty or fitness is implied. The information provided is on an "as is" basis. The authors and the publisher shall have neither liability nor responsibility to any person or entity with respect to any loss or damages arising from the information contained in this book.

Executive Editor
Michael Stephens

Acquisitions Editor
Todd Green

Development Editor
Michael Watson

Managing Editor
Charlotte Clapp

Project Editors
Elizabeth Finney
Katelyn Cozatt

Copy Editor
Margaret Berson

Indexer
Sandra Henselmeier

Proofreader
Suzanne Thomas

Technical Editors
Steve Heckler
Peter Horadan

Team Coordinator
Lynne Williams

Interior Designer
Gary Adair

Cover Designer
Gary Adair

Page Layout
Rebecca Harmon
Cheryl Lynch
Stacey Richwine-DeRome

Contents at a Glance

Introduction 1

Part I   Introduction to WebLogic Workshop

   1   Introduction to Web Services 7
   2   The WebLogic Workshop 17
   3   Building an Application in WebLogic Workshop 37
   4   Developing Conversant Applications 49

Part II   Building Applications in WebLogic Workshop

   5   Controls 75
   6   The Database Control 93
   7   Debugging 113

Part III Declaring Maps and Controls

   8   Creating a Map 127
   9   Messaging Using JMS 151
  10   Including an EJB Control 165
  11   Accessing Web Services from Java 183
  12   @jws JavaDoc Tags 189
  13   An Online Ordering System 199

Part IV   Appendixes

   A   Java Essentials 229
   B   XML 253
   C   Web Service Description Language (WSDL) 273
   D   SOAP 295

      Index 303

Table of Contents

Introduction   1

Part I   Introduction to WebLogic Workshop

1   Introduction to Web Services   7

What Are Web Services? 7

Examples of Web Services 7

Advantages of Web Services 10

Disadvantages of Web Services 11

The Web Service Protocols 12

    XML 12

    SOAP 13

    WSDL 13

    UDDI 13

Why Use WebLogic Workshop? 14

2   The WebLogic Workshop   17

Verify That Everything Is Functional 17

    Open the Samples Project 17

    Testing HelloWorld 19

    Starting the WebLogic Server 19

    Starting the HelloWorld Service 20

    Running HelloWorld 20

    Understanding the Output 20

Overview of the Workshop Environment 22

    The Project Tree 22

    Structure Pane 23

    Hide and Show Panes 24

    Design View 24

    Test View 28

Changing the Workshop Environment 30

    Changing the Display Properties 31

    Changing the Editor Settings 32

    Changing Colors 34

    Configuring System Paths 34

3 Building an Application in WebLogic Workshop   37

Creating a Project 37

Creating the HelloWorld Service 37

Add a Method 38

Go to Source of Message 39

Return a Value 39

Define Response 41

Testing Your New Service 41

Build the File 41

Run the Service 42

Stop the Service 43

Passing Information to the Service 43

Build and Rerun the Program 44

The JWS File 44

Adding Methods in Code 44

JavaDoc Comments 44

Creating an Operation Method 45

Creating the helloByHand() Method 45

Adding a Description 46

Adding Method Descriptions 46

Adding a Description for the Whole Service 47

4 Developing Conversant Applications   49

Conversations 49

A Two-Stage Conversation 50

Starting a Conversation 50

Declaring a Class Variable 51

Edit the Method 51

Workshop JavaDoc Variables 53

Continuing a Conversation 53

Finishing a Conversation 53

Testing HelloConversation 55

Continuing the Conversation 56

Finishing the Conversation 56

Begin a New Conversation 56

Why Is Asynchronous Activity Different from Synchronous

Activity? 57

Diagrams of Synchronous Activity Versus Asynchronous

Activity 58

Appropriate Situations to Use Asynchrony 59

Limitations and Advantages 60

    Advantages 60

    Limitations 61

What Makes HelloConversation Synchronous? 62

HelloConversation as an Asynchronous Conversation 63

    Creating a Buffered Message 63

    Buffer JavaDoc Comments 64

Adding a Callback 64

    Calling the Callback Method 66

Testing HelloConversationAsync 67

    Refreshing the List 68

Buffering a Callback 68

Timeout Parameters 69

    Defining the Entire Lifetime of a Conversation 69

    Defining the Idle Timeout Values 69

    Changing the Timeout Values in Code 69

Cleaning Up After Your Conversation Ends 70

    Creating an onFinish() Method 71

Part II   Building Applications in WebLogic Workshop

5   Controls   75

Using a Timer 75

Creating HelloDelayed 75

    Adding the Timer Control 76

    Starting the Timer 77

    Defining onTimeout 77

Testing HelloDelayed 78

Stopping the Timer 78

Defining a Timer Control in Code 79

    The @control Tag 79

    The @jws:timer Tag 79

    Specifying Time in Workshop 80

    Repeated Firing 81

    Coalesce of Events 81

Adjusting Timing Defaults Programmatically 82

    Changing the Timeout Time 82

    Obtaining Current Timeout 83

    Changing/Obtaining the Repeats-Every Value 83

    Toggling Coalesce Events 84

Restarting the Timer 84
Obtaining Time at Event 84
Broadcast Date Example 84
HelloWorld as a Service 86
    Creating the Control File 87
    Using a CTRL in Another Service 87
    Accessing a CTRL File That Is Not in the Current Package 91
    Using a CTRL File from a Different Project 91
Handling Callbacks from CTRLs 92

6   The Database Control   **93**

Creating a Database Control 93
Defining a Database Connection 94
Creating an SQL String 95
    Selecting Values 96
    Updating Values 97
    Inserting Values 97
    Deleting Values 97
    Joining Tables 97
Including Variables 98
Getting a Result Set 98
    Returning a Variable 98
    Returning a Row of Results 99
    Returning a Class 99
    Returning a `HashMap` 100
    Returning a Multiple Row Result Set in a Container 101
Executing Multiple Statements 101
A Sample Application 102

7   Debugging   **113**

Debugging in WebLogic Workshop 114
Debugging a Web Service 114
    Start 114
    Setting Breakpoints 115
    Stepping Through Code 117
    Continue 120
Variables 120
    Locals 121
    Watching Variables 122
The Call Stack 123

Part III   Declaring Maps and Controls

8   Creating a Map   127

Customizing XML Content 127

Building XML Maps Using Workshop 127

   Input Maps 128

   Output Maps 131

XML Map Elements 132

   <xm:value> 132

   <xm:attribute> 133

   Mapping Java Objects 133

   Declaring Map Variables 135

   Including Multiple Elements 136

Storing Maps in External Files 137

Using XMLScript 138

   ECMAScript Overview 139

   XML Scripts 140

   ECMAScript and XML 140

   Extracting Parameters from XML Data 144

   Mapping XML into Java with ECMAScript 145

9   Messaging Using JMS   151

Connections and Connection Factories 152

Sessions 153

Sending and Receiving 153

Using the JMS Control 153

   Sending Queue Messages 154

   Receiving Queue Messages 155

   Sending Topic Messages 157

   Receiving Topic Messages 159

JMS JavaDoc Options 160

Sending XML Messages 160

10   Including an EJB Control   165

EJB Overview 165

Including an EJB in Your Workshop Project 169

An EJB Control Example 171

EJB JavaDoc Options 181

11   Accessing Web Services from Java   **183**

The Client Side of Web Services 183

Java Proxy Details 184

JavaServer Pages and the Java Proxy 185

Using the Proxy Outside the WebLogic Environment 186

Changing the Web Service Location 186

12   @jws JavaDoc Tags   **189**

Method Tags 189

   @jws:conversation—Define Conversation Boundaries 189

   @jws:operation—Label a Method as a Web Service Method 190

   @jws:parameter-xml—Define Incoming XML Format 190

   @jws:return-xml—Define Outgoing XML Format 191

   @jws:sql—Define SQL Statement 191

   @jws:target-namespace—Specify Namespace for Outgoing

     Messages 192

Control Tags 192

   @jws:connection—Define a Database Connection 192

   @jws:ejb—Specify an EJB Home Interface 192

   @jws:jms—Configure a JMS Control 192

   @jws:jms-header—Specify the Format of a JMS Header 193

   @jws:jms-message—Specify the Format of a JMS Message 193

   @jws:jms-property—Specify JMS Message Properties 193

   @jws:timer—Configure a Timer Control 193

Defining Filewide Enhancements 194

   @jws:conversation-lifetime 194

   @jws:define—Create Inline Files 194

   @jws:protocol—Specify Web Service Protocols 195

   @jws:schema—Use an XML Schema 196

   @jws:wsdl—Use a WSDL File 197

   @jws:xmlns—Specify an XML Namespace 197

13   An Online Ordering System   **199**

Designing an Ordering System 199

Working with the Database 201

   Creating the Database Tables 202

   Creating the Database Control 203

Creating the OrderEntry Service 219

Creating the OrderTracking Service 222

Part IV   Appendixes   **227**

A   Java Essentials   **229**

Your First Java Program 229
Declaring Variables 232
    Values 233
    Object References 234
Operators 235
Conversions 238
Classes and Objects 238
Control Flow 241
    if-else 241
    while 242
    for 243
    switch 243
    continue and break 244
    return 245
Exceptions 245
Interfaces 247
Packages 248
Common Java Packages 250
    java.lang 250
    java.io 250
    java.util 251
    java.net 251
    java.sql 251
Where to Go from Here 251

B   XML   **253**

What Is XML? 253
    Why Use XML? 254
XML Basics 255
    Elements 255
    Attributes 256
    Comments 257
    Data 257
    Document Type Definitions 258
XML Schema 261
    XML Schema Basics 261
    Using XML Schema in a JWS File 267

Related XML Specifications 269
    XML Namespaces 269
    XSL 270
    XPath 271

C Web Service Description Language (WSDL)   273

History of WSDL 273
WSDL in Workshop 273
Obtaining the WSDL Definition for Any Service in Workshop 274
    Generate a WSDL for Your Service 274
    View Current WSDL for Service 274
Utilizing an External Web Service When You Have Its WSDL URL 274
Creating a Service That Complies with a WSDL File 275
WSDL Definition 276
Communication Processes 276
Types 277
    Creating the Address Type for the WSDL Document 278
Messages 280
    Using Elemental Form to Create Messages 280
    Using Types to Create Messages 281
Operations 283
    Types of Operations 283
    Creating a One-Way Operation 285
    Creating a Request/Response Operation 285
    Creating a Notification Operation 286
    Creating a Solicit/Response Operation 286
Port Type 286
    Creating a Port Type with a One-Way Operation 287
Binding 287
    Binding myMethod to SOAP over HTTP 288
    Binding myMethod to Multiple Transports 288
Port 290
    Defining a Port 290
Service 290
    Declaring the Service 291
    Combining Port Types Within a Service 293

D   SOAP   **295**

SOAP Message Exchange 295

Web Services and SOAP 297

SOAP Message Format 297

SOAP Data Encoding 299

SOAP over HTTP 300

SOAP Headers 302

Index   **303**

Preface

Web services have attracted much attention recently as the next "big thing" in computing technology. Vendors of all shapes and sizes have announced their support for Web services technologies, and every month a new Web services conference is popping up somewhere on the globe. With all this hype and attention, sometimes it's difficult to really discover what Web services are, where they fit in your company, what the business case is, and how you can actually get started taking advantage of this technology.

BEA has been working with customers to answer many of these questions, and provide solutions that enable companies to easily construct Web services that meet their needs today. Contrary to the common conception of Web services as a consumer-focused technology, Web services may have the greatest potential as a technology inside enterprises—as a new way of tying disparate applications together using standards-based technologies. To make Web services really work in the enterprise, however, it's essential that they meet core enterprise requirements: Web services applications have to exist in a constantly changing IT environment where different applications are built and modified by different people on different schedules. They must accommodate everything from modern J2EE-based applications, to legacy systems, to applications at business partners. They must be able to handle rich and complex information and transmit it between internal and external applications. They must easily interact with other applications to leverage existing investments. They must be robust, reliable, and they must perform. Perhaps most important of all, they have to be easy to build. For Web services to flourish within an organization, all developers will need to be able to build Web services that meet these requirements.

BEA WebLogic Workshop Kick Start introduces you to BEA's new WebLogic Workshop product—a development tool and runtime framework that makes it easy to build powerful Web services that take advantage of the robust, enterprise features of the WebLogic J2EE application server. WebLogic Workshop provides a graphical tool that makes it easy to visualize, develop, and test Web service applications and visual controls that dramatically simplify access to existing resources like databases, packaged applications, Enterprise Java Beans, and other Web services. The Workshop framework provides out-of-the-box support for building Web services that are loosely coupled so that the internal implementation details of an application can be cleanly separated from the "public contract" that a Web service offers to other applications. This makes Workshop Web services flexible in the face of a constantly changing IT environment. Workshop also provides built-in support for asynchronous messaging so that Web service applications can carry on rich, two-way conversations with their clients and accommodate interaction with legacy systems and human users. Finally, Workshop supports easy manipulation of coarse-grained messages so that rich documents can be handled without resorting to tedious XML DOM programming.

All of these capabilities can be accessed in a simple, declarative fashion that enables all developers—not just J2EE experts—to get started building Web services today.

Even if you are new to the Java programming language, or have never built a J2EE application before, I think you'll be surprised how easy it is to get started with Workshop. Working inside the WebLogic Workshop environment, you can focus on the procedural business code that is important to getting your applications built and leave all of the details of Web service and J2EE plumbing to the application framework. *BEA WebLogic Workshop Kick Start* will give you an introduction to Web services in general, and teach you the few Java and J2EE concepts you'll need to know along the way. Rich with examples, this book illustrates the power of Web services, and will help you realize the value they can bring to your company.

Carl Sjogreen
Product Manager
WebLogic Workshop
BEA Systems, Inc.

About the Authors

Joseph Weber is a software architect, manager, and consultant from Wisconsin. Mr. Weber has been an outspoken champion of Java and related technologies since their public birth in 1995. During his career he has provided senior leadership in software definition, research, development and implementation to numerous Fortune 200 and large government organizations. Currently Mr. Weber is a Senior Software Engineer and Project Manager for UltraVisual Medical Systems, where he is helping to develop next-generation medical imaging software (PACS). Mr. Weber is also the founder and sole official member of the Green Sky Society dedicated to irradiating the social misunderstanding that the sky is blue and not green. *BEA WebLogic Workshop Kick Start* marks Joe's 11th book. He recently outlined and contributed to Sams' *Java Web Services Unleashed* (0-672-32363-X) and co-wrote Que's *Special Edition Using Java 2* (2000 edition: 0-7897-2468-5). Mr. Weber can be reached at jlweber@hotmail.com or via his occasionally active Web site: http://www.fluidimagination.com.

Mark Wutka has been programming since the Carter administration and considers programming a relaxing pastime. He managed to get a computer science degree while designing and developing networking software at Delta Air Lines. Although he has been known to delve into areas of system and application architecture, he isn't happy unless he's writing code—usually in Java. As a consultant for Wutka Consulting, Mr. Wutka enjoys solving interesting technical problems and helping his coworkers explore new technologies. He has taught classes, written articles and books, and given lectures. His first book, *Hacking Java*, outsold Stephen King at the local technical bookstore. He's also known for having a warped sense of humor.

Most recently, Mr. Wutka contributed to *Java Web Services Unleashed,* and wrote *Special Edition Using JavaServer Pages and Servlets* (ISBN: 0-7897-2441-3) and *Special Edition Using Java 2 Enteprise Edition* (ISBN: 0-7897-2503-7) He plays a mean game of Scrabble, a lousy game of chess, and is the bane of every greenskeeper east of Atlanta. He can be reached via email at mark@wutka.com. You can also visit his company Web site at http://www.wutka.com.

Dedication

From Joseph Weber

To Emma and Andrew, who have blessed me beyond my ability to put into words.

From Mark Wutka

To Samantha and Kaitlynn

Acknowledgments

From Joseph Weber

Although an author is capable of sculpting the initial structure of a book, the entire beast cannot be complete without an army of help. That help comes in so many forms, it is absolutely amazing, and humbling to behold.

The entire team at Sams, as always, has been a joy to work with. You have put up with my schedule, my quirks, and my (not so occasional) inability to write sensible English. I am so happy to have worked with such a talented group.

I would like to acknowledge my coauthor Mark Wutka. Mark, you stepped up to the plate when I had to step down. I'm forever astounded by your skill and determination. Thank you for making this book possible.

Thank you to the tech editors: Steve Heckler, Peter Horadan, and Michael Abbott. Without your work this book would not be nearly as valuable.

To Todd Green, thank you for working with me again, even as it must have become trying to do so. A big thank you to Michael Watson for extracting the best out of this book, and to Elizabeth Finney for getting it put together. To all the other people at Sams whose names I never learned but who worked to put some polish on a very rough stone.

To the WebLogic Workshop team for putting together such a good project (I like the name Jellybeans by the way). Thank you to BEA for providing us such great access.

Thank you to my children, Emma and Andrew, who, without having any say in the matter, gave up having a dad around for so many hours. You two have brought so much meaning to my life that I could never have imagined possible. May you both always reach for the stars and follow your dreams.

Finally, the greatest acknowledgement goes to my wife Kim, who never receives enough credit. Without your support I would not have been able to do any of this. I love you. I love you, and I love you more.

From Mark Wutka

I'd like to thank the Academy, but before I do, I'd just like to say to Tom Hanks, Harrison Ford, and Denzel Washington—"Better luck next year, guys." Wait… wrong speech…

Although only two authors are listed on the cover of this book, there are so many other people who worked very hard to make this book a reality. Some of these people, like Todd Green, Michael Watson, Steve Heckler, and the other folks at Sams, are listed just inside the front cover. I'd like to thank them for their patience and dedication in getting this book done.

Carl Sjogreen and Pete Horadan from BEA have been extremely helpful in getting us copies of the software and in answering our questions. Their enthusiasm over this product really showed in our conversations with them and we share it.

I'd like to thank Samantha and Kaitlynn for allowing me a little time on my computer to get this book written. I am always grateful to my mom for the example she has given me—it keeps me going. Finally, I'd like to thank my wife Ceal; I don't really have enough room here to express just how grateful I am to you. Thanks, Sweetie!

Tell Us What You Think!

As the reader of this book, *you* are our most important critic and commentator. We value your opinion and want to know what we're doing right, what we could do better, what areas you'd like to see us publish in, and any other words of wisdom you're willing to pass our way.

As an executive editor for Sams Publishing, I welcome your comments. You can email or write me directly to let me know what you did or didn't like about this book—as well as what we can do to make our books better.

Please note that I cannot help you with technical problems related to the *topic* of this book. We do have a User Services group, however, where I will forward specific technical questions related to the book.

When you write, please be sure to include this book's title and author as well as your name, email address, and phone number. I will carefully review your comments and share them with the author and editors who worked on the book.

Email: feedback@samspublishing.com

Mail: Michael Stephens
            Executive Editor
            Sams Publishing
            201 West 103rd Street
            Indianapolis, IN 46290 USA

For more information about this book or another Sams Publishing title, visit our Web site at www.samspublishing.com. Type the ISBN (excluding hyphens) or the title of a book in the Search field to find the page you're looking for.

Introduction

Who Should Buy This Book

This book is for developers who want to learn to use WebLogic Workshop quickly and get the most out of it. This book is not an introduction to programming—you should know how to program in some programming language. It also helps if you are familiar with a graphical development environment.

Although this book doesn't assume you know Java, the introduction to Java in the back of the book is merely a starting point. If you know nothing about Java, you will probably want to get a more comprehensive book on Java before undertaking a large-scale project, but this book should give you just enough background to get you going. C++ developers usually have the easiest time adjusting to Java because of the similarity between the languages. Microsoft's new C# language is similar enough to Java that C# developers have little trouble picking up Java as well. If you primarily use Visual Basic, Delphi, or Cobol, you may want to go ahead and get a Java book. Sams Publishing has several good Java books. *Teach Yourself Java 2 in 21 Days* is fairly popular and provides a good introduction to the language. You might also try *Pure Java 2* or *Java 2 for Professional Developers*.

WebLogic Workshop is a development environment for writing Web services. If you've heard a lot about Web services and want to experiment with them, WebLogic Workshop is the product for you, and this is the book for you. WebLogic Workshop makes it incredibly easy to develop Web services, and this book shows you how.

If you don't know what Web services are, this book will teach you some of the basics. Briefly, Web services are programs that can be invoked over the Web using a simple protocol called SOAP (Simple Object Access Protocol). Because SOAP is a simple, easy-to-implement protocol, it is easy to use Web services from many different programming languages. Microsoft's new Visual Studio .NET environment makes it very easy to write applications that can access Web services, and Java is getting more and more support for Web services. WebLogic Workshop gives you an environment to write services that can be accessed by a large number of potential clients.

Although you can write Web services in Java using any development environment, WebLogic Workshop was designed specifically for writing Web services and provides a tremendous amount of value. First, WebLogic Workshop handles all the SOAP protocol coding for you. You just write simple Java code, and Workshop handles the rest. Second, Workshop can automatically run and debug your Web services—something that is not easy in other development environments. Third, Workshop provides special controls that simplify many other complex tasks (like interfacing with a database), making it even easier to develop Web services.

How This Book Is Organized

This book is divided into four sections. In the first section, you'll learn about the basics of WebLogic Workshop—how to install it, run it, and build basic applications. This section includes

- Introduction to Web Services
- Installing WebLogic Workshop
- Overview of the WebLogic Workshop Development Environment
- Building your first WebLogic Workshop application
- Running a Web service from WebLogic Workshop
- Debugging a Web service

In the second part, you'll learn about some of the useful controls Workshop provides that really make development easy. This section includes

- Creating conversations
- Accessing a database
- Using a timer
- Accessing Enterprise JavaBeans
- Using the Java Message Service control

The third section focuses on some of the lower-level aspects of Workshop. There are times when you need to customize some of the things that Workshop does for you automatically. This section shows you what all your options are. This section includes

- Creating a custom XML map
- Using XML Script
- JavaDoc tags for customizing a Web service

The fourth section consists of appendixes that give you an overview of some of the technologies that WebLogic Workshop includes. It gives you a brief overview of Java, XML, and some of the XML-related protocols like SOAP and WSDL. This section includes

- Introduction to Java

- Overview of XML

- Overview of SOAP

- Overview of the Web Services Description Language (WSDL)

Conventions Used in This Book

This book uses certain conventions to help make the book more readable and helpful:

- Code listings, methods, elements, functions, and other code terms appear in a `monospace` font.

- Placeholders (words with substitutes for what you actually type) appear in a `monospace italic`.

- Sometimes a code line that should be one line is unable to fit on a single line in this book. When this happens, the line is broken and continued on the next line, preceded by a ➥character.

In addition, this book uses special sidebars that are set apart from the rest of the text, including Notes, Tips, and Cautions.

Source Code and Updates

For updates to this book, and to download the source code and examples presented in this book, visit `http://www.samspublishing.com`. From the home page, type this book's ISBN (0672324172) into the search window, and click on Search to access information about the book and a direct link to the source code.

System Requirements

WebLogic Workshop runs on Windows 2000, Windows NT, Solaris 8.0, and Linux (RedHat 7.1). You also need the BEA WebLogic Server, which comes bundled with WebLogic Workshop. You don't necessarily need Java installed on your system ahead of time because Workshop comes with its own Java environment. The combination of Workshop and the WebLogic Server is pretty memory-intensive. Although it may run with 128MB of RAM, it is better to have 256MB or more. Aside from installing WebLogic Workshop, you shouldn't need any additional tools in order to edit, compile, and run the examples from this book.

PART I

Introduction to WebLogic Workshop

IN THIS PART

1 Introduction to Web Services

2 The WebLogic Workshop

3 Building an Application in WebLogic Workshop

4 Developing Conversant Applications

1

Introduction to Web Services

IN THIS CHAPTER

- What Are Web Services?
- Examples of Web Services
- Advantages of Web Services
- Disadvantages of Web Services
- The Web Service Protocols
- Why Use WebLogic Workshop?

Although the term "Web services" has been one of the latest buzzwords floating around, many people have difficulty defining exactly what Web services are. One of the reasons for the difficulty is that Web services are very new and some of the standards used to implement them are still being defined.

What Are Web Services?

Speaking very generally, a Web service is a set of operations that can be invoked remotely over the Web. When you dive deeper into Web services, you find that they aren't much different from other remote services. For example, the Common Object Request Broker Architecture (CORBA) enables you to write applications that can be accessed over the network, and so does Java's Remote Method Invocation (RMI).

A Web service uses simple, common protocols like XML and SOAP (which you'll learn more about shortly). The simplicity is one of the most attractive aspects of Web services.

Examples of Web Services

Web services are frequently used for Business-to-Business (B2B) applications. In these cases, a business needs to interact directly with another business without human intervention. That is, a program sends a request to another program. In the past, the businesses might have used CORBA or RMI, but many of them used the Web. The problem with using the Web for B2B communications is that the Web was designed for reading hypertext documents. Even the idea of submitting forms to a central server was an afterthought. In general, it is the capability of sending form data to a Web server that makes B2B communication even possible.

When a Web server processes form data, it typically uses various server-side programming technologies. One of the oldest server-side technologies is the Common Gateway Interface (CGI), which enables developers to write simple form-handling programs in almost any language—usually C or Perl. CGI has several disadvantages. First, the Web server executes a CGI program to handle each request, which takes extra time and usually more memory. Second, when writing out an HTML response, CGI programs usually contain print statements of some form or another. Editing HTML embedded within another language is inconvenient at the least.

Java servlets provide some of the capabilities of CGI, but don't require a separate program to handle each request. Servlets generally have a faster startup time and have become a popular Java-based alternative to CGI. Servlets still have the disadvantage of requiring print or some equivalent for writing HTML. Technologies like Active Server Pages (ASP), JavaServer Pages (JSP), and Hypertext Pre-Processor (PHP) solve the HTML problem by allowing you to embed server-side code within HTML pages.

Although the various server-side technologies make it easy for users to interact with Web servers, they are not suited well for B2B communication. The problem is that these technologies are still geared toward browsers, with the data embedded into HTML. Any programs that want to retrieve data must parse through the HTML to locate the data. If the format of the HTML changes, the programs that parse the HTML must also change. For example, back in 1998, a company was shipping a large number of packages via UPS and needed to track packages. They wrote a custom program that parsed data from the UPS online tracking system and updated a local database.

Web services provide an alternate way to access data over the Web. The key difference between Web services and traditional Web applications is that Web services are not display-oriented. You don't need to parse through HTML just to access the data you need.

Companies are now beginning to offer Web service access to many of the services they previously offered to Web browsers. Now, their customers can automate more of their interactions with these companies. For example, a manufacturing company can allow customers to place orders via a Web service. In fact, online ordering is one of the most common types of Web service. Where a traditional Web application might display a catalog of available products and require frequent customer interaction, a Web service typically accepts a compact order that already contains all the correct quantities and product codes. A warehouse might use a manufacturer's Web service to automatically reorder parts whenever they are in short supply.

Web sites are beginning to use Web services to hand data off from one site to another. The idea here is that several Web sites maintain customer data that they may want to share—addresses, credit card numbers, passwords, and so on. These sites don't necessarily want to store this data in the browser. Instead, the sites pass data between themselves via Web services without the involvement of the browser. For example, one site may keep a digital wallet containing your bank account and credit card information. When you visit an online shopping site, the site accesses your digital wallet via a Web service in order to validate payment. Although this kind of interaction is possible through the browser in a traditional Web application, there is less possibility for fraud because the credit information is never stored on the browser. You don't have to worry about the data being stored accidentally in a browser cache somewhere on your PC. This also reduces the possibility of fraud because the critical data is never in the hands of the user where it could be changed.

Figure 1.1 illustrates this kind of data exchange.

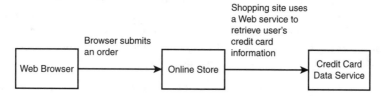

FIGURE 1.1   Web sites can use Web services to exchange data without involving the browser.

Many shipping companies currently allow customers to track packages online, and they have also begun to offer libraries that allow programs to track the packages. These tracking systems are ideal candidates for Web services. The companies don't need to send out custom libraries; they simply publish the specifications for their Web service. You can find a Web service that can track both FedEx and UPS packages at http://www.xmethods.net.

Google, the popular search engine, has created a Web service interface for searching. This interface enables companies to integrate Web searching into their products without the need of a Web browser. You can find more information about the service, including a WSDL (Web Service Description Language) file describing the various SOAP functions available at http://www.google.com/apis/. Basically, you sign up for a special Google account, and then when you invoke one of the Google SOAP services, you pass your account information along with the information you are searching for. You have a limited number of free searches available per day.

Advantages of Web Services

Web services give you an advantage over other technologies because of this technology's simplicity and standardization. In the past, if you were implementing a CORBA or RMI solution, you were limited to languages with support for these technologies. For RMI, you were mainly limited to Java, whereas for CORBA you had a choice of many languages like Java, C, C++, Perl, and so on. Microsoft's equivalent of CORBA or RMI is DCOM (the distributed version of the Component Object Model). Like CORBA, DCOM supports many different languages. Unfortunately, it is generally limited to only Microsoft packages, although there has been some work to make DCOM available on non-Microsoft platforms.

Since both parties in the transaction must use the same protocol, RMI requires that both parties use Java. Although Java is very popular, some companies still don't want to use it, so an RMI-based solution may not cover everyone. Many CORBA implementations are fairly expensive and customers may balk at installing an expensive package just to do business with your company.

Both CORBA and DCOM are particularly cumbersome because they require you to create special Interface Definition Language (IDL) files that describe the format of the remote functions and data structures. In fact, although CORBA and DCOM both use the name "IDL," they use different formats for these files. Maintaining these IDL files in addition to the CORBA or DCOM code places more of a burden on developers than RMI, which works strictly off Java files.

Because Web services use simple, standard protocols, you can use a larger number of languages. For one thing, you can use any of the .NET-based languages because Microsoft is a huge supporter of Web services. The simplicity of the Web service protocols makes them easier to implement and therefore more attractive to developers. For Java developers, Microsoft's Web service support is a big win. Java has really grown in popularity for server applications. Unfortunately, Java hasn't been as popular on the client side. Many development shops prefer to use Microsoft's development tools for their client-side applications. Because Microsoft doesn't directly support CORBA or RMI, it is difficult to make a Microsoft application communicate with a Java server application. If the server application makes itself available as a Web service via the SOAP protocol, however, it is easy to use the various .NET languages (Visual Basic .NET, C#, C++ .NET, ASP.NET) communicate with the Java application.

Another advantage of Web services comes from the way that companies protect their networks. A typical business uses one or more firewalls that block many incoming requests. These firewalls usually allow common Internet protocols like SMTP (email) and HTTP (Web). Because Web services typically use the Web protocols, they can pass through firewalls. Custom protocols like RMI and CORBA's IIOP require special firewall modifications, or special libraries to send requests over the Web protocols.

Finally, the simplicity of the Web service protocols makes them easy to read, understand, and debug. You can look at a series of Web service requests and immediately see all the data being sent—the protocols use plain text. Other protocols like RMI use a binary encoding that is difficult to interpret without the aid of a decoder program.

Disadvantages of Web Services

Although the simplicity of Web services is an advantage in some respects, it can also be a hindrance. Web services use plain text protocols that use a fairly verbose method to identify data. This means that Web service requests are larger than requests encoded with a binary protocol. The extra size is really only an issue over low-speed connections, or over extremely busy connections.

Although HTTP and HTTPS (the core Web protocols) are simple, they weren't really meant for long-term sessions. Typically, a browser makes an HTTP connection, requests a Web page and maybe some images, and then disconnects. In a typical CORBA or RMI environment, a client connects to the server and might stay connected for an extended period of time. The server may periodically send data back to the client. This kind of interaction is difficult with Web services, and you need to do a little extra work to make up for what HTTP doesn't do for you.

The problem with HTTP and HTTPS when it comes to Web services is that these protocols are "stateless"—the interaction between the server and client is typically brief and when there is no data being exchanged, the server and client have no knowledge of each other. More specifically, if a client makes a request to the server, receives some information, and then immediately crashes due to a power outage, the server never knows that the client is no longer active. The server needs a way to keep track of what a client is doing and also to determine when a client is no longer active.

Typically, a server sends some kind of session identification to the client when the client first accesses the server. The client then uses this identification when it makes further requests to the server. This enables the server to recall any information it has about the client. A server must usually rely on a timeout mechanism to determine that a client is no longer active. If a server doesn't receive a request from a client after a predetermined amount of time, it assumes that the client is inactive and removes any client information it was keeping. This extra overhead means more work for Web service developers.

Table 1.1 summarizes some of the differences between RMI, CORBA, DCOM, and Web services.

TABLE 1.1 Differences Between RMI, CORBA, DCOM, and Web Services

	RMI	CORBA	DCOM	Web Service
Multiple Languages	No	Yes	Yes	Yes
Multiple Operating Systems	Yes	Yes	No	Yes
Open Standard	No	Yes	No	Yes
IDL Required	No	Yes	Yes	No
Stateful/Stateless	Stateful	Stateful	Stateful	Stateless

The Web Service Protocols

Web services rely on a set of services that perform much of the underlying work. To write a Web service, you often just implement the actual service and then rely on the underlying libraries to do all the translation and communications.

XML

The Extensible Markup Language (XML) is the real core of Web services. Most of the other Web service protocols are based on XML. Put simply, XML provides a way to represent structured data using plain text. A snippet of XML data might look something like this:

```
<person>
    <name>Samantha Tippin</name>
    <age>9</age>
    <address>
        <street>123 Barbie Lane</street>
        <city>Gymtown</city>
        <state>GA</state>
        <zip>30123</zip>
    </address>
</person>
```

Even without knowing the rules of XML, you can figure out what the data represents just by looking at it. If you have never seen or used XML before, Appendix B, "XML," gives you a general overview of XML.

XML is the main reason that Web services have such a simple protocol. Because of its easy-to-understand plain text syntax, XML is easy to implement in most programming languages, making it easy for programs in different languages to exchange data. Because XML is a popular and open standard, it makes an attractive choice for implementation because so many companies already support it. There are plenty of XML tools available, reducing the amount of custom work needed to implement an XML-based solution.

SOAP

The Simple Object Access Protocol (SOAP) enables you to send requests from one program to another over a network. All SOAP requests and responses are XML documents, making SOAP a human-readable protocol. Typical SOAP implementations use the Web protocol HTTP to send and receive data, but SOAP is not limited to this one protocol. There are SOAP implementations that use the email protocol SMTP to transmit requests, and other implementations that use the Java Message Service (JMS).

Most Web services are built directly on top of SOAP—that is, SOAP is the main technology used to implement Web services (apart from XML, which SOAP is built on top of). Appendix D gives you an overview of SOAP.

WSDL

The Web Service Description Language (WSDL) describes the functions that a Web service supports, as well as the structure of the data it accepts and returns. It can also describe the protocols supported by the service and the network address or addresses of the service. As with many Web service protocols, WSDL files are actually XML documents.

Although WSDL may play a role in locating a service, it doesn't play a role in the actual invocation of a Web service. That is, you don't use WSDL to actually send or receive a Web service request. Appendix C gives you an overview of WSDL.

UDDI

The Universal Description, Discovery, and Integration (UDDI) protocol provides a lookup mechanism for Web services. Basically, it is a way for businesses to locate available Web services. In UDDI's early implementation, people, not programs, mainly use UDDI. A UDDI browser enables users to look for particular companies or services and then explore the various offerings. As UDDI matures, however, programs will use UDDI more often to locate services. One of the things a UDDI directory may provide is the location of the UDDI file that further describes a Web service. As with the other common Web service protocols, UDDI is based on XML and also on SOAP. You use SOAP to perform UDDI lookups. In fact, you can consider UDDI to be a Web service itself.

Because UDDI isn't really used by programs yet, you don't need to use it when you create Web services with WebLogic Workshop, so it is not covered any further in this book. You can find more information about UDDI at http://www.uddi.org and also http://uddi.microsoft.com.

Why Use WebLogic Workshop?

At first glance, the Web service protocols may look a little scary. Although XML and its related protocols are easy to read, you don't necessarily want to learn all of them just to implement a simple Web service. That's where WebLogic Workshop comes in.

In the past, developing a Web service in Java meant writing a lot of code to interface with a SOAP library and possibly with WSDL or UDDI. WebLogic Workshop relieves you of that burden, allowing you to focus on implementing the service itself. For example, Figure 1.2 shows the code editor for WebLogic Workshop with a simple Web service method. You generally just write the Web service methods and let WebLogic Workshop handle the Web service protocols.

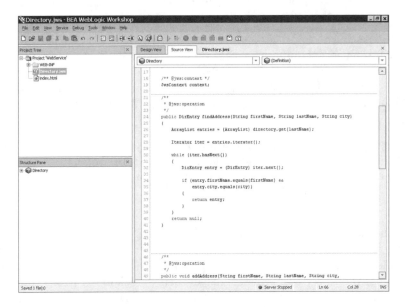

FIGURE 1.2   WebLogic Workshop lets you focus on implementing methods, instead of the underlying protocols.

Not only does Workshop make it easy to create Web services, but it also makes it easy to deploy and test the methods. Without an automated tool, it is often difficult to deploy a Web service. You often need to copy files to various places, edit configuration files, and sometimes even restart the server. With Workshop, you deploy your service by clicking on the Run icon or by selecting Run from the menu.

When you run a Web service, Workshop automatically creates a test page, allowing you to test your service from a Web browser using a simple form interface. Without Workshop, you would need to write your own test programs. This simple feature can save you hours of work. Figure 1.3 shows the test page for the Web service method you saw in Figure 1.2.

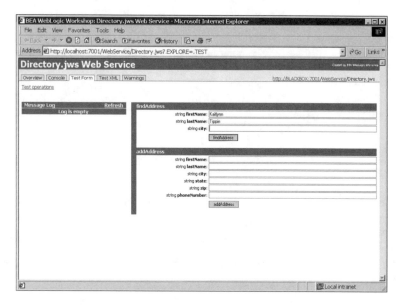

FIGURE 1.3   WebLogic Workshop's testing page lets you quickly test your Web service.

Debugging is another nightmare for Java Web service developers. It is often difficult to run a SOAP service within a Java development environment, and remote debugging is often difficult to set up. Workshop has built-in support for debugging—you simply click the Debug icon or select Debug from the menu. Again, this may save you hours of work. Figure 1.4 shows the Workshop debugger in action.

There is more to developing a Web service than just making some methods available via SOAP. You may need to keep track of client sessions, or you may need to access a database or an Enterprise Java Bean or the Java Message Service. Workshop contains a number of tools called *controls* that handle many of these tasks for you, letting you focus on implementing the Web service method instead of trying to integrate several technologies together.

UDDI is very useful for exchanging information about a Web service, but the language itself is somewhat cumbersome. It could take you all day just to write a UDDI file for one Web service. Workshop can generate a UDDI file in a matter of seconds. It can also read UDDI files for existing Web services, allowing you to access these other services from within your own Web service. In other words, you can use Workshop to build new services on top of existing ones.

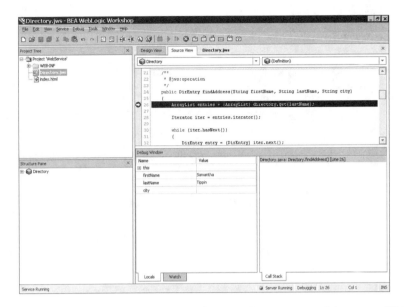

FIGURE 1.4   The WebLogic Workshop debugger makes it easy to debug your Web services.

Overall, WebLogic Workshop is an exciting and simple way to create Web services. You only need to be able to write a little Java code to implement a Web service with Workshop, and yet you can create some very powerful services in a short amount of time. Workshop will revolutionize the development of Web services in Java.

2

The WebLogic Workshop

IN THIS CHAPTER

- Verify That Everything Is Functional
- Overview of the Workshop Environment
- Changing the Workshop Environment

Verify That Everything Is Functional

The first step to using Workshop is obviously to run through the setup program provided with Workshop. Once you have Workshop installed, the next step is to make sure that everything is functional. To verify Workshop's install, the easiest thing to do is run a simple test service. In this case, the test you will run is to execute the HelloWorld service from the Samples project. In Chapter 3, "Building an Application in Workshop," we will actually build the HelloWorld service from scratch. For now, you will just execute the version that should have been installed with Workshop.

Open the Samples Project

Groups of files in WebLogic are grouped together into bundles called *projects*. When you first launch Workshop, the project that is open will be the Samples project. If the Samples project is not open, you must first open it. You can do this by clicking on File, Open Project. This will bring up the Project browser, which looks like Figure 2.1.

Using the Project browser, you can switch to any project you have built in Workshop. In this case we want to switch to the Samples project. So select the Samples entry and click the Open button.

With the Samples project open, you should see the base Workshop environment. The Project tree on the left can be used to navigate to or create new source files. If you have opened Workshop for the first time, HelloWorld.jws is selected in this tree. If not, double-click on the icon labeled HelloWorld.jws to open the HelloWorld service.

FIGURE 2.1   The Project browser.

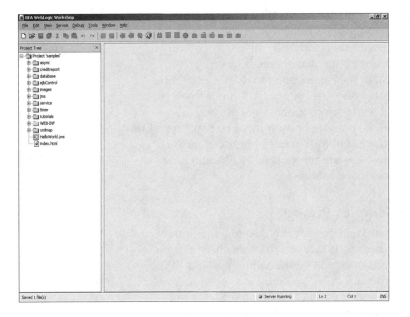

FIGURE 2.2   The Workshop environment.

At this point you should have the HelloWorld file open and Workshop should now look like Figure 2.3. You will notice that several things were added to the environment between Figure 2.2 and Figure 2.3. We will be going through each of these in different sections later in this chapter.

The most important thing to look at now is the panel in the center of the screen. In the middle you see what is called the Design view. The Design view provides a graphic representation of the HelloWorld service you are about to run. Notice the arrow pointing from the Client to the box labeled HelloWorld. The arrow represents a message that can travel from the client to the HelloWorld service.

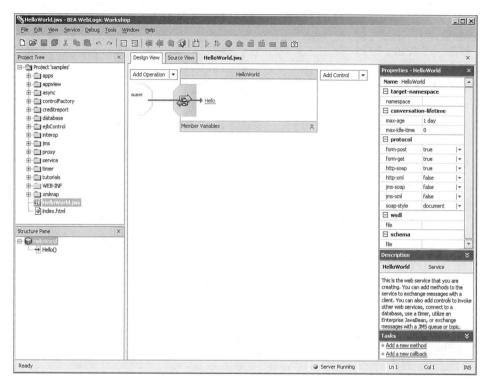

FIGURE 2.3   Workshop with HelloWorld open.

Testing HelloWorld

Now that you have HelloWorld loaded, it's time for you to test it to make sure
WebLogic will actually be able to run the service.

Starting the WebLogic Server

Before you can run any service, the first thing that you must do is make sure that
the WebLogic server is started. When the server is not running, you will see a red
light with the label Server Stopped in the status bar on the bottom of the
Workshop screen. To start the server, go to Tools, Start WebLogic Server. This will
cause a progress bar to appear, and WebLogic will start to run.

NOTE

You can also let Workshop start WebLogic for you. When you run or debug a service,
Workshop will automatically check to see whether WebLogic is running. If WebLogic is not
running, Workshop will automatically start it for you.

Do not be alarmed if it seems to take a long time for WebLogic to start up. This is normal. When the server starts up, it is preloading a lot of information, and this process can take quite a while.

Starting the HelloWorld Service

When WebLogic has started, you can run the service by clicking on Debug, Start. Alternatively, you can press Ctrl+F5. When you do this, a Web browser window will open and look like Figure 2.4.

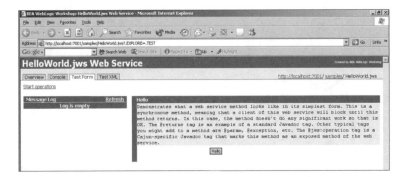

FIGURE 2.4   Test framework in Workshop.

The browser window that opened is a test bed for running your Web services and is called the *test view*. Throughout this book you will become more and more familiar with utilizing the test view in order to run the services that you create.

Running HelloWorld

The last item in the right-hand window is a button labeled Hello. To actually execute the HelloWorld service, click on the Hello button. When you do, you should see a Web page similar to Figure 2.5.

If your output does in fact look like Figure 2.5, congratulations! You have successfully run your first Web service in Workshop.

Understanding the Output

The output window of the test form can be rather daunting at first. As you go through this book, you will learn about different aspects of the output. Concentrate for the moment on the portion of the table labeled Service Response.

The service response displays some of the critical information about the communication the client had with the service. The first line just indicates when the conversation took place. Under the Hello label you can see the message that was sent back from the service.

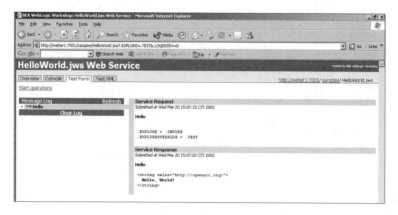

FIGURE 2.5   Result of testing the HelloWorld service.

In the case of HelloWorld, the response was the following XML document:

```
<string xmlns="http://openuri.org/">
  Hello, World!
</string>
```

XML is one of the cornerstones of all Web services, because an XML document can be understood by any computer language and by any type of system. Each element in an XML document is usually enclosed in a tag. A tag opens with a less than symbol (<), and (forward slash and greater than symbol)> (forward slash and greater than symbol), XML end tag>), XML end tag> (forward slash and greater than symbol)>), XML end tag>ends with a greater than symbol (>). Most XML tags come in pairs including a start tag and an end tag. The end tag starts with a less than symbol and a slash (</). In between the start and end tags is the value of the element. A customer invoice in XML might look like this:

```
<INVOICE>
  <CUSTOMER>
    <NAME> George Smith </NAME>
    <ADDRESS>
      <STREET_ADDRESS>123 Anywhere St.</STREET_ADDRESS>
      <CITY>Madison</CITY>
      <STATE>WI</STATE>
    </ADDRESS>
  </CUSTOMER>
  <MANIFEST>
    <PRODUCT>
      <NAME>Wing Nut</NAME>
      <PRODUCT_CODE>2345</PRODUCT_CODE>
```

```
        <PRICE>.45</PRICE>
        <QTY>25</QTY>
    </PRODUCT>
    <PRODUCT>
        <NAME>Bolt</NAME>
        <PRODUCT_CODE>2365</PRODUCT_CODE>
        <PRICE>.65</PRICE>
        <QTY>25</QTY>
    </PRODUCT>
    </MANIFEST>
</INVOICE>
```

For more information about XML, refer to Appendix B, "XML."

In this case the element that is open and closed is a string, and the value is Hello, World!.

> **NOTE**
>
> It is not strictly the case that XML must include start and end tags. In Chapter 8, "Creating a Map," you will learn more about different XML constructs that allow you to use attributes within a tag, and tags that are singular. These tags can look like this:
>
> `<CUSTOMER name="George Smith" customerid="2345"/>`

Overview of the Workshop Environment

Now that you have seen how to execute a service, it's helpful to take a closer look at the entire Workshop IDE. The Workshop environment is broken up into different panels. Each panel gives you access to a different part of the development process.

The Project Tree

The Project tree, shown in Figure 2.6, is your access to all of the files in a project. Using the Project tree, you can switch between files, add new files to your project, move files around in your project, add files from other parts of your hard drive, or copy files from Workshop to your hard drive.

As you right-click on various files in the tree, you will find that you can perform additional actions on them. Throughout this book you will be introduced to all these actions.

To add source files that you didn't create in Workshop to the project, you can drag and drop them from your operating system's browser. For instance, in Windows you can open Windows Explorer and drag a file from the Explorer window to the Project tree. This will copy the source file into the Workshop project just as if you were copying it using Windows Explorer. This is helpful if you want to use sources from a different project you've built in a different IDE, or sources you've picked up from a third party.

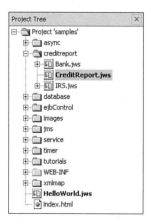

FIGURE 2.6   The Project tree.

The CreditReport Example

To see more of the features of Workshop, it's helpful to look at a more full featured service than HelloWorld. First, make sure that you are still in the Samples project. When you have the Samples project open, find the folder called creditreport. Open the creditreport folder and select the file labeled CreditReport.jws.

Structure Pane

Below the Project tree, you will see another panel called the Structure pane. The Structure pane is designed to let you see the various elements involved in your service. As shown in Figure 2.7, in the case of the CreditReport service, a good number of items are listed. You can see all the methods, callbacks, services, and all the member variables of the service. If you aren't familiar with each of these concepts, don't worry; you'll cover all of them as you go through the book.

The Structure pane is designed to allow you to switch quickly to each of these elements.

FIGURE 2.7   The Structure pane.

Hide and Show Panes

It is convenient at times to use different combinations of the various panes. To hide (or show) any of the panes, select the View menu and check the panes you want to hide or show. You can also hide a pane by clicking on the close box (X) in the upper right corner of the pane.

Design View

To the right of the Project tree and Structure pane is a section that contains either the Design view or the Source view. These two views are where you will do all the work of developing your services.

Structural View of the Service

The largest portion of the Design pane is dedicated to the structural view of the service, as shown in Figure 2.8. Chapters 3 through 6 will walk you through using the features in the Design pane.

In the center of the Design pane is a large box that shows the service that you are working on. There are two sections to the box. When you are working on a service, in the top part are message links. The arrows from the message links indicate communication from the service to the client or to other controls.

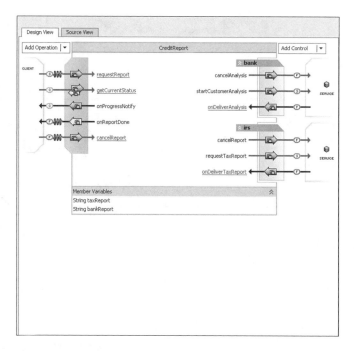

FIGURE 2.8   The graphical view of your service.

The methods that appear as hyperlinks are methods of the service. A method is a function or operation in the service. The other methods are methods that actually exist in the external client or service.

The bottom half of the service box contains the member variables of the class. You can use this to see what other variables the service might be using.

On the left side of the Design pane is a bubble that represents the client. On the right are bubbles for each of the services that are used by the service.

Properties Pane

To the right of the Design view are several panels. The top panel is the Properties pane (see Figure 2.9). When you select elements in the graphical view of the Properties pane, it will give you access to the attributes of the selected item. The Properties pane is context sensitive, so the values in the Properties pane will change constantly. For example if you click on a method arrow, the Properties pane will give you access to the properties of the method. If you click on the service box, you will have access to the properties of the service.

FIGURE 2.9   The Properties pane.

Description

Below the Properties pane is the Description pane (see Figure 2.10). As you select items throughout the Design view, the Description pane will show you some context-sensitive help about the item you've selected. This is particularly helpful when you are selecting items in the Properties pane because you can see a description of each element.

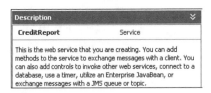

FIGURE 2.10   The Description pane.

Tasks

The Tasks pane is directly below the Description pane. Certain common functions in WebLogic Workshop can be created with a single click, by clicking on links in the Tasks pane. These links are an additional way to perform frequently used functions. The Tasks pane, shown in Figure 2.11, shows options available when the service is selected in the Structure pane.

FIGURE 2.11   The Tasks pane.

Source View

The majority of your work in WebLogic Workshop will actually take place in the Source view. To get to the Source view, click on the Source View tab. As shown in Figure 2.12, the Source view is the editor for actual source code of your files.

FIGURE 2.12   The Source view.

One somewhat unique feature about the way that WebLogic Workshop's Source view is designed is the Variable and Method selectors at the top of the source editor shown in Figure 2.13. Using these combo boxes, you can quickly jump to an individual method or variable in the source. When you do, WebLogic will also set the method off in a different color to highlight it.

FIGURE 2.13   The Variable and Method selectors.

Test View

As you saw earlier, Workshop comes with an easy-to-use test view. which acts as a ready-made test harness for your services. You will learn more about the test harness as you progress though this book. For now you should just familiarize yourself with the functions of each of the tabs on the test view.

When you first run or debug an application in WebLogic Workshop, the test view will open to the *test form*, which is shown in Figure 2.14. You have already seen how the test form works earlier in this chapter.

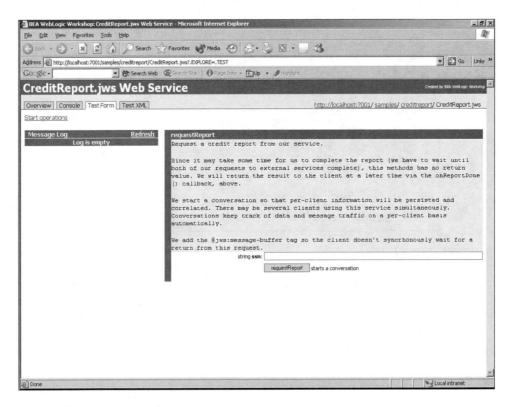

FIGURE 2.14   The test form.

In addition to the test form, there are three other tabs in the test view framework. The tab on the left, shown in Figure 2.15, is the Overview tab. The Overview tab is designed to give you quick access to details about the service necessary for others to take advantage of the service.

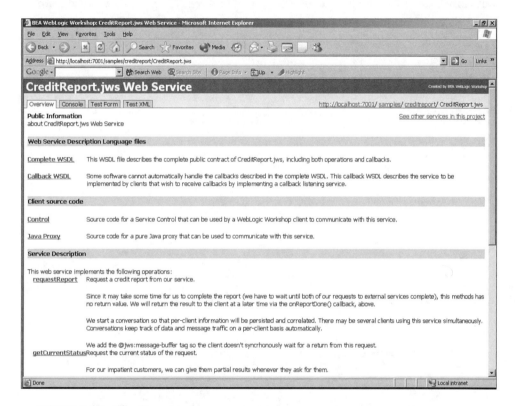

FIGURE 2.15   The Overview form.

The Console tab, shown in Figure 2.16, enables you to configure how the test environment works.

The last tab, Test XML, shown in Figure 2.17, allows you to specify the input XML for the service directly. This is very helpful if the XML your service needs is more complicated than a single string or int.

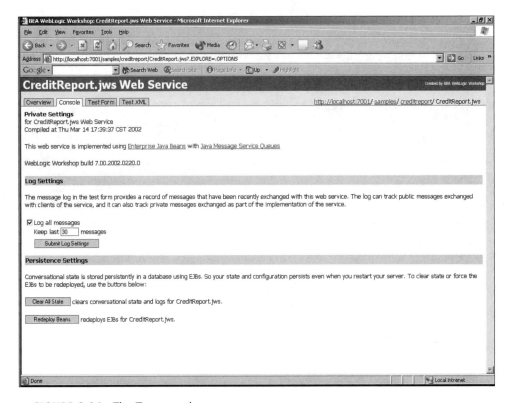

FIGURE 2.16   The Test console.

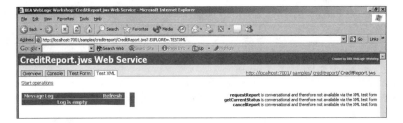

FIGURE 2.17   The Test XML form.

Changing the Workshop Environment

One other nice feature of Workshop that you may want to work with right away is the environment configuration. Everybody has their own preferences as to how they want to work in an environment. Many people like the current standard of black text on a white field. Some, like this author, like to have a high contrast dark blue field with white text. You might also want to change the location where various files are located. The Tools Preferences dialog box allows you to change all of these settings.

To open the Tools Preferences dialog box, go to the Tools menu and select the Preferences option.

Changing the Display Properties

When the Tools Preferences dialog box comes up, the first tab that is selected is the Display settings, as shown in Figure 2.18. The Display tab gives you access to several different types of display settings.

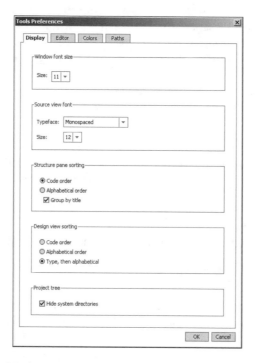

FIGURE 2.18   The Display properties.

The Window Font Size setting changes the fonts for the Workshop environment—in other words, the text that appears on buttons, tabs, items on the Project tree, Structure pane, and so on. You will have to restart Workshop for changes you make in the Window Font Size box to take effect.

As you can see from the second group of settings labeled Source View Font, the typeface settings for the source code viewer can be changed independently of the window font.

The Structure Pane Sorting settings, of course, change the settings for the way that things are displayed in the Structure pane. Initially most people find that an alphabetical order is easiest to manage. After a while some developers would prefer to have them in the order that the elements appear in the code. The radio box group for Structure Pane Sorting allows you to have elements ordered strictly in alphabetical order, or code order. The check box labeled Group by Title first groups by the type of element (method, callback, and so on), and then by the alphabetical or code order based on the radio button selection.

One of the settings you might want to change is the way that methods and callbacks are displayed in the Design view. You will learn about methods and callbacks in Chapters 3 and 4. By default, methods are grouped by their type and then alphabetically. Methods and callbacks are sorted together. Within the methods and callbacks, they are sorted by their conversational state (which you will learn about in Chapter 3). Only after this are the groups then sorted by alphabetical order. This setting is designed to allow you to quickly see the functionality of a service in a logical order. However, you may prefer to have yours grouped either by strict alphabetical order or by the order they appear in the code. The radio buttons in the Design View Sorting group allow you to select the sort order.

Changing the Editor Settings

The editor settings allow you to change the nature of the way the source code editor works. These settings, shown in Figure 2.19, allow you to customize the way that the source looks.

Design View Sorting

The flags in the Design View Sorting area have the following impact.

The Show Line Numbers value toggles the display of the line numbers as the left-hand column in the editor.

The Show Whitespace value changes whether or not you can see markers for whitespace characters. Toggling whitespace on will allow you to visually see the whitespace characters, such as a space, as shown in Figure 2.20. This can be very helpful when working on XML in WebLogic Workshop. Sometimes an extra space can throw you off completely.

The Draw Lines Between Functions option will toggle the appearance of a gray line between individual methods in the class. If you are used to a Visual Basic environment, you probably leave the lines on. If you are used to Java, you will probably just find it a convenient visual marker between methods. However, if you find the lines a nuisance, you can disable them by unchecking this box.

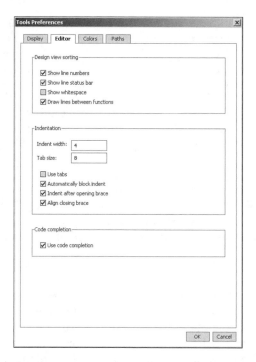

FIGURE 2.19   The editor properties.

```
19  * <p>Conversations represent resources; they shouldn't be left around.</p>
20  *
21  * @jws:conversation-lifetime max-idle-time="30 minutes"
22  */
23  public class CreditReport
24  {
25     ....
26     /*
27      * <p>ReportResult is an inner class used to represent a complete
28      * credit report.  It is used to return report responses to
29      * the client.</p>
30      *
31      * <p>Inner classes that are used outside the parent class
32      * MUST be declared "public static" and they MUST have
33      * a public no-argument constructor.</p>
34      */
```

FIGURE 2.20   Source with whitespace showing.

Indentation

The Indentation section deals with indentation rules. Every organization has its own set of rules regarding indentation. This setting allows you to have WebLogic Workshop comply with most of those rules.

The first two settings, Indent Width and Tab Size, allow you to define how far WebLogic Workshop indents either between nested braces or when you press the Tab key.

The Use Tabs option indicates whether tabs or spaces are actually placed in the source file when you press the Tab key. In most environments you will want to insert a certain number of spaces when you press Tab. This allows code to be formatted consistently in all editors. However, in some organizations a tab character (\t) is perfectly acceptable.

The Indent After Opening Brace setting changes the location of the opening brace of a method. When the Indent After Opening Brace option is checked, Workshop will automatically indent the code inside of a method that it creates.

Code Completion
The final editor setting is the ability to turn on and off code completion. Using code completion, Workshop will start to help you as you start writing code. For instance, when you start typing the name of a method, code completion will start to look for methods that start with the same letters and suggest the methods to you.

Changing Colors

Each different type of element in the source code can be individually adjusted for color. The colors are designed to allow you to see the nature of the code at a glance. Some people consider changing the colors used by the system to represent different text and art. By changing the colors to meet your own personal preferences, you can create an environment you will be more comfortable working in. Figure 2.21 shows the color choices for different Workshop elements.

Configuring System Paths

The last tab in the Tools Preferences dialog box is the Paths tab (see Figure 2.22). The Paths tab is designed to allow you to configure Workshop's interaction with the WebLogic server. Fortunately, the default settings are usually sufficient, so you will probably not have to make many modifications to this tab.

WebLogic Development Server
The Name value specifies the name of the WebLogic server itself. This will be localhost when you start initially, but WebLogic is a fairly resource-hungry application. It is possible that you will want to run it on an external computer even during development. The Name field should be changed to the name or IP address of that machine.

The Port setting represents the TCP/IP port that Workshop should use to connect to WebLogic. You configure this when you set up WebLogic; by default it is 7001.

The Config Directory represents the location where the configuration for your deployed Web services files will reside.

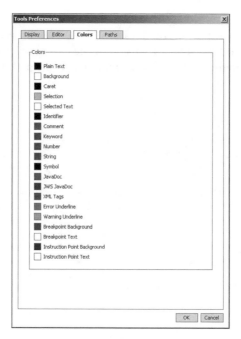

FIGURE 2.21   Changing the system colors.

FIGURE 2.22   The system paths.

Browser Path

The Browser Path value specifies the location of the Web browser that you want to use when testing your Web services. Although the easiest solution under Windows is to use the default Internet Explorer, you can also set this path to your Netscape installation.

3

Building an Application in WebLogic Workshop

In Chapter 2, "The WebLogic Workshop," you ran the HelloWorld service included as part of the WebLogic Workshop install. In this chapter you will go through the process of creating HelloWorld from scratch by yourself. The goal is to learn how to write the most basic application using the tools Workshop gives you. If you are not familiar with the Java programming language, it might be a good idea to first read Appendix A, "Java Essentials," and then to refer to it as you read the book.

Creating a Project

In Workshop, files are organized in projects. Therefore the first step you must take before creating any new set of files is to first create a project for them to reside in. To create a project, choose File, New Project. You will first be prompted for the name of the project. Enter Training and click the OK button (or simply press Enter).

Creating the HelloWorld Service

Workshop is smart enough to know that you probably do not want to create an empty project, so when you create a new project, Workshop will immediately prompt you to create a new file for the project. You can use the Create New File dialog box, as shown in Figure 3.1, to create a new Web service or other application file. The goal at this point is to create the HelloWorld Web service, so select Web Service and change the filename to HelloWorld.

Now that you have opened the new service on the left, you will see the Project tree, which you learned about in

IN THIS CHAPTER

- Creating a Project
- Creating the HelloWorld Service
- Testing Your New Service
- Passing Information to the Service
- The JWS File
- Adding Methods in Code
- Adding a Description

Chapter 2. To the right of that, and filling the majority of the screen, is a view called the Design view. There are three general areas to the Design view:

- On the left are client operations. This section shows all the messages that are traveling to and from the client of your service.

- In the center is the class you are working on (in this case, the HelloWorld service).

- On the right is an area for external controls. When your service starts to communicate with other services or controls, the messages to and from your service to the controls will appear here (more on this in Chapter 4).

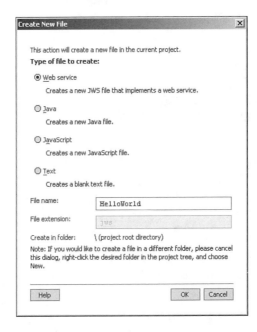

FIGURE 3.1 Creating a new Web service.

Add a Method

All interaction with a Web service must be started by a client. So to start the HelloWorld service, you must add a method to HelloWorld. To do this, click on the Add Operation combo box and select Add Method.

When you do this, as shown in Figure 3.2, an arrow will be created pointing from the client to the HelloWorld class. The arrow indicates that there is a message that can be sent from the client to your service. In this case the message goes to the new method you just created.

In the text field next to the arrow is the name of the method you've just added. Change the name of the method to `Hello`.

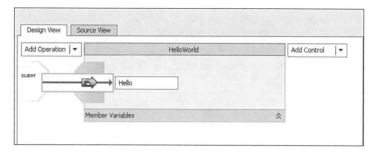

FIGURE 3.2   Adding a method.

Go to Source of Message

The actual work of the `Hello` method will be done in the source code of the method. To get to the source of the `Hello` method, click on the Hello link that appeared after you changed the name. Workshop will then display the source declaration of the `Hello` method. The code that you see in the Source view is standard Java source code. If you are not familiar with Java syntax, you can refer to Appendix A for a quick overview of the language. For now you need to know just two things. First, an operation in Java is known as a method. Second, a method begins with what is known as a *method signature*. A line similar to the first one you see in the source code defines the method signature:

```
public void Hello()
```

For now you can ignore the `public` keyword; it is simply indicating that all classes can call the `Hello` method. The other two keywords, however, are important. The `Hello` keyword defines the name of the message. The keyword `void` indicates that your method will not return any values.

Return a Value

If you look back at the Design view, you will notice that the arrow that points from the client to the service is actually made up of two arrows. The first arrow is a thin arrow that stretches the entire distance from the client to the service. The second arrow is a larger arrow icon, which is in the middle of the thin arrow. The arrow icon appears as a single arrow pointing to the right. This icon indicates that this message is one-way, from the client to the service. This type of message would provide a message from the client to the service with no response coming from the service afterwards. In the case of HelloWorld, you want the service to return a message back to the client to say 'Hello World'. This means that you want the larger arrow to point in both directions, and the message to flow in two directions—first from the client to the service and then from the service back to the client.

The fact that it says void is why the message flow arrow indicated that the message only goes in one direction. The term void indicates that the method does not return any values. If instead the method returns a String, the arrow will change to two-directional. Back in the Source view, change the word void to String so that it reads as follows:

```
public String Hello()
```

The method signature now indicates that the method will respond with a String. Click on the Design View tab to switch back to the graphic view. The large arrow on the message should now be pointing in two directions as shown in Figure 3.3.

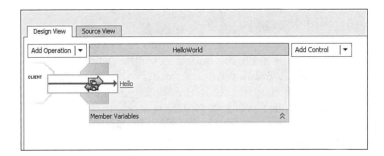

FIGURE 3.3   The Hello message is a bidirectional message.

NOTE

Although it is convenient for Workshop to graphically represent that the void message flows in a single direction, this is technically misleading. When the void response contains no values, Workshop will always send a response to the client acknowledging that the message has been processed, or received (see Chapter 4, "Creating Conversant Applications," to learn about buffered methods).

By always sending a response, WebLogic ensures its end of transactional security on the process. If the client never receives the acknowledgement, it means that WebLogic was either unable to finish the resulting processes, or never received the message in the first place.

Therefore, do not confuse the single direction, bidirectional message distinction in Workshop with WSDL's one-way versus request/response or solicit/response versus notify operations.

Define Response

Until now, the method signature has been modified to indicate that it will return a `String`, but the actual implementation of the response has not been defined. To define the body of the method, return to the source code either by clicking on the Hello link, or by clicking on the Source View tab.

In Java, as well as many other languages, blocks of code are defined by curly braces (`{}`). As such, the source of the `Hello` method is delineated by the two curly braces that you can see below the method signature. Between those two braces is where you can do the work of the method. You have already told Workshop that you want to return a `String` object, so now you just need to tell it the `return` value, which ultimately will be placed in the response message.

Change the method to read:

```
public String Hello()
{
    return "Hello, World!";
}
```

This will cause the message 'Hello, World!' to be sent back to the client.

Testing Your New Service

Congratulations, you have just completed writing your first Web service in WebLogic Workshop. Now all that's left to do is make sure that it actually works.

Build the File

The first step in testing your application is to compile it. You can do this three different ways.

- Select Debug, Build.

- Press Ctrl+B.

- Click the Build icon on the toolbar.

If you are still on the Source View tab, a new panel should open up under the source code. The panel is the Output panel. This panel will display the entire output message from the compiler.

If you have correctly entered all of the code, the panel should now display the message:

```
Build complete - 0 error(s), 0 warning(s)
```

CAUTION

If you are not used to Java, you may have encountered an error message that said

```
';' expected
```

Unlike languages like JavaScript or Visual Basic, in Java all lines of code must be terminated with a semicolon (;), so what has probably happened is that you have missed the ; at the end of the return line.

Run the Service

The final step is to actually execute the application. To do this, you'll follow the same steps as you did running the sample HelloWorld in Chapter 2.

To start the application you can do one of three things:

- Select Debug, Start.
- Press Ctrl+F5.
- Click the Start icon.

NOTE

If the WebLogic Server is not started, starting the service will cause Workshop to start the server. It is normal for this to take a while.

Remember from Chapter 2 that you can tell whether the server is running or not based on the green or red light on the status bar.

NOTE

When you start the service, WebLogic will automatically build the source for you. So you do not actually need to build the code before clicking Start.

The test form that comes up, shown in Figure 3.4, will look a lot like the test form that came up when you ran the HelloWorld service from the samples package (see Figure 2.4 in Chapter 2).

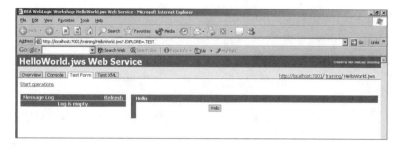

FIGURE 3.4   Test form for your HelloWorld service.

To actually execute the HelloWorld service, click the Hello button in the lower right panel. The results should look identical to the output you saw in the sample version of HelloWorld in Chapter 2.

Stop the Service

At this point you are done with running the HelloWorld service. To stop the service, you can do one of four things:

- Select Debug, Stop.

- Press Shift+F5.

- Click the Stop icon.

- You can just close the browser window and WebLogic will stop it for you.

Passing Information to the Service

Now that you have gotten the standard version of HelloWorld up and running, the next step is to enhance the HelloWorld program to take a parameter from the client.

Insert String name in between the parentheses () on the method declaration line. By placing this text between the parentheses, you are defining a parameter to be passed into the message.

Change the return line so it all looks like this:

```
public String HelloWorld(String name)
{
    return "Hello, "+name;
}
```

Build and Rerun the Program

Next you need to recompile the program and run it.

This time, when the test form comes up you will see a text field above the Hello button. Enter "Joe" or your name into the text field labeled `string` **name** and click the Hello button.

The output in the service response window should now read:

```
<string xmlns="http://openuri.org/">
  Hello, Joe
</string>
```

The JWS File

In traditional Java programming, developers create files with the .java extension. Several other variations on the .java file have already been introduced, such as .jsp. Workshop is designed to work with a new type of file called a .jws file.

As you have seen, Workshop generally has two development modes represented by the Design view and the Source view. The Design view allows you to create the .jws files visually.

JWS files are very similar to standard .java files with a couple of differences. The most important difference between the JWS file and a Java file is that the JWS file is compiled when it is deployed, and certain operations are performed on the file during the compilation process. The only syntactical difference between a JWS file and a Java file is the addition of @jws tags in the comments of JWS files. These tags guide the WebLogic server to build the service for you. Each of the @jws tags directs WebLogic to perform a myriad of tasks that would otherwise require detailed Java programming.

Adding Methods in Code

When you become familiar with the way that Workshop works, you will probably start adding methods directly in code rather than always switching to the Design view. Adding methods by hand requires adding @jws tags to the source code in JavaDoc comments.

JavaDoc Comments

In Java there are three different ways to add a comment. The first two are line comments and block comments.

Line comments (//) turn the remainder of that line into a comment. For example:

```
//This line is a comment
```

A block comment (/* ended with a */) is a combination similar to block comments available in many languages. The values between the two markers are turned into comments and ignored by the compiler.

```
/*This section
   is a comment
*/
```

The third comment is called a JavaDoc comment. JavaDoc comments are similar to the traditional block comment, but are differentiated by beginning with two stars instead of one. The code between the /** and */ is used to generate documentation about the class or method. The JavaDoc rendering tool will go through the class and use the JavaDoc comments on each method or variable to document it.

```
/**
 * This is a JavaDoc comment
 */
```

Creating an Operation Method

To expose a method to the client, WebLogic must know that the method should be available as a message. For a method to be a valid message method, WebLogic needs to find an operation JavaDoc tag in the method's JavaDoc comment. The tag that WebLogic expects looks like this:

```
@jws:operation
```

Creating the helloByHand() Method

To try this, go into the source window and create a new version of the hello method by hand. Just type

```
    /** @jws:operation
     */
    public String helloByHand(String name)
    {
        return "Hello, "+name;
    }
```

Now switch back to the Design view and you will see that Workshop has automatically added the `helloByHand` method to the list of published methods the client can send messages to.

Adding a Description

You may have noticed one difference in the way that the test view looked in Figure 3.4 compared with the version you saw in Chapter 2 (in Figure 2.4). In the version from the Samples project, there was a description above the Hello button. In your version of HelloWorld, the Hello button is completely unadorned. This difference is caused by the fact that you have not added any description for your service yet.

Adding Method Descriptions

When you added the `Hello` method, Workshop added a part of a JavaDoc comment to the `Hello` method so that it could include the `@jws:operation` tag. In order for the test view to display information about the method, you need to expand the JavaDoc comment and add the description of the method as shown in Listing 3.1.

LISTING 3.1   HelloWorld.jws

```
public class HelloWorld
{

    /** @jws:context */
    weblogic.jws.control.JwsContext context;


    /**
     * This operation will greet you with a friendly salutation <p>
     *
     * Please provide the operation with your name <br>
     * @jws:operation
     */
    public String Hello(String name)
    {
        return "Hello, "+name;
    }
}
```

When you run the service, the test view will show the description you've entered above the Hello button as shown in Figure 3.5. The description will also be written into the WSDL file for your service. For more information on WSDL, see Appendix C, "Web Service Description Language (WSDL)."

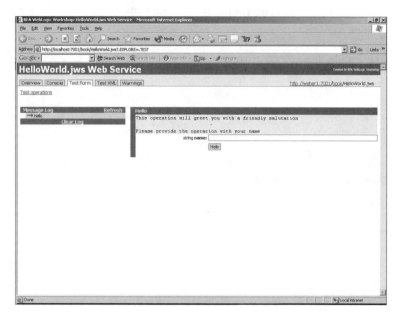

FIGURE 3.5   Description exposed to test view.

Adding a Description for the Whole Service

You can also add a comment to the whole service by adding a comment above the class definition as shown in Listing 3.2.

LISTING 3.2   Adding a Comment

```
/**
 * The HelloWorld service will send you a friendly greeting when you call the
➥Hello method
 */
public class HelloWorld
{

    /** @jws:context */
    weblogic.jws.control.JwsContext context;
```

LISTING 3.2   Adding a Comment

```
/**
 * This operation will greet you with a friendly salutation <p>
 *
 * Please provide the operation with your name <br>
 * @jws:operation
 */
public String Hello(String name)
{
    return "Hello, "+name;
}
}
```

The class's JavaDoc will appear on the Overview tab of the test view as well as the
WSDL description of your service.

4

Developing Conversant Applications

In the Hello World example from Chapter 2, the communication with the server was contained within a single message. This chapter discusses a conversation that continues over several messages.

Conversations

One of the central elements involved in developing applications in WebLogic Workshop is the concept of a *conversation*. A conversation takes place any time you want your application to have several stateful interactions with the server. A *stateful* interaction occurs when you have (at least) two messages transmitted from the client where the second message assumes that the server already has the data created in the first.

For instance, in the case of a billing system, the first message might be "start a new bill for Mr. Smith." The second message can be "add Fifty Wizbang Poppers." The conversation requires state because the server needs to know that this conversation is taking place in the context of the bill for Mr. Smith.

WebLogic Workshop makes developing applications that have prolonged dialog extremely easy. In WebLogic you create asynchronous services by using a concept called a conversation. Essentially a conversation has a fairly simple lifecycle. It begins, continues for a while, and finally ends. Figure 4.1 illustrates the nature of the lifecycle of a conversation.

IN THIS CHAPTER

- Conversations
- A Two-Stage Conversation
- Testing HelloConversation
- Why Is Asynchronous Activity Different from Synchronous Activity?
- Limitations and Advantages
- What Makes HelloConversation Synchronous?
- HelloConversation as an Asynchronous Conversation
- Adding a Callback
- Testing HelloConversationAsync
- Buffering a Callback
- Timeout Parameters
- Cleaning Up After Your Conversation Ends

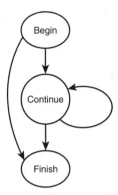

FIGURE 4.1   The lifecycle of a conversation.

The entire body of the communication is known in WebLogic as a conversation. A conversation is directly analogous to a session, but to differentiate from HTTP sessions, BEA chooses to call them conversations. Throughout the conversation WebLogic maintains the values, and keeps information gathered in the conversation grouped together for you.

A Two-Stage Conversation

The most basic conversation you can have with a service is one that simply has two steps. To do this we will rewrite the HelloWorld listing to take place over two operations. The first operation will obtain the name of the caller. The second will provide the actual greeting.

Starting a Conversation

Any message that the client sends to the server can start a conversation with the server. Begin by creating a new file. The file will be a Web service called HelloConversation. Add a method called setName.

Next, classify the method as the start of the conversation. To do this, click on the arrow that represents the setName message (for example, the arrow pointing to the setName hyperlink). On the right side of the screen, you should see a panel labeled "Properties – setName." In the Properties list there is an item labeled conversation. Select the conversation and change the phase to start. As you can see in Figure 4.2, when you change the phase to start, WLW will place an S icon on the operations arrow. The S indicates that a conversation is started when this operation is called.

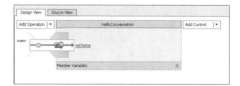

FIGURE 4.2   The S indicates that the conversation is started.

NOTE

If you have the message selected, you can jump to the Conversational Phase combo box by clicking on the `Make this method participate in a conversation` link in the Tasks panel, or the `Change the conversation phase of this method` link if the method is already part of a conversation.

Declaring a Class Variable

This time instead of simply passing the name back as part of the greeting, you are going to "save" the value. You are going to set the value up as a class value. To do this you must first declare a class member variable, also known as a *field*. Member variables are available across all methods. To add the variable, you need to right-click on the Member Variables area at the bottom of the `HelloConversation` box. Add a new variable called `name` and set the Type to String as shown in Figure 4.3.

FIGURE 4.3   Add the name variable.

Edit the Method

The next step is to edit the `setName` method. Click on the `setName` link. Alter the signature of the method to take the name as a parameter just as you did in Chapter 3, "Building an Application in WebLogic Workshop." Then assign the member variable to the value that the client provides. The method should now look like this:

```
/**
 * Start the conversation by stating your name
 * @jws:operation
 * @jws:conversation phase="start"
 */
public void setName(String yourName)
{
    name= yourName;
}
```

CAUTION

If you have a method variable with the same name as a class member variable, everywhere you use the variable name within the method, it will refer to the method variable.

When this happens, you can refer to the class variable using the `this` value. Consider the following example:

```
public class HelloConversation
{
    public String name;

    /** @jws:context */
    weblogic.jws.control.JwsContext context;

    /**
     * @jws:operation
     * @jws:conversation phase="start"
     */
    public void setName(String name)
    {
    //This will do nothing, it just reassigns the variable to itself.
    name = name;

    //this will assign the class member to the variable
        this.name=name;
    }
}
```

In this case, when you just use `name`, it is just referring to the variable that was passed into the method. You need to say `this.name` to refer to the class member.

Workshop JavaDoc Variables

When you look at the source for the method, you may have noticed the addition of a JavaDoc comment above the method, which reads:

```
* @jws:conversation phase="start"
```

Workshop uses this comment to indicate that the method is the start of a conversation. The three valid phases are start, continue, and finish.

Continuing a Conversation

After a conversation is started, the server will create a conversation session, which will hold the state variables for that conversation. As part of that session WebLogic will maintain an instance of the HelloConversation as something called an Enterprise JavaBean (EJB). With the EJB mechanism, WebLogic will make sure that the name variable (and its value) is available throughout the conversation. Each different conversation session has its own instance of name and each is guaranteed to get the correct version.

To see an example of using the name value, add another method to the HelloConversation. This time call the method getGreeting and set the conversation phase to be continue. Notice that Workshop has placed an icon with the letter C on the operations arrow.

When you use the continue phase, you are indicating to the Workshop that you want getGreeting to be part of the original conversation. This will mean that getGreeting will have access to the same instance of the name variable as the setName method.

Edit the method to read as follows:

```
/**
 * @jws:operation
 * @jws:conversation phase="continue"
 */
public String getGreeting()
{
    return "Hello there "+name;
}
```

Finishing a Conversation

After all the communication has taken place between the client and the server, it is important to end the conversation. This will tell WebLogic that it can free the conversation and all the resources that have been allocated to it. As a result, it's important to make sure that you always have a finish method.

Create a third method called goodBye and set the conversation phase to finish. You will notice that Workshop has placed an icon with the letter F on the operations arrow as shown in Figure 4.4.

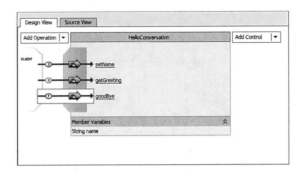

FIGURE 4.4   A conversation with all three phases.

Edit the goodBye method to return a salutation, and the whole class should now look like Listing 4.1.

LISTING 4.1   HelloConversation.jws

```
public class HelloConversation
{
    /**
     * The name of the caller
     */
    public String name;

    /** @jws:context */
    weblogic.jws.control.JwsContext context;

    /**
     * Start the conversation by stating your name
     * @jws:operation
     * @jws:conversation phase="start"
     */
    public void setName(String yourName)
    {
        name= yourName;
    }

    /**
     * Get a friendly greeting
     * @jws:operation
```

LISTING 4.1   Continued

```
     * @jws:conversation phase="continue"
     */
    public String getGreeting()
    {
        return "Hello there " + name;
    }

    /**
     * Say goodbye and finish the conversation
     * @jws:operation
     * @jws:conversation phase="finish"
     */
    public String goodBye()
    {
        return "Good bye for now "+name;
    }
}
```

Testing HelloConversation

Now it's time to run your new Web service. When you run the service, enter your name and click the setName button.

This time when the results come back you will see an additional link labeled Continue this conversation in the upper left corner as shown in Figure 4.5. If you click on the Conversation ID field, it will also take you to the continuation form.

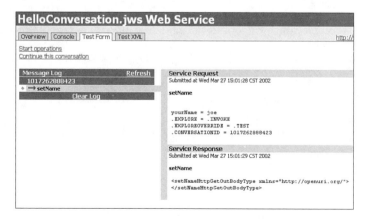

FIGURE 4.5   Click the Continue this conversation link.

You will also notice that this time there is a large number listed in the message log. This number is the conversation ID for the conversation. As you create more conversations (by running the setName operation), the list will continue to grow.

Continuing the Conversation

When you click on the Continue this conversation link, as shown in Figure 4.6, you will have the other two operations available to you.

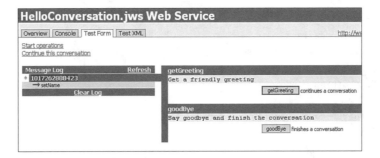

FIGURE 4.6   Continuing the operation.

Go ahead and click on the getGreeting link, and you will see predictable results. You can continue to repeat the cycle of clicking on Continue and getGreeting to get as many greetings as you would like.

Finishing the Conversation

When you have had enough "hellos," you can finish the conversation and click on goodBye.

Now that the conversation has finished, WebLogic will free all the resources it was holding for your session. You will not be able to call getGreeting or goodBye any longer.

Begin a New Conversation

If you want to have a new conversation with the service, you can do so by clicking on the Start operations link. As you can see in Figure 4.7, because the conversation is occurring inside a session, your new conversation is grouped under a new SessionID heading.

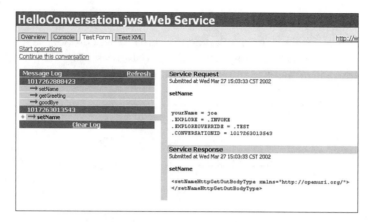

FIGURE 4.7   Each new conversation gets a new SessionID.

Why Is Asynchronous Activity Different from Synchronous Activity?

When most developers look at building applications, they naturally think of applications in terms of synchronous activity. In a synchronous environment, you send a message and receive the response back all in one continuous timeline.

The key difference between asynchronous and synchronous activity is the fact that, in an asynchronous conversation, the timeline between the request and the response are completely independent. In addition, you're not necessarily guaranteed of the order of the responses to multiple requests.

One of the key differences between standard programming practices and Web services is that often responses cannot, or should not, be synchronous. Frequently you want a client to be able to say to the server, "when you have some free time, could you look up the history of the world and send me a synopsis?" If this type of activity had to occur synchronously, the client would effectively need to sit around waiting for the server's answer.

If this was a Web site, that might be exactly what you want to have happen. A user is unlikely to be willing to wait until tomorrow for a Web page to show up. Many applications that access Web services aren't so impatient.

Applications think in terms of multiple threads and processes. They tend to want to do many things at once. They are usually not concerned about which pieces of the puzzle get placed first, so long as in the end all the pieces get assembled.

Diagrams of Synchronous Activity Versus Asynchronous Activity

In Figure 4.8 you see a diagram of asynchronous and synchronous activity. Notice that in the synchronous environment the client always knows what state the server is in. In the asynchronous example the client cannot be certain.

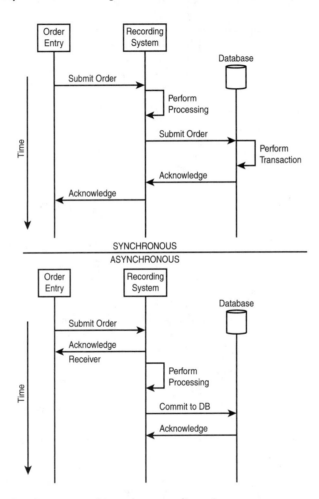

FIGURE 4.8   Synchronous and asynchronous discussions.

A Political Debate as an Example

To understand the difference between synchronous and asynchronous, it's helpful to think about it in terms of human conversation. Most conversations that people have are asynchronous. The two people can speak at any time and interrupt each other at will.

To think of a synchronous conversation, you have to be a bit creative. One example is a political debate.

For purposes of illustration, think of a debate between two different candidates. As in Figure 4.9 you can see that there are really three actors, the two candidates and a moderator.

Each candidate has a period of time to talk and then the moderator gives the "floor" to the next candidate for an equal amount of time. Both of the candidates agree beforehand on a moderator and a format for the communication. Key to all debate, however, is that only one candidate is speaking at a time. The key to making this synchronous is that somebody is controlling the flow of the conversation, namely the moderator.

Appropriate Situations to Use Asynchrony

WebLogic Workshop defines two different development modes for synchronous and asynchronous activity. The HelloConversation example you built earlier in the chapter was a synchronous version. Another version of HelloConversation can be developed asynchronously.

In the asynchronous solution the response from the server might come immediately, but it might just as easily come in five hours. Like the situation with email, the asynchronous pattern allows the client to say "okay, whenever you get around to it, can you say Hello?"

FIGURE 4.9   The players in a debate.

Limitations and Advantages

Before you start building applications using the asynchronous pattern, you should first consider advantages and limitations inherent in the asynchronous pattern.

Advantages

The advantages to using an asynchronous pattern to develop your Web service are primarily based on the fact that neither the server nor the client needs the conversation to be immediately interactive.

NOTE

Typical development environments require considerable design and hand-coding to take advantage of asynchronous communications. WebLogic Workshop simplifies development by eliminating the need to code for multithreaded processes during asynchronous communication and by creating fairly seamless communication processes.

Clients Don't Have to Wait

When the client knows that the server might not respond right away, the client will be developed to go along its merry way and continue doing other things while the server ponders the request. This is ideal when the processing work on the server is bound to take a while.

This also means that the client can ask the server to start working on a piece of the problem before the client has its act together. For instance, let's assume that you are building a system that interacts between a manufacturer, whom we'll call FooBars, Inc., and its parts supplier, Washers On the World (WOW).

During the week FooBars is constantly consuming washers and reordering as soon as their supply gets low. The problem is that FooBars is never sure if WOW will have enough or when the washers will be delivered.

You are going to construct a new Web service that allows FooBars to order washers, and WOW will notify FooBars about the progress of their shipment interactively.

In this situation, if the application at FooBars had to wait for the updates from WOW, it would be waiting an awfully long time. Instead FooBars will simply issue the order and receive asynchronous updates from WOW.

More Transport Protocols Available

Another advantage of designing your service using an asynchronous protocol is that it opens up more protocols for you to use. In particular you can use JMS (Java Messaging System), which just queues up messages and delivers them whenever a client is ready for them. This allows you to set up your system so that the applications do not even need to be directly interactive.

An executive at FooBars can place an order while he's on the airplane and the order will go into his "outbox." He'll actually transmit the order the next time he connects to the network.

Alternatively, FooBars might be tracking the progress of the washers coming into the factory. The executive can still receive the updates from WOW, even if his laptop isn't connected when WOW sends the update. He'll just pick up the status operations when he gets on the ground.

Limitations

The advantages of asynchronous communication do not come without a cost. Not all applications should be developed using an asynchronous pattern due to some equally weighty limitations.

Not Supported by All Web Service Platforms

Probably the most important limitation of asynchronous operations is that not all Web service platforms support the asynchronous operations at this time. Supporting the asynchronous communication is not difficult, but the methods for maintaining a conversation are not standardized. As a result, consumers of your Web service might have to do a fair number of tasks to create their own support for the conversation ID and other issues related to asynchrony.

If the consumers of your Web service are not using Workshop, the first requirement they will have to deal with is the ability to create the equivalent of a SessionID. Workshop passes these values in `conversationID` and `callbackID` elements in its operations. So it's perfectly legitimate to document this information and pass it along to your clients. Nonetheless, it does create a point of failure if your clients fail to implement it correctly.

The more difficult requirement is that your clients will have to maintain the `conversation ID` in a way that allows them to connect up the different messages from the server. This is similar to what you need to do in a synchronous conversation, but a key difference exists: In the synchronous communication everything is happening in a single thread. So maintaining the value is simple. You can have a method that looks like the following pseudocode:

```
{
    Results values = HelloConversation.setName("Joe");
    String salutation = HelloConversation.getGreeting(values.getConversationID());
}
```

Notice that there is no complex programming required to connect the conversation IDs together.

Clients Usually Must Be Multithreaded

One of the advantages of asynchronous dialog is that you can send individual operations whenever and however often you like. Unfortunately this is also a limitation. Sending operations without any timing means that in order for the client to function correctly, it usually must be multithreaded. The only exception is if the client acts as if the operations are synchronous and waits around for each message. Although this is possible, it is not very effective.

The problem with the demand on the client to be multithreaded is that not all programmers are comfortable working in a multithreaded environment. Even the majority of Java developers are not truly efficient with all the issues of multithreaded programming. You need to recognize that you are creating an added burden on their programs as well.

Blocking Responses Are Difficult

Sometimes a client really needs to wait until it receives the response from the server. In this case asynchronous communication is simply not effective. For instance, if you were creating a gas pump purchasing system, you might need to wait for the credit card to be verified before allowing the gas to be pumped. In this case the client program (the pump) is forced to create a series of monitors and controls to handle multithreaded processing when, in reality, it buys the client nothing because it can't do anything while it's waiting to receive the authorization.

Fortunately, if the client is using Workshop the entire process will be completely seamless to them.

What Makes HelloConversation Synchronous?

Before we continue, it's important that even the setName method of HelloConversation is in fact a synchronous method. This is because the client will always receive a response from the server only after the server has finished the body of the setName method. Take a look at the upper sequence diagram in Figure 4.10; it shows how the server is completing the activity of setting the name value prior to sending back an acknowledgement to the client.

In the case of the HelloConversation class, the effect of waiting until the setName function has been processed is pretty minor. The real overhead actually comes from the time it takes WebLogic to create a new instance of HelloConversation, and even that time is very small. The impact really comes when setName is performing a long-running task. For instance, imagine that you had a very long loop included in the setName function.

In an asynchronous response the server will respond immediately to the client. It is acknowledging that it has received the client's request and will continue with the processing. This is illustrated in the lower sequence diagram of Figure 4.10.

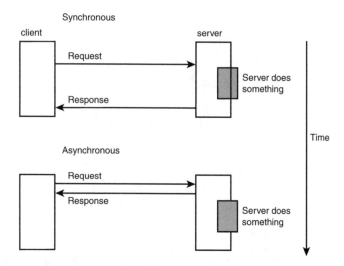

FIGURE 4.10   Synchronized and asynchronous responses to the client.

HelloConversation as an Asynchronous Conversation

To make a method respond asynchronously, you need to tell WebLogic to acknowledge the receipt of the request immediately. This is done by adding a buffer to the message. When a method is buffered, WebLogic will actually respond to the client before it even starts to process the method. Don't worry—WebLogic will guarantee that the method gets called.

Creating a Buffered Message

Start by creating a new Web service called HelloConversationAsync, and add a method called getGreeting, which starts a conversation.

This time make getGreeting a buffered message. To do this, first click on the arrow for the getGreeting method.

Then click on the link labeled "Buffer this method so that it returns to the service immediately".

Alternatively, you can also buffer the method by changing the Message-Buffer values in the Properties panel.

Now that you have buffered the image, as in Figure 4.11, you will notice the little spring icon added to the message arrow. The icon signifies that the message has been buffered.

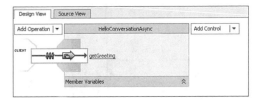

FIGURE 4.11   Message buffers are indicated by a spring icon.

Buffer JavaDoc Comments

If you look at the source for getGreeting, you will see that Workshop has added a new JavaDoc comment to the code. The new comment looks like this:

```
@jws:message-buffer enable="true"
```

The new comment is how Workshop is maintaining the buffered state. As you become more familiar with Workshop, you can also specify that a message is buffered by just adding this JavaDoc comment to any method.

Adding a Callback

A buffered message must not attempt to return a value to the client. The return type must be void. This is because if the method is buffered, WebLogic returns back to the client right away and has no way to know what it would return.

To get the value back to the client, there are two approaches. The first is to use the same technique you used in HelloConversation with the client polling the server for a response (by clicking the getGreeting button). This is not a very practical approach most of the time because you don't want the client to have to actively search for the information. Instead you want the server to send the response back to the client directly. This type of method is called a *callback*. Callbacks function exactly the same way that standard methods do, with one major exception. When you execute a method on a callback, the method is being called on the client, not on the server.

To add a callback, click on the Add Operations combo box and select Add Callback. This will cause a new operation to be added just like the Add Method. This time, however, the message arrow points from the service out to the client. Change the name of the method to sendGreeting just as you would change a method name. In addition, make the method part of the conversation and set the phase to finish.

Changing the Parameters of the Callback

Right now the sendGreeting method doesn't allow you to pass any information. Because you want the sendGreeting to actually send the same greeting to the client they would have gotten from the HelloConversation example, you need to edit the parameters. To do this, right-click on the sendGreeting link and select Edit Maps and Interface.

Your goal now is to change the signature of the method so that you can pass in the greeting as a parameter. The Edit Maps and Interface dialog box serves two purposes. The first is to allow you to change the nature of the XML that is passed back and forth from the client to the server. You will learn more about this in Chapter 8, "Creating a Map." For now you are only concerned about the Java field. Edit the method as shown in Figure 4.12.

FIGURE 4.12   Change the signature of the callback method.

Editing the Callback Manually

You can also edit the callback code manually. Editing the callback is a bit less straightforward than editing the method signatures as you have done up until now. This is because the actual code representation of the callback is as an interface (see Appendix A, "Java Essentials," if you are not familiar with Java). The callback interface serves to give your service a "view" to the client, but there is no code there for you to edit.

To get to the callback interface, right-click on the callback method and select Go to Code. You can also just switch to the Source view directly. At the top of the class you will see an Interface called Callback declared. At this time Callback will have one method, namely the sendGreeting method. All you have to do is change the signature to reflect the String being passed in.

```
public interface Callback
{
    public void sendGreeting(String greeting);
}
```

Calling the Callback Method

The last step to finishing the HelloConversationAsync is to actually call the callback method. In the next chapter you will learn how to use more interesting constructs. However, for now what we'll do is just put the call directly in the getGreeting method.

If you look at the code for the entire HelloConversationAsync class, you will notice that Workshop has added a member variable called callback. The callback variable is your handle to the client. To execute sendGreeting() on the client, you simply need to add the following line to the getGreeting() method.

```
callback.sendGreeting("Hello, World!");
```

> **NOTE**
>
> If the getGreeting() method had not been buffered, WebLogic would not allow you to call sendGreeting from the getGreeting() method. This is because only one message can be transacted at a time. You must finish sending a response to the request *prior* to sending a new message.
>
> This is legal in this situation: Because the method is buffered, WebLogic responded to the client before the method even begins processing. If you attempted to call sendGreeting in the getGreeting method, the code will compile, but when you actually execute the call to the method, you will get an error in the response.

At this point the only thing that the getGreeting() method will do is immediately turn around and issue the method call back to the client. To make life a little bit more interesting, you can add a loop in the method. The loop serves no purpose other than to "tie up" the server for a little bit during the getGreeting method. In the end your entire class will look like Listing 4.2.

LISTING 4.2 `HelloConversationAsync`

```
public class HelloConversationAsync
{

    public Callback callback;

    public interface Callback
    {
        /**
         * @jws:conversation phase="finish"
         */
        public void sendGreeting(String greeting);
    }
    /** @jws:context */
    weblogic.jws.control.JwsContext context;

    /**
     * @jws:operation
     * @jws:message-buffer enable="true"
     * @jws:conversation phase="start"
     */
    public void getGreeting()
    {
        //this will concatonate 's' onto a string 20,000 times.
        //depending on your machine it should take about a second.
        String dummyString = "s";
        for (int x=0;x<20000;x++){
            dummyString = dummyString + "s";
        }
        callback.sendGreeting("Hello, World!");
    }
}
```

Testing HelloConversationAsync

Now that you have HelloConversation finished, it's time to take it out for a whirl. Build the code and run it just as you have before. This time when you click on the getGreeting button, you will notice that the results are essentially like the results you saw with HelloConversation. This time, however, there is no way for you to continue the conversation manually.

Refreshing the List

Because the server acknowledged the receipt of the `getGreeting` message prior to actually sending out a response, the greeting doesn't appear in your message log yet. To get it to appear, click the `Refresh` link. If you've waited long enough, the list should now look like Figure 4.13. Notice that there are now two messages, and the `callback.sendGreeting` message appears with an arrow pointing to the left indicating that it was sent to the client. If you click on `callback.sendGreeting`, you will see the message digest sent from the client containing your greeting.

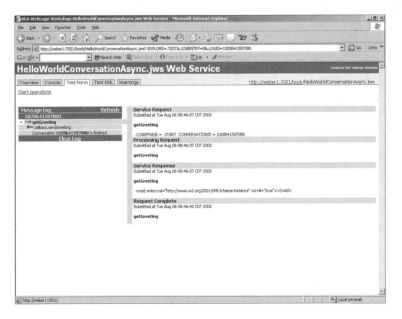

FIGURE 4.13 Two-way communication in the text platform.

Buffering a Callback

It might not have occurred to you, but you can also buffer a callback. When you buffer a callback, your service is able to continue functioning at full speed even while the message is being delivered to the client. This avoids the roundtrip costs associated with the transaction. It also is more reliable. With the callback buffered, WebLogic is responsible for ensuring that the message gets delivered. If the client is down or busy, a callback would normally fail. If the callback is buffered, however, WebLogic will resend the message to the client until it is delivered.

Timeout Parameters

Conversations do not (or should not) live indefinitely. The Web, like applications in general, is volatile and there is nothing you can do to guarantee that the client will always finish the conversation gracefully by calling one of your finish methods.

To avoid this situation, it's important to specify timeout parameters. WebLogic Workshop has two different timeout values you can control. When the timeout is reached, WebLogic will expire the conversation, and it will no longer be accessible.

Defining the Entire Lifetime of a Conversation

You can specify the maximum amount of time that you are going to allow the conversation to take. This is the maximum time from when the client first sends a request to the server to the time that the last message must be received by. Typically you want this to be a fairly long time.

To set the timeout parameters, click on the class in the Design view (for example, on the HelloConversationAsync box). In the Properties panel you should see an item labeled `conversation-lifetime`. You can set the value for the entire lifetime of the conversation by changing the `max-age` parameter. When you do this, Workshop will add a JavaDoc to the class, which looks like this:

```
@jws:conversation-lifetime max-age="2 days"
```

See Chapter 5, "Controls," for a complete listing of how to specify time in Workshop.

Defining the Idle Timeout Values

The second type of timeout that WebLogic observes is the idle timeout. The idle timeout specifies the maximum amount of time that can occur between messages—in other words, the maximum amount of time between when a client sends one message and the time it sends the next one (or the server sends out a message). The idle time can be changed by setting the `max-idle-time` value and will result in Workshop adding the following JavaDoc tag.

```
@jws:conversation-lifetime max-idle-time="2 minutes"
```

Note that the `max-idle-time` and the `max-age` appear on the same tag if both values are set.

Changing the Timeout Values in Code

The values that you specify in the parameter list via the JavaDoc comment are initial values for the timeout. There are times when you want to change these values temporarily. For instance, you might have a particular message sequence that you know will take an unusually long time.

Setting the Idle Time

To handle this situation, you can change the timeout values programmatically. If you look at the top of the source for the class, you will see that there is a variable called context. The context variable is the variable that WebLogic uses to control the information about an individual conversation.

To set the maximum idle time to five minutes, use either of the following. In the second example, you are specifying the idle time in seconds.

```
context.setMaxIdleTime("5 minutes");
```

```
context.setMaxIdleTime(300);
```

You can also obtain the current idle time by calling

```
long seconds = context.getMaxIdleTime();
```

You can also reset the idle clock manually by calling

```
context.resetIdleTime()
```

Setting Maximum Age

To change the maximum age value of the context, you can either specify the time as a string:

```
context.setMaxAge("1 day");
```

Or you can create a date object that corresponds to the time you want the maxAge to end by:

```
        long TIME_IN_MS_IN_AVG_DAY = 86400000;
        Date endDate = new Date(System.currentTimeMillis() +
TIME_IN_MS_IN_AVG_DAY);
        context.setMaxAge(endDate);
```

Please note that in order to use the Date class, you must add an import to the top of the class:

```
import java.util.Date;
```

Cleaning Up After Your Conversation Ends

When a conversation ends, it is important that you clean up the mess that the conversation created. You want to leave a nice clean environment for the next set of conversations.

Creating an `onFinish()` Method

Whenever a conversation finishes, either because a `finish` message was sent or because one of the conversation timeout values was exceeded, WebLogic will unload the context and its members. Before it unloads the conversation, it will first attempt to call the `onFinish()` method.

Not all classes must have an `onFinish()` method, but those that tie up additional resources should. For instance, if you are opening a database connection manually or otherwise creating resource handles, it is a good idea to close them gracefully.

One unique thing about the `onFinish` method is that its name is not constant. The name of the `onFinish` method is actually based on the context. It must be `context_onFinish` where `context` is replaced with the name of the `context` variable. Ordinarily the `onFinish` method will actually be `context_onFinish()`, but there are times when this will change.

PART II

Building Applications in WebLogic Workshop

IN THIS PART

5 Controls

6 The Database Control

7 Debugging

5

Controls

One of the major concepts in Workshop is the idea of a control. A control is any external set of operations (like another Web service) that you can access from Workshop. Controls make programming your services even easier, because they look and act as if your service is a client to the control.

Using a Timer

One of the simplest controls is the timer control. The idea with the timer control is to be able to schedule activity for some time in the future, possibly recurring every once in a while. The timer works like an alarm clock. For instance, if you wanted to push the latest price of a stock out to your client every minute, you can user a timer to trigger the push.

In Chapter 4, "Developing Conversant Applications," you built the asynchronous `HelloConversationAsync` application. That application wasn't all that interesting because it simply allowed you to perform some long-running function during the `getGreeting` method. In this section you will take that concept one step further. Instead of just performing some long-running function, this time you will intentionally delay the whole process for 5 seconds.

Creating `HelloDelayed`

Begin by creating a class called `HelloDelayed`. Add a method called `getGreeting` and a callback called `sendGreeting (String msg)` just as you did in the previous chapter. Be sure to make them both part of a conversation. This time, however, don't put anything in the body of `getGreeting()` yet; you'll do that later in the next couple of sections.

IN THIS CHAPTER

- Using a Timer
- Creating HelloDelayed
- Testing HelloDelayed
- Stopping the Timer
- Defining a Timer Control in Code
- Adjusting Timing Defaults Programmatically
- Restarting the Timer
- Obtaining Time at Event
- Broadcast Date Example
- HelloWorld as a Service
- Handling Callbacks from CTRLs

Adding the Timer Control

On the right side of the `HelloDelayed` service box is a combo box labeled Add
Control. From that menu, select Add Timer Control as shown in Figure 5.1.

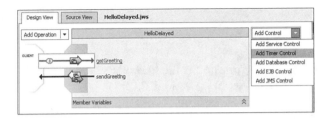

FIGURE 5.1   Adding a timer control.

Adding a timer will cause the Create Timer Control dialog box to appear. This dialog
box has three fairly intuitive values. The first value is the name of the control. This
name will correspond to the variable name that the control will be given in the
source code. For this instance, name the timer control `delayedTimer`.

The second and third values correspond to values specific to the timer control. As
you have no doubt guessed, the `timeout-in` value tells Workshop how long to wait
from the time you start the timer to the time that it will fire. The `repeats-every`
value tells the timer to time out again and again at the specified interval period. In
this case both values have been set to be 10 seconds.

After you click the Create button (or press Enter), you will see the timer control
added to the right of the `HelloDelayed` box. As in Figure 5.2, you can see that there
are message arrows for all of the exposed methods of the timer control, just as the
arrows exist from the `CLIENT` box and the `HelloDelayed` box. With controls, arrows
pointing to the right are methods that you can call, and arrows to the left are
methods that `Timer` expects `HelloDelayed` to implement.

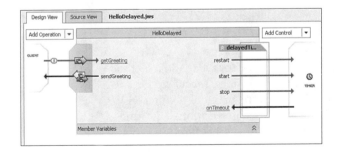

FIGURE 5.2   A timer control added to the service.

Starting the Timer

In `HelloDelayed` you want to start the timer each time the client calls the `getGreeting` method. Edit the code of the `getGreeting` method to start the timer by calling the `start()` method on `delayedTimer`.

```
/**
 * Call this method to get HelloDelayed to send you a greeting.  After
 * calling getGreeting you will receive a greeting from HelloDelayed
 * every 10 seconds (asynchronously).
 * @jws:operation
 * @jws:conversation phase="start"
 */
public void getGreeting()
{
    delayedTimer.start();
}
```

Defining `onTimeout`

The timer is now set to fire every 10 seconds after the client sends the `getGreeting` message. When the timer fires, it sends a message along the `onTimeout` path marked by the arrow pointing back at the service. The result is to make a call to an `onTimeout` service method in HelloDelayed. To add HelloDelayed's `onTimeout` method, switch back to the Design view and click on the `onTimeout` link that the timer's arrow is pointing to.

In this case, from the timer's perspective, the `onTimeout` method is a callback method. To support this, HelloDelayed must implement an `onTimeout` method for the `delayedTimer` to call. To create the method, click on the timer's callback method (the `onTimeout` hyperlink located inside HelloDelayed). Clicking on the callback will cause Workshop to add the new method to the `HelloDelayed` class to service messages from the timer.

When the timer fires, you want to send the greeting back to the client. You can accomplish this with HelloDelayed's callback method, just as you did in Chapter 4.

```
private void delayedTimer_onTimeout(long time)
{
    callback.sendGreeting("Hello, World");
}
```

Notice that the method that's created is actually called `delayedTimer_onTimeout`. Workshop names the callback for controls based on the name of the control. This allows you to have two timers, one called `delayedTimer`, and another called `oneHourTimer`. Each timer will call a different method when its callback is fired.

Testing HelloDelayed

To test the HelloDelayed service, switch to the test mode by running the service. After you run the HelloDelayed service, click on the getGreeting button. Initially you will have just a single getGreeting link in the message log. However, if you wait a little while and click the Refresh link, you will see the sendGreeting message appear below the getGreeting link. If you continue to click on Refresh, you will see that the messages continue coming every 10 seconds.

NOTE

If you never receive the greeting, it is probably because you did not make the getGreeting and sendGreeting messages part of a conversation.

NOTE

If you see only one message, remember to click the Refresh link. If that still doesn't work, check two things. First, make sure that the conversational state of sendGreeting is set to continue. If it is set to finish, the first call to sendGreeting will end the conversation (more on this in the next section). Second, check to make sure that you included a repeat value on the timer. To verify this, go to delayedTimer's declaration and verify that the line reads:

```
* @jws:timer timeout="10s" repeats-every="10s"
```

If the repeats-every="10s" portion is missing, the timer is set to fire only once.

Stopping the Timer

You have probably noticed that there is one rather large flaw with HelloDelayed as it stands right now. The flaw is that the service will never stop sending out messages to the client and the client has no way to stop this activity.

To solve this problem, you need to add another method to the service. The new method will have a conversation phase of finish, and will stop the timer. For the sake of simplicity, just add another method called stop, which should look like this:

```
/**
 * @jws:operation
 * @jws:conversation phase="finish"
 */
public void stop()
{
    delayedTimer.stop();
}
```

The next time you test the HelloDelayed service, you will see another continuation method called Stop. Executing Stop will cancel the inflow of new greetings.

Defining a Timer Control in Code

Like everything in WebLogic Workshop, timers can be created manually in code as well as by using the Design view. To do this, you need to add a new weblogic.jws.control.TimerControl variable to the class with some additional JavaDoc tags.

In general, to declare the timer you use the following format:

```
/**
 * @jws:control
 * @jws:timer
 *      timeout="5 s"
 *      repeats-every="5 s"
 *      coalesce-events=true
 */
TimerControl timer;
```

> **NOTE**
>
> When using a TimerControl, make sure you've imported weblogic.jws.control.TimerControl into the class.

The @control Tag

The first tag (@jws:control) tells Workshop that the timer is a control. All controls regardless of what type they are will have the @jws:control tag. The tag does three things for you:

- It tells Workshop to display the timer as a control in the Design view.
- It tells Workshop to create all the underlying plumbing to connect the control up to its source.
- Without the tag, calls to the control will result in a null pointer because the timer will never be initialized.

The @jws:timer Tag

The second tag (@jws:timer) tells Workshop the nature of the timer it should instantiate for the timer object. The values timeout, repeats-every, and coalesce-events detail how the timer should behave.

The `timeout` value specifies how long the timer should wait from the time you start the timer to when it will fire.

Specifying Time in Workshop

WebLogic Workshop tries to make specifying time fairly easy. Time is generally specified by an integer followed by the name of the time period, a letter that starts the time period, or a series of letters (all case insensitive). For instance, to specify 5 seconds you can write:

```
"5 s"
"5 Sec"
"5 seconds"
```

or even

```
"5 SeCoN"
```

Workshop is smart enough to figure out that you mean 5 seconds in all four cases.

The valid time units are

- Years

- Months

- Days

- Hours

- Minutes

- Seconds

Unfortunately, because you can truncate the units down to their first letter, there is some ambiguity in the letter M. Does it mean minutes or months? WebLogic solves this two ways. First, by itself m means months. However, if you place the letter t before the time, it becomes minutes. Consider the following examples:

`"5 m"` is equivalent to "5 months"

`"t5 m"` is equivalent to "5 minutes"

In addition, if you place the letter P before the time unit, the whitespace between the number (5) and the type (seconds) must be removed, and the time must be written in the form p#y#m#d#t#h#m#s. So you can also write 5 days and 5 seconds like this:

```
"p0y0m5dt0h5m0s"
```

Getting the Timer to Fire Immediately

Sometimes it is useful to get the timer to fire immediately. Usually you would do this just to facilitate some asynchronous activity that doesn't really need a delay. If you want the timer to fire right away, you can set it to 0 seconds.

```
"0 seconds"
```

Repeated Firing

The second option of the timer tag is the `repeats-every` value, and it is optional. The `repeats-every` value indicates how often the timer should continue to fire (if at all) after it fires the first time. For instance, if you want to periodically send status messages to the client, you can have the timer repeat every 20 seconds. The `repeats-every` value specifies only the amount of time to wait after the first fire.

Coalesce of Events

The final value of the `@timer` tag is called `coalesce-events`. What `coalesce-events` does is specify whether or not each time the timer fires the event should be guaranteed to be processed, or if any of the event is missed, should that event and the subsequent event just be treated as one.

Here's how this works: Let's assume that you have a timer set up to fire every 3 seconds. Each time the timer fires, the service will perform a database query and send the current results to the client. Occasionally, because the database takes too long, the process takes longer than 3 seconds. When the timer fires during the query, the service is busy, so the timer can't actually send a message to the service. The new `onTimeout` message instead gets differed (queued up). If the query actually takes 7 seconds, the sequence will work like this:

- At time 0, the timer fires the first event, and the database query starts.

- At time 3 seconds, the timer fires again, but the service is busy, so the event gets differed.

- At time 6 seconds, the timer fires a third time; the service is still busy, so this event gets differed as well.

- At time 7 seconds, the query finishes and the service accepts the first event.

Here's where coalescing comes in: When the message is differed, you can tell the timer to do one of two things. First you can make each timeout cause an event. In the case of an "every 3 seconds" timer, that means that if 7 seconds transpire there will always be two events. However, if you are coalescing events, the timer will instead function like this:

At time 7 seconds, Workshop will look at the fact that you have two events queued, but they are allowed to coalesce. Therefore it will process the onTimeout method once and consider both events to have been satisfied.

Which option you choose depends on your situation. In the case of the status update it's likely that you really don't care to have a specific number of messages so much as a periodic update. On the other hand sometimes you just want to break up the transaction across time. In that case you certainly don't want to skip a step in the transaction; it's very important to make sure that the same number of messages always get sent. Set the value by adding one of the following;

```
coalesce-events=true
```

```
coalesce-events=false
```

If coalesce-events is not specified (it's optional), it will default to false.

Adjusting Timing Defaults Programmatically

The values specified for the timer in the JavaDoc are the initial default values for the timer. You can still adjust these times programmatically using the timer's methods.

Changing the Timeout Time

The timeout can be changed in one of three ways.

First, the timeout can be changed by calling the setTimeout() method and providing it with a String just as in the JavaDoc:

```
timer.setTimeout("3 minutes 6 seconds");
```

Second, the timeout can be changed by calling the setTimeout() value and just giving it the number of seconds to wait as an integer:

```
timer.setTimeout(186);
```

Finally, you can also specify a specific date and time when the timer should fire by using the setTimeoutAt(Date) method. To do this you need to create a standard Java object called a Date. Creating a Date correctly is a bit tricky. The problem is that there are a surprisingly large number of ways to calculate what time it is. To combat this, Java has another class called a Calendar. Thus the actual code for creating a date involves first obtaining a Calendar object. Let's say that you want to set a timer to fire on January 1, 2005. To do this, use the following code.

First, you need to import the Calendar and Date classes into the service. At the top of the class, add the following:

```
import java.util.Calendar;
import java.util.Date;
```

In the method for which you want to set the date, add the following code:

```
// obtain a Calendar object
Calendar calendar = Calendar.getInstance();
//set the date of the calendar (year, month, date, hour, minute)
calendar.set(2005,1,1,12,30);
//get the date object represented by this calendar
Date time = calendar.getTime();
delayedTimer.setTimeoutAt(time);
```

NOTE

Creating and manipulating dates beyond this point is beyond the scope of this book. If you want to learn more about Calendar, Date, or another useful object called a SimpleDateFormat, you can read Que's *Special Edition Using Java 2 Platform*.

Obtaining Current Timeout

It is often useful to know what the current timeout values are set to. You can obtain the current timeout value by using the getTimeout() method. The timeout will actually be returned as a long number that represents the number of seconds.

You can also obtain the TimeoutAt value (if it has been set) by using the getTimeoutAt() method. If the specific date/time has not been set, this method will return null.

Changing/Obtaining the Repeats-Every Value

Just as with the timeout value, the repeats-every value can be set and obtained programmatically. The following methods mirror the setTimeout methods:

```
void setTimeout(String period)
```

```
void setTimeout(long periodInSeconds)
```

Interestingly, although the getTimeout() method returns the amount of the time as a long, the getRepeatsEvery() method returns the value as a String.

```
String getRepeatsEvery();
```

Toggling Coalesce Events

By default, events are not coalesced. You can set them to be combined by using the `coalesce-events=true` in the timer's JavaDoc tag. You can also toggle the value on and off using the `setCoalesceEvents(boolean)` method:

```
delayedTimer.setCoalesceEvents(true);
```

You can obtain the current coalesce status by calling the `boolean` `getCoalesceEvents()` method as follows:

```
boolean status = delayedTimer.getCoalesceEvents();
```

Restarting the Timer

As you have seen, the time between when the timer is started and the amount of time it will delay after that are independent. The timer could be instructed to wait just 2 seconds before it starts, but wait 10 seconds thereafter.

It is sometimes convenient to tell the timer to restart and fire based on the `timeout` value rather than the `repeats-every` value. To do this, you call `restart()` as in the following:

```
delayedTimer.restart();
```

Obtaining Time at Event

You might have noticed that the `onTimeout` method had a parameter passed into it called `time`. The `time` value can be used to know what time the timer actually fired. The number itself is a number in milliseconds. So if you check the number between two calls, the difference will be the number of milliseconds that have transpired. The specific number will seem rather high. This is because it is actually the number of milliseconds since midnight on January 1, 1970, in UTC time.

Broadcast Date Example

To tie all of this together, you can write a class to broadcast the current date. Using the `time` value in the `onTimeout` method, you can obtain the current time. Just to make the example more fun, you can also reset the timer every other time it fires. If you change the `timeout` and `repeats-every` values to be different, this will result in messages being sent out at different times.

LISTING 5.1   HelloDelayed

```java
import weblogic.jws.control.TimerControl;
import java.util.Date;
import java.util.Calendar;
public class HelloDelayed
{

    /**
     * @jws:control
     * @jws:timer timeout="2 seconds" repeats-every="10 seconds"
     */
    private TimerControl delayedTimer;

    public Callback callback;

    /**
     *  Value to track alternative timeouts of the timer
     */
    boolean onAlternateTimeout = false;

    public interface Callback
    {
        public void sendGreeting(String greeting);
    }
    /** @jws:context */
    weblogic.jws.control.JwsContext context;

/**
     * Call this method to get HelloDelayed to send you a greeting.  After
     * calling getGreeting you will receive a greeting from HelloDelayed
     * every 10 seconds (asynchronously).
     * @jws:operation
     * @jws:conversation phase="start"
     */
    public void getGreeting()
    {
        delayedTimer.start();

    }

    /**
     * Stop receiving new greetings
```

LISTING 5.1   Continued

```
 * @jws:operation
 * @jws:conversation phase="finish"
 */
public void stop()
{
    delayedTimer.stop();
}


/**
 * Method called by timer each time the timer 'fires'
 */
private void delayedTimer_onTimeout(long time)
{
    //Create a new date object at the current time
    Date currentDate = new Date(time);
    //Create the calendar object
    Calendar calendar = Calendar.getInstance();
    //Set the calendar to the current time
    calendar.setTime(currentDate);
    callback.sendGreeting("Hello, World it is now " +calendar);

    //Every other time, restart the timer
    if (onAlternateTimeout){
        delayedTimer.restart();
    }
    //"flip" the onAlternateTimeout value
    onAlternateTimeout = !onAlternateTimeout;
}


}
```

HelloWorld as a Service

Any service you create in WebLogic Workshop can also be used as a service to your application just like the timer control. In Chapter 3 you created the HelloWorld Web service. You can now use this service as part of a new server.

Creating the Control File

In order to use any JWS file as a control in Workshop, you must first create a file called a Control (CTRL) file. The Control file essentially defines the nature of the plumbing needed to interact with the service, such as the methods that can be called and the scope of the methods. All controls with the exception of the timer are implemented in CTRL files.

> **NOTE**
>
> A CTRL file is a proprietary file used in WebLogic Workshop. The CTRL file contains the information necessary to define the public standard WSDL interface. In addition, the CTRL file serves as a Java `interface`, which can be exposed via EJB (and as a Workshop service).

To create the control file for HelloWorld, you can either right-click on the `HelloWorld.jws` file in the Project tree, and select Generate CTRL from JWS, or you can select Generate CTRL from JWS from the Service menu.

Using a CTRL in Another Service

After you create the CTRL, you will find a new icon on the Project tree under the HelloWorld icon, as shown in Figure 5.3. The new icon labeled "HelloWorldControl" represents the CTRL file.

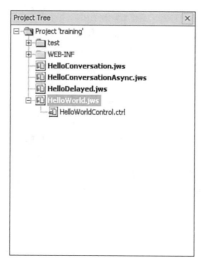

FIGURE 5.3   The CTRL icon.

Drag and Drop from Project Tree

The simplest way to utilize the control file is to drag the CTRL file from the Project tree and drop it onto the Design panel. To try this, declare a new service called `HelloAggregate`. The goal is going to be to simply use the `HelloWorldControl` to provide the return value to the client. This is a simple example of a very powerful technique called aggregation. At a minimum, aggregation allows you to partition the logic of your application. At best it can provide you with significant flexibility in design.

With the `HelloAggregate` class declared, drag and drop the HelloWorldControl icon onto the Design view. As shown in Figure 5.4, Workshop automatically detects the Hello message and provides access from HelloAggregate to HelloWorld's `Hello` method.

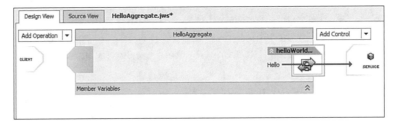

FIGURE 5.4   HelloAggregate with the HelloWorldControl added.

Adding the Control from the Design Panel

In addition to using the drag-and-drop technique, you can also add the HelloWorld control by selecting Add Service Control from the Add Control drop-down list on the Design panel. In the resulting dialog box, you need to first specify the name of the variable you want to use for the control.

From the Add Service Control dialog box, click Browse and select the control file. Normally your Project tree will be much larger than the one displayed, and at that point it might be easier to find the control you are looking for than to use the drag-and-drop mechanism. The results are very similar to the result in Figure 5.4, except that you can provide a variable name for the control using this method. With the drag-and-drop technique, Workshop automatically selects a name for the variable (though you can still change it by modifying the code directly).

Invoking CTRL Methods

Invoking a method on a CTRL object is just as easy as invoking a method on the
`Timer` control. In the case of HelloAggregate, simply add a method called `Hello` and
return the value of `helloWorldControl.Hello()`. The entire listing is shown in
Listing 5.2.

LISTING 5.2 HelloAggregate

```
/**
 * HelloWorld Service which returns results from another Workshop service
 */
public class HelloAggregate
{

    /**
     * @jws:control
     */
    private HelloWorldControl helloWorldControl;
    /** @jws:context */
    weblogic.jws.control.JwsContext context;

    /**
     * Get a nice little salutation
     * @jws:operation
     */
    public String Hello()
    {
        return helloWorldControl.Hello();
    }
}
```

Testing HelloAggregate

Testing HelloAggregate is as simple as testing HelloWorld. The result of running the
HelloAggregate `Hello` method contains a little bit more data. As you can see in
Figure 5.5, clicking the Hello button causes the test view to have an extra node. The
new node is how the test view shows the methods passing from the client to
HelloAggregate and then from HelloAggregate to HelloWorld.

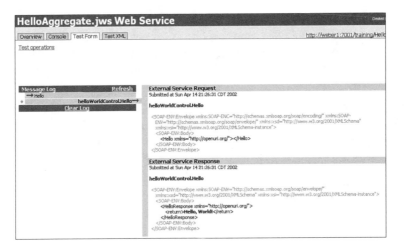

FIGURE 5.5   Aggregate method calls show up in test run.

Including a CTRL in Code

As with the Timer control, it is also possible to include the HelloWorld control by
simply typing the code into the source view. If you look at the declaration of the
helloWorldControl variable in Listing 5.2, it looks like this:

```
/**
 * @jws:control
 */
private HelloWorldControl helloWorldControl;
```

In general the variable is declared much like any other variable in Java, with two key
notable differences:

- The control contains the @jws:control tag in the JavaDoc for the variable.

- The variable is declared for a Java class that does not really exist. The
  HelloWorldControl is actually an interface, which is declared in the CTRL file
  that Workshop automatically generated for you (HelloWorldControl.ctrl).

The @jws:control tag causes Workshop to accomplish two key things for you under
the hood. First, it tells Workshop how and where to obtain the HelloWorldControl
interface (namely from the CTRL file). Second, Workshop will modify the code to cause
it to instantiate a new version of HelloWorldControl, which will be generated by effectively causing HelloWorld to implement HelloWorldControl. This means that although
you don't see it, the code will function similarly to the more traditional Java code:

```
private HelloWorldControl helloWorldControl = new HelloWorld ();
```

Exceptions from CTRL Methods

The designer of a CTRL method can declare that the method will throw an exception, just as any Java method can throw an exception. When the CTRL throws an exception, you are required to catch the exception and handle it or to continue to throw the exception upward.

In addition to the exceptions that the CTRL explicitly declares, the framework that WebLogic places around the CTRL can also cause the method to throw another type of exception. Any CTRL method can throw the exception `weblogic.jws.control.ControlException`. It is not absolutely necessary for you to catch the `ControlException` because it extends from `RuntimeException`. However, if you do not catch the `ControlException` when it is thrown, the service will fail and the exception will be sent back out to the client, which will probably not know what to do with it. As a result, you should consider catching `ControlExceptions` in most cases.

Accessing a CTRL File That Is Not in the Current Package

In the HelloWorldAggregate example, the HelloWorldControl is conveniently placed in the current package. As a result, the code for the class was readily available. In many situations this won't be the case.

If the HelloWorldControl was in a different package, the process would be very similar to the case where it's in the current package. In fact, if you use the drag-and-drop technique and drag the icon from the Project tree to the Design view, Workshop will take care of all the details for you.

If you are hand-coding the use of the service, the only difference is that you need to remember to import the class as well. If you do, the package name is the same as the directory structure of the control file in the project. If you had a service called `ImportService` and it was located in the `test` folder, you would need to add the following `import` statement to utilize the control:

```
import test.ImportServiceControl;
```

Using a CTRL File from a Different Project

When you want to use a CTRL file from a project other than your current one, you must copy the CTRL file from its project. Workshop does not currently have any way to access the CTRL file unless the CTRL is actually within the project.

Fortunately, you can copy the CTRL file to either the directory of the current Web service, or if you'd prefer, you can copy it to a central package and use the techniques discussed in the previous section to import it from that package.

CAUTION

When you copy a CTRL file, you should remember that you are copying the file itself, not a reference to the file. This means that if the original CTRL file changes, the changes will not be reflected in your copy. You can still copy the CTRL file again, but if you fail to do this the changes will not be reflected and you might have issues as a result.

Handling Callbacks from CTRLs

Many services that you will create, such as the HelloWorldAsync class you declared in Chapter 3, "Building an Application in Workshop," and the timer control, have callbacks. In order for your service to handle a callback from the control, it must have a callback handler. You can create a callback handler by clicking on the Callback link in the Design view (as you did for the timer), or you can declare a callback handler method by hand.

A callback handler has the name *variableName_methodName* where *variableName* is the name you gave to the control variable followed by an underscore followed by the name of the callback method.

6

The Database Control

IN THIS CHAPTER

• Creating a Database Control

• Defining a Database Connection

• Creating an SQL String

• Including Variables

• Getting a Result Set

• Executing Multiple Statements

• A Sample Application

Many Web services act as a front end to a database. That is, some Web services simply act as a means to store data in the database and to retrieve it. Other Web services use a database as part of the overall application functionality. In these cases, the database can contain vital application data, but the Web service provides data validation and additional business logic. Because database operations are very common and often tedious, Workshop provides a database control that handles the tedious parts.

Creating a Database Control

To add a database control to your application, select Service, Add Control, and Add Database Control. You will see the Add Database Control dialog box, as shown in Figure 6.1.

As with other controls, you must give the control a variable name and then either specify an existing control, or create a new control. When you create a new control, you must also specify a data source. A data source is a factory for creating JDBC database connections, similar to the JDBC DriverManager class. One of the advantages of a data source is that you can locate it using JNDI, giving you a central place to keep your database URLs. Data sources were introduced as part of Java 2 Enterprise Edition and represent a cleaner way to access database connections.

A data source gets its connections from a JDBC connection pool. A connection pool can keep several database connections open at one time. Without a connection pool, you might encounter delays while the JDBC driver sets up a new connection each time you need one. Because the pool maintains a group of reusable connections, your program is more efficient when allocating a connection.

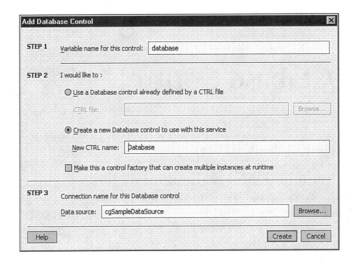

FIGURE 6.1   You can add a database control to handle database access.

Defining a Database Connection

To use the database control, you must define a data source. To define a data source in WebLogic, you must first define a connection pool. The easiest way to define a connection pool is through the WebLogic server console. Figure 6.2 shows the page for creating a connection pool. Notice that you must supply the JDBC connection URL and the JDBC driver class.

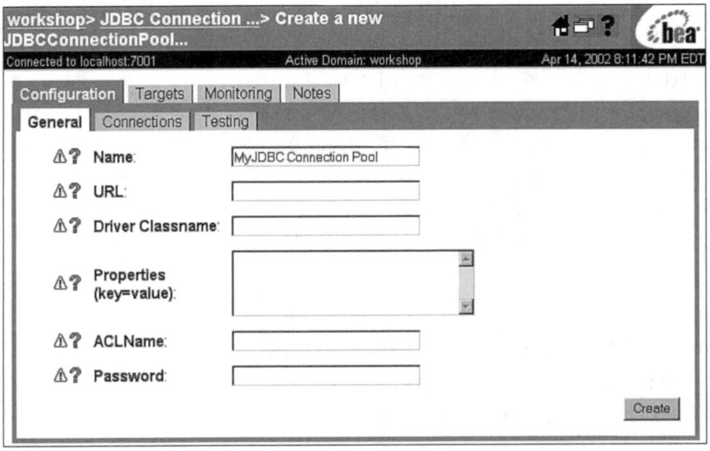

FIGURE 6.2   You can create connection pools using the WebLogic console.

After you create a connection pool, you can create a data source that uses the connection pool. The WebLogic console makes it easy to create connection pools, as shown in Figure 6.3. Simply give the data source a name and enter the name of the connection pool that the data source should use to obtain database connections.

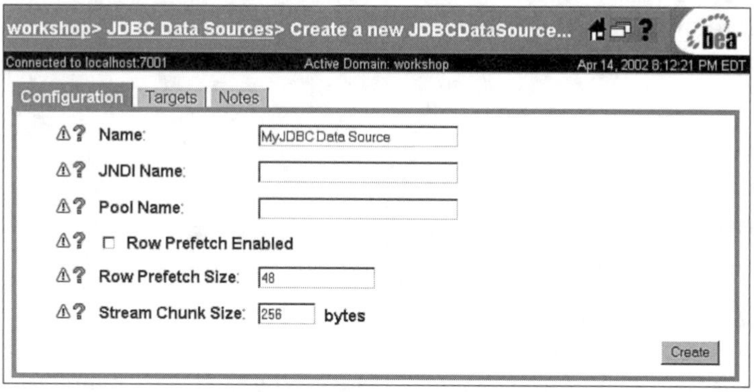

FIGURE 6.3   You can create data sources using the WebLogic console.

The WebLogic samples server includes a sample data source that you can use for test programs. The data source name is cgSampleDataSource. You can use this data source to create new database tables and then execute SQL statements to manipulate these tables.

Creating an SQL String

To execute database statements from a database control, you first create a method that accepts any parameters you want to pass to the database statement. For example, you might want to pass an order number to search for, or a customer's new address. Next, you use the @jws:sql JavaDoc tag to create the database statement.

NOTE

You can find more information on SQL, including a tutorial and links to the SQL specification, on the support page for this book at http://www.samspublishing.com.

The only attribute in the @jws:sql tag is statement, which contains the database statement. For example:

```
/**
 * @jws:sql statement="select * from accounts"
 */
```

If a statement is long, you can split it across multiple lines. Instead of enclosing the statement in quotes, use the statement:: form of the attribute using :: to end the statement, like this:

```
/**
 * @jws:sql statement:: update personnel set
 *     title='Manager', department='Toys'
 *     where id='123456'
 * ::
 */
```

Selecting Values

The general format for the SQL SELECT statement is

```
SELECT fields FROM table
```

The fields can either be * to indicate all fields in the table, or a comma-separated list like first_name, last_name, city, state, zip.

One of the most common clauses in a SELECT statement is the WHERE clause, which narrows the selection. The WHERE clause contains a Boolean expression, which can contain comparison operators like =, <, and >. You can also combine multiple expressions with AND, OR, and NOT. To test whether a column has no value, use IS NULL. Here are some sample queries:

```
SELECT * FROM personnel WHERE department='123456'
SELECT * FROM personnel WHERE spouse IS NULL
SELECT * FROM orders WHERE status='SHIPPED' or status='BACKORDERED'
```

You can add an order by clause to sort the results. The order by clause takes a list of fields to sort by. For example, to sort first by last name and then by first name, use the following query:

```
SELECT * FROM personnel ORDER BY last_name, first_name
```

By default, ORDER BY sorts items in ascending order. You can use the DESC keyword after a field to sort that field in descending order. You can use the ASC keyword to explicitly specify ascending order for a field, which for complex ORDER BY clauses might improve readability. To sort by last name, then first name, then by age in descending order, use the following query:

```
SELECT * FROM personnel ORDER BY last_name, first_name, age DESC
```

Updating Values

The UPDATE statement updates values in a table. The general format is

```
UPDATE table SET column=value, column=value, ... WHERE where-clause
```

For example:

```
UPDATE personnel SET department='Marketing', manager_id='987654' WHERE id='123456'
```

Inserting Values

The INSERT statement inserts values into a table. The general format is

```
INSERT INTO table (columns) values (column-values)
```

For example:

```
INSERT INTO personnel (id, first_name, last_name)
    VALUES (1, 'Kaitlynn', 'Tippin')
```

Deleting Values

The DELETE statement deletes values from a table. The general format is

```
DELETE FROM table WHERE where-clause
```

For example:

```
DELETE FROM personnel WHERE id='321654'
```

Joining Tables

One of the most powerful aspects of SQL is the ability to coordinate data from multiple tables. This technique is called *joining*. You join tables by comparing values from two different tables in a WHERE clause. When the tables have duplicate column names, you can prefix the field name with the table name, using the form *table.field*, for example: personnel.first_name.

Because your SELECT statement might get cluttered with long table names, you can create aliases for tables in the FROM clause. Simply list the alias after the table name. For example, if the FROM clause is FROM personnel p, you can refer to fields in the personnel table with p.*field* in the FROM clause. You can also use the *table.field* form when you list the fields you want to select.

The following SELECT clause locates all items ordered by customers in Atlanta—locating customers in a particular city, orders whose customer ID matches the customer's ID, and the products whose order ID matches the order's ID:

```
SELECT p.* FROM customer c, products p, orders o
    WHERE p.order_id = o.id AND o.customer_id = c.id
        AND c.city = 'ATLANTA'
```

Including Variables

The database control uses the same variable substitution mechanism that you use to map incoming XML values to method parameters and vice versa. That is, you can include an incoming methods parameter in a database statement by surrounding it with {}s. You don't need to include the quotes for string fields, WebLogic Workshop handles that for you. For example, suppose you create a method that updates personnel information, like this:

```
public void updatePersonnel(String id, String firstName, String lastName);
```

You can substitute the parameters into an update statement like this:

```
/**
 * @jws:sql statement::
 *    UPDATE personnel UPDATE first_name={firstName}, last_name={lastName}
 *        WHERE id={id}
 */
public void updatePersonnel(String id, String firstName, String lastName);
```

Getting a Result Set

Although the database control has an easy way to map incoming parameters into an SQL statement, mapping SQL return values into method return values is more difficult. The problem is that a Java method can only return a single value—a primitive type or an object.

Returning a Variable

If a SELECT statement returns a single value, the database control can automatically return the result, like this:

```
/**
 * @jws:sql statement="SELECT last_name FROM personnel WHERE id={id}
 */
public String getLastName(String id);
```

The INSERT, UPDATE, and DELETE statements each return an integer value indicating the number of rows that have been inserted, updated, or deleted. You can return this value from a database control method:

```
/**
 * @jws:sql statement="DELETE FROM personnel WHERE id={id}"
 */
int delete(String id);
```

In this case, the return value of the DELETE method is the number of rows actually deleted.

Returning a Row of Results

If a statement returns multiple values for a single column (as opposed to multiple columns), you can return an array of all the values:

```
/**
 * @jws:sql statement="SELECT last_name FROM personnel"
 */
String[] getAllLastNames();
```

You can limit the number of items returned in an array with the array-max-length attribute:

```
/**
 * @jws:sql statement="SELECT last_name FROM personnel"
 *      array-max-length="25"
 */
String[] getFirst25LastNames();
```

By default, the database control limits the number of rows returned to 1,024. Use "all" with array-max-length to force the control to return all values no matter how many there are.

Returning a Class

Returning single values or an array of values from a single column isn't very useful in a large application. You usually need to retrieve many values. The database control can map column values to fields in a Java class, as long as the field names match the column names.

For example, to retrieve id, first_name, and last_name from the personnel table, you can use the following class:

```
public class Personnel
{
    public String id;
    public String first_name;
    public String last_name;

    public Personnel()
    {
    }
}
```

Now, to retrieve all the values from the personnel table, use the following declaration:

```
/**
 * @jws:sql statement="select * from personnel"
 */
public Personnel[] getAllPersonnel();
```

Returning a HashMap

If you don't want to write new classes for every variation of columns that you might retrieve, you can simply return a HashMap (a Java data structure that associates keys with values) or an array of HashMaps (if you want to return multiple database rows). The database control stores each column value in the HashMap using the column name as the key, for example:

```
/**
 * @jws:sql statement="select * from personnel"
 */
public HashMap[] getAllPersonnel();
```

To fetch the value of the "firstName" column for the first row returned by the getAllPersonnel method, you could use a statement like this:

```
HashMap[] personnel = getAllPersonnel();
String firstName = (String) personnel[0].get("firstName");
```

Returning a Multiple Row Result Set in a Container

For managing large data sets, you might want to use a Java iterator instead of returning an array of values. To use an iterator, you must use the `iterator-element-type` attribute to specify what kind of object the iterator should return.

To iterate through the `personnel` table, use the following declaration:

```
/**
 * @jws:sql statement="select * from personnel"
 *     iterator-element-type="Personnel"
 */
public java.util.Iterator getAllPersonnel();
```

The database control can also return an iterator that returns `HashMaps`. Simply specify `java.util.HashMap` as the iterator element type. To access each of these iterators, you could do something like this:

```
Iterator iter = getAllPersonnel();
while (iter.hasNext())
{
    HashMap row = (HashMap) iter.next();
    String lastName = (String) row.get("lastName");
    // do something with lastName
}
```

Executing Multiple Statements

Sometimes you need to execute multiple database statements as part of a single transaction. Even though you can only execute a single SQL statement from a database control method, you can still execute several statements within a single transaction. Because of the way WebLogic Workshop creates Web service methods, each Web service method executes as a single transaction. Any database operations you perform during the Web service method are part of the same transaction. If any one of the operations fail, they all do. This way, you don't need to worry about reversing previous operations if another operation fails—it happens automatically.

You can also invoke a stored procedure from a database control, using the stored procedure syntax for your specific database (the syntax varies from database to database). Although stored procedures are occasionally useful, the fact that there is no standard for stored procedures makes it difficult to switch databases. Stored procedures do have their own unique advantages. They tend to run a series of statements faster because all the statements are already on the database. They can provide additional security because they are self-contained and residing on the database, eliminating the possibility that someone could tamper with intermediate results.

Although some application architects make heavy use of stored procedures, putting much of the business logic into them, other architects use them only as a last resort to solve some specific performance or security problem.

JDBC includes a special syntax for calling stored procedures, but unfortunately you can't use it in a WebLogic Workshop database control. Instead, you must use a database-specific syntax. For example, suppose your data uses the following syntax:

```
CALL updatePersonnel('Samantha', 'Tippin', 123456)
```

You might define the following function in a WebLogic Workshop database control to invoke the procedure:

```
/**
 * @jws:sql statement="CALL updatePersonnel({firstName}, {lastName}, {id});
 */
public int updatePersonnel(String firstName, String lastName, String id);
```

A Sample Application

Suppose you want to allow customers to check on whether their orders have shipped. Assuming you have a database table that indicates order status, you really only need a table of customers and their order status to provide this service.

For this example, you can use the sample database and data source in the WebLogic samples server. WebLogic comes with a pure-Java database server called PointBase. Although you can use the PointBase console for maintaining your database, this example uses the database control to create the sample tables and insert test data values.

Listing 6.1 shows the database control that creates tables, inserts test data, and allows you to query for status information. The control contains methods for creating and dropping tables because the WebLogic Workshop doesn't provide any tools to manage its built-in PointBase database. In a typical production environment, you wouldn't include these types of methods because you often have a database administrator who is responsible for creating and dropping the tables. The other methods in the control simply perform the kinds of SQL statements that the application needs— inserting customers and order status, and querying for customers.

LISTING 6.1   Source Code for OrderStatusCtrl.ctrl

```
import weblogic.jws.*;
import weblogic.jws.control.*;
import java.sql.SQLException;
```

LISTING 6.1   Continued

```java
/**
 * Defines a new database control.
 *
 * The @jws:connection tag indicates which WebLogic data source will be used by
 * this database control. Please change this to suit your needs. You can see a
 * list of available data sources by going to the WebLogic console in a browser
 * (typically http://localhost:7001/console) and clicking Services, JDBC,
 * Data Sources.
 *
 * @jws:connection data-source-jndi-name="cgSampleDataSource"
 */
public interface OrderStatusCtrl extends DatabaseControl
{
    /**
     * @jws:sql statement::
     *    create table orderStatus(
     *        orderId INTEGER,
     *        customerId INTEGER,
     *        orderStatus VARCHAR(255),
     *        orderStatusCode INTEGER)
     * ::
     */
    void createOrderStatusTable();

    /**
     * @jws:sql statement="drop table orderStatus"
     */
    void dropOrderStatusTable();

    /**
     * @jws:sql statement::
     *    insert into orderStatus (orderId, customerId, orderStatus,
     *        orderStatusCode) values ({order.orderId}, {order.customerId},
     *            {order.orderStatus}, {order.orderStatusCode})
     * ::
     */
    void insertOrderStatus(OrderStatus order);

    /**
     * @jws:sql statement::
     *    create table customer(
```

LISTING 6.1   Continued

```
 *          customerId Integer,
 *          address varchar(255),
 *          city varchar(64),
 *          state varchar(32),
 *          zip varchar(10),
 *          userName varchar(32),
 *          password varchar(32))
 * ::
 */
void createCustomerTable();

/**
 * @jws:sql statement="drop table customer"
 */
void dropCustomerTable();

 /**
  * @jws:sql statement::
  *     insert into customer (customerId, address, city, state, zip,
  *         userName, password) values ({cust.customerId}, {cust.address},
  *         {cust.city}, {cust.state}, {cust.zip}, {cust.userName},
  *         {cust.password})
  * ::
  **/
void insertCustomer(Customer cust);

/**
 * @jws:sql statement="select * from customer where userName={userName}"
 */
Customer getCustomerByUserName(String userName);

/**
 * @jws:sql statement::
 *     select * from orderStatus where
 *         customerId={customerId}
 * ::
 */
OrderStatus[] getCustomerOrders(int customerId);

/**
 * @jws:sql statement::
```

LISTING 6.1   Continued

```
*       select * from orderStatus where
*           customerId={customerId} and
*           orderId={orderId}
* ::
*/
OrderStatus getOrderStatus(int customerId, int orderId);
}
```

Before you can run the example, you must first create the tables and insert data. Listing 6.2 shows the Admin service that allows you to create the tables, insert data, and delete the tables. Again, the only reason for the Admin service is that there is no tool in WebLogic Workshop to manage the built-in database. In a production environment, you would do these kinds of operations using a database tool (or leave them up to the database administrator). In this case, the tool creates the necessary tables and populates them with data using the OrderStatusCtrl database control from Listing 6.1.

LISTING 6.2   Source Code for Admin.jws

```
import weblogic.jws.control.JwsContext;

public class Admin
{

    /**
     * @jws:control
     */
    private OrderStatusCtrl orderStatus;
    /** @jws:context */
    JwsContext context;

    /**
     * @jws:operation
     */
    public void initializeTables()
    {
        orderStatus.createCustomerTable();
        orderStatus.insertCustomer(
            new Customer(1, "Samco",
                "123 Main St.", "Lithonia", "GA", "30038",
```

LISTING 6.2   Continued

```
            "sammy", "barbie"));
    orderStatus.insertCustomer(
        new Customer(2, "Katy World",
            "6 Reader Lane", "Lithonia", "GA", "30038",
            "katy", "katy"));

    orderStatus.createOrderStatusTable();
    orderStatus.insertOrderStatus(
        new OrderStatus(1, 1, "Shipped: 1 Box of 1024 Crayons",
            OrderStatus.ORDER_SHIPPED));
    orderStatus.insertOrderStatus(
        new OrderStatus(2, 1, "Backorder: 3 Reams Multi-color card stock",
            OrderStatus.ORDER_BACKORDERED));
    orderStatus.insertOrderStatus(
        new OrderStatus(3, 2, "Processing: 1 Copy Ozzie's World",
            OrderStatus.ORDER_IN_PROCESS));
    orderStatus.insertOrderStatus(
        new OrderStatus(4, 2,
            "Partial: Shipped-Where The Wild Things Are; "+
            "Backorder-Hop On Pop", OrderStatus.ORDER_PARTIAL_SHIPPED));
}

/**
 * @jws:operation
 */
public void removeTables()
{
    orderStatus.dropOrderStatusTable();
    orderStatus.dropCustomerTable();
}

/**
 * @jws:operation
 */
public void removeOrderStatusTable()
{
    orderStatus.dropOrderStatusTable();
}

/**
 * @jws:operation
```

LISTING 6.2   Continued

```
    */
    public void removeCustomerTable()
    {
        orderStatus.dropCustomerTable();
    }
}
```

To retrieve or insert data, you usually need to define classes to contain table data (if you don't use a HashMap). Listing 6.3 shows the class that represents a customer. You can compare this Customer class to the customer table defined by the createCustomerTable in the OrderStatusCtrl database control in Listing 6.1. Notice that there is a field in the Customer class for each column defined in the customer database.

LISTING 6.3   Source Code for Customer.java

```
public class Customer
{
    public int customerId;
    public String name;
    public String address;
    public String state;
    public String city;
    public String zip;
    public String userName;
    public String password;

    public Customer()
    {
    }

    public Customer(int aCustomerId, String aName, String anAddress,
        String aState, String aCity, String aZip, String aUserName,
        String aPassword)
    {
        customerId = aCustomerId;
        name = aName;
        address = anAddress;
        state = aState;
        city = aCity;
        zip = aZip;
```

LISTING 6.3   Continued

```
        userName = aUserName;
        password = aPassword;
    }
}
```

Listing 6.4 shows the class that represents an order status. You can compare this class to the orderStatus table defined in the createOrderStatusTable method in Listing 6.1. As with the Customer class, the OrderStatus class contains a field for each column in the orderStatus table. In addition, the class defines numeric constants (the public static final int fields) to represent the various order status codes that can be stored in the database.

LISTING 6.4   Source Code for OrderStatus.java

```
public class OrderStatus
{
    public static final int ORDER_IN_PROCESS = 1;
    public static final int ORDER_SHIPPED = 2;
    public static final int ORDER_BACKORDERED = 3;
    public static final int ORDER_PARTIAL_SHIPPED = 4;
    public static final int ORDER_SUSPENDED = 5;

    public int orderId;
    public int customerId;
    public String orderStatus;
    public int orderStatusCode;

    public OrderStatus()
    {
    }

    public OrderStatus(int anOrderId, int aCustomerId,
        String anOrderStatus, int anOrderStatusCode)
    {
        orderId = anOrderId;
        customerId = aCustomerId;
        orderStatus = anOrderStatus;
        orderStatusCode = anOrderStatusCode;
    }
}
```

If you want to require customers to log in before they check their order status, you need your Web service to maintain a conversation. The `login` method initiates a conversation, and the `logout` method terminates the conversation. During the life of the conversation, you keep track of the customer's ID so you can use it for any status queries.

Listing 6.5 shows the main order status Web service. In addition to the `login` and `logout` methods, the `Orders` Web service includes methods to retrieve all available orders (using the customer ID determined during the `login` method), and also to get the status for a particular order. These data retrieval methods simply make use of the `OrderStatusCtrl` database control from Listing 6.1, and also the `OrderStatus` data object from Listing 6.4.

LISTING 6.5   Source Code for Orders.jws

```
import weblogic.jws.control.JwsContext;

public class Orders
{
    public int customerId;

    /**
     * @jws:control
     */
    private OrderStatusCtrl orderStatus;
    /** @jws:context */
    JwsContext context;

    /**
     * @jws:operation
     * @jws:conversation phase="start"
     */
    public String login(String userName, String password)
    {
        Customer cust = orderStatus.getCustomerByUserName(
            userName);

        if (cust != null)
        {
            if (!cust.password.equals(password))
            {
                customerId = -1;
                context.finishConversation();
```

LISTING 6.5   Continued

```
                    return "Invalid password";
            }
            else
            {
                customerId = cust.customerId;
                return "Login successful";
            }
        }
        else
        {
            customerId = -1;
            context.finishConversation();
            return "Invalid user-id";
        }
    }

    /**
     * @jws:operation
     * @jws:conversation phase="continue"
     * @jws:return-xml xml-map::
     *      <getAllOrdersResponse xmlns="http://openuri.org/">
     *      <order-statuses>
     *      <order xm:multiple="o in return" xmlns:xm="http://bea.com/jws/xmlmap"
     *          id="{o.orderId}">
     *          <status>{o.orderStatus}</status>
     *          <statusCode>{o.orderStatusCode}</statusCode>
     *      </order>
     *      </order-statuses>
     *      </getAllOrdersResponse>
     *
     * ::
     */
    public OrderStatus[] getAllOrders()
    {
        if (customerId >= 0)
        {
            return orderStatus.getCustomerOrders(customerId);
        }
        else
        {
            return null;
```

LISTING 6.5   Continued

```
        }
    }

    /**
     * @jws:operation
     * @jws:conversation phase="continue"
     * @jws:parameter-xml xml-map::
     *      <getOrderStatus xmlns="http://openuri.org/">
     *      <order-id>{orderId}</order-id>
     *      </getOrderStatus>
     *
     * ::
     * @jws:return-xml xml-map::
     *      <getOrderStatusResponse xmlns="http://openuri.org/">
     *      <order id="{return.orderId}">
     *          <status>{return.orderStatus}</status>
     *          <statusCode>{return.orderStatusCode}</statusCode>
     *      </order>
     *      </getOrderStatusResponse>
     *
     * ::
     */
    public OrderStatus getOrderStatus(int orderId)
    {
        if (customerId >= 0)
        {
            return orderStatus.getOrderStatus(customerId, orderId);
        }
        else
        {
            return null;
        }
    }

    /**
     * @jws:operation
     * @jws:conversation phase="finish"
     */
    public void logout()
    {
    }
}
```

Although the database control might not solve all your database needs, it should certainly be sufficient for smaller applications. In larger, more complex applications, it becomes more difficult to manage your code. The reason for this is that there is often logic in your Java code that implements business rules on top of the data. For example, you might have a rule that says that a customer ID can never start with '9'. When you have several Web services that manipulate the customer data, you might find that you are enforcing these rules in several places.

To help manage the complexity of business rules, developers often make "business objects" that manage data in the database and also maintain business rules. In this kind of scenario, any Web service that needed to update the `customer` table would use methods in a special `Customer` business object that would perform any special processing or validation of the customer data.

Enterprise JavaBeans (EJBs) are a special case of business object. The EJB architecture provides a standard way to represent these business objects and also provides powerful mechanisms for storing these objects in a database and retrieving them. You will learn how to access EJBs in Chapter 10, "Including an EJB Control."

7

Debugging

IN THIS CHAPTER

- Debugging in WebLogic Workshop
- Debugging a Web Service
- Variables
- The Call Stack

Debugging Web services and other code running on an application server has traditionally been difficult. Most debuggers work fine with standalone code, but need special configuration parameters or proxy objects to debug code running within another application.

For example, the Java Virtual Machine includes a debugging interface called JPDA—the Java Platform Debugging Architecture. To use JPDA, you must place the JVM into debug mode, which typically requires several command-line parameters like `-Xdebug` and `-Djava.compiler=NONE`. Servers like the ones you use to run Web services typically have startup scripts that contain a number of additional JVM parameters. You often need to edit these startup scripts in order to put the server into debug mode. Even then, when the server is in debug mode, you need a debugger that can perform remote debugging—that is, you need a debugger that can connect to another JVM and debug programs in the other JVM.

Another option is to run the entire server within an Interactive Development Environment (IDE) that has a built-in debugger (most commercial IDEs also support remote debugging). Because most servers have complicated startup scripts, you need to make sure the IDE performs the same startup steps that the script would. This process could take several hours to finally get right.

If you can't run a debugger on the code, your next best option is to print as much information as you can to a log file and then try to figure out the error from the log file. In fact, this might be your only resort in some cases. For example, an application might only encounter a particular error as a result of a heavy load or because several users have performed an unusual series of requests. It is difficult to catch these kinds of errors with a debugger because a debugger usually slows down the execution of the server (Java's just-in-time compiler, which speeds up execution, can't operate when the JVM is in debug mode). In some cases, the error only occurs in a production environment, where you can't really afford to stop the server and run a debugger on it.

When you have to debug by log messages (or `println` statements), try to provide as much information as you think is necessary—print out relevant variable values and indicate what part of the program is generating the message. Sometimes it is useful to include a stack trace to indicate where the error is occurring. One quick-and-dirty way to print a stack trace is just to do this:

```
(new Exception()).printStackTrace();
```

In this case, you don't have to throw an exception; you just print a stack trace indicating exactly where the current thread is executing. Stack traces are useful when multiple methods can call a particular method that is having the error. If all of the errors occur as a result of a call from one specific method, you might be able to narrow down the cause of the error.

Debugging in WebLogic Workshop

WebLogic Workshop includes a built-in debugger that lets you debug your Web services without any of the pains of putting a JVM in debug mode. One limitation of Workshop is that it currently doesn't support remote debugging. You might see this option in future versions, however. With the Workshop debugger, you can stop at a particular point in a program, display the value of variables, and trace through the execution of various methods to see what statements are actually executed.

If you happen to use the XML scripting capabilities described in Chapter 8, "Creating a Map," you can even debug ECMAScript scripts —which is something the normal Java debugger won't allow (these scripts aren't actually Java code).

Debugging a Web Service

When you debug a Web service, Workshop gives you several menu options and buttons. You can start a debug session, set and clear breakpoints, and step through your code.

Start

To start a debug session, either choose Debug, Start and Debug from the menu, or click the Start and Debug icon on the toolbar, as shown in Figure 7.1.

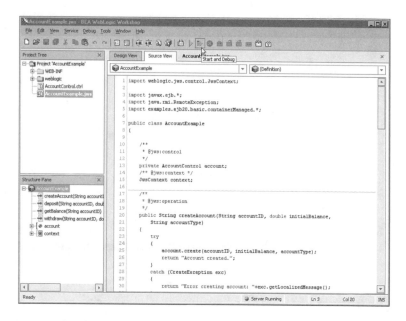

FIGURE 7.1   The Start and Debug icon starts a Web service in debug mode.

Setting Breakpoints

When debugging a Web service, you usually want to make the debugger stop at a particular place. Typically, you choose to put a breakpoint on a particular line because the server is reporting errors occurring around that line. In other cases, you find that your Web service is coming up with incorrect values in some calculation and you set a breakpoint at the place where the calculation is performed. There are really three main reasons for setting a breakpoint at a particular place in the code—you want to see the value of variables at that point, and/or you want to see what statements get executed after the breakpoint, and/or you want to see if the code even hits that breakpoint.

To set a breakpoint, you can click in the breakpoint area for the line you want to debug. The breakpoint area is just to the left of the line numbers, as shown in Figure 7.2.

As you can see in Figure 7.2, when you click in the breakpoint area, a red dot appears and the line is highlighted. If you click on the dot again, the breakpoint is removed.

If the cursor is on a line, you can press F9 to add a breakpoint for that line, or select Debug, Toggle Breakpoint from the menu. If you press F9 or select the Toggle Breakpoint menu option and there is already a breakpoint on the line, the breakpoint is removed.

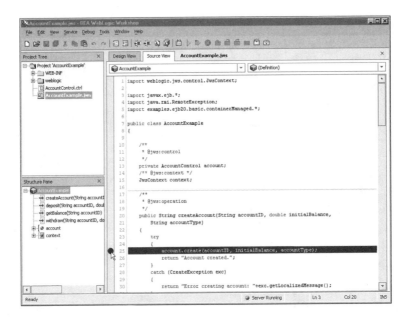

FIGURE 7.2   The breakpoint area shows active breakpoints, and you can set or clear breakpoints.

You can also toggle a breakpoint by clicking the Toggle Breakpoint icon, as shown in Figure 7.3.

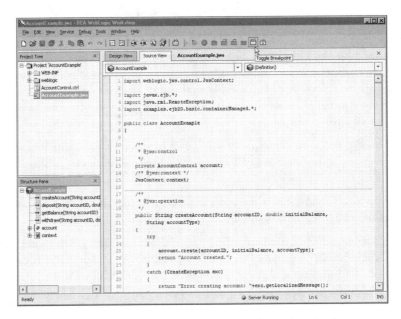

FIGURE 7.3   The Toggle Breakpoint icon can set or clear a breakpoint.

You can remove all breakpoints by pressing Ctrl+Shift+F9 or selecting the Debug, Clear All Breakpoints menu option. You can also click the Clear All Breakpoints icon, as shown in Figure 7.4.

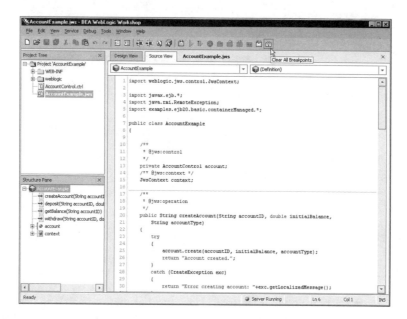

FIGURE 7.4   The Clear All Breakpoints icon removes all breakpoints in a Web service.

Stepping Through Code

When debugging code, you often want to follow the execution to see exactly what statements are executed. For example, you might want to see whether a particular if statement gets executed or skipped, or how many times a for loop gets executed. WebLogic Workshop supports three different stepping options—"step into," "step out," and "step over."

Step Into

As you step through individual lines of code, you sometimes come to a method call and you want to trace through the individual lines in that method. You can use the Debug, Step Into menu option to step into a method, press F11, or click the Step Into icon, as shown in Figure 7.5.

If you try to step into methods where there is no source code available, Workshop will stay on the current line. Use the Step Over feature for these lines.

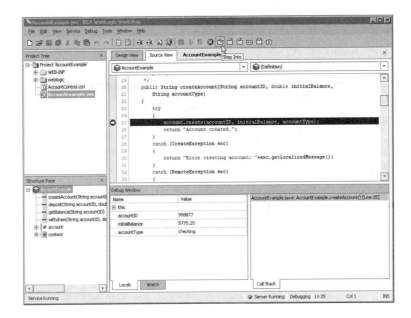

FIGURE 7.5   The Step Into icon lets you debug each line of a method.

When a method call involves a constructor or another method call, the debugger will step into the constructor or the other method call first, which can be a little confusing at first. For example, suppose you have the following line:

```
orders.getOrders(new OrderStatus("PENDING"));
```

The call to getOrders here involves the creation of a new OrderStatus object. Before the JVM executes the call to getOrders, it must first create a new OrderStatus object and call the OrderStatus constructor. When you click the Step Into button, you will suddenly jump to the OrderStatus constructor. You can then either step through the constructor, or just click the Step Out button. When you step out of the constructor, you will be back on the original line:

```
orders.getOrders(new OrderStatus("PENDING"));
```

This time, when you click Step Into, you will jump to the getOrders method.

Step Out

Sometimes, when debugging a method, you see what you were looking for and you just want to finish executing the method and then go back to the next line in the code that called the current method. The Debug, Step Out method finishes executing the method, and then goes back to the previous method. You can also press Shift+F11, or click the Step Out icon, as shown in Figure 7.6.

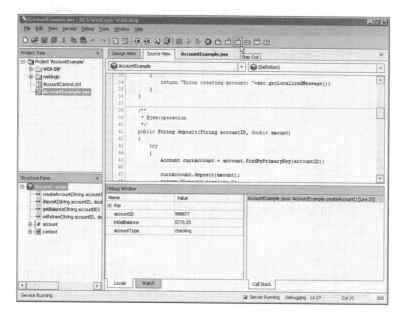

FIGURE 7.6   The Step Out icon finishes executing the current method.

Step Over

If you don't want to step into a method, but just execute it and go on to the next line, press F10 or select Debug, Step Over from the menu. You can also click the Step Over icon, as shown in Figure 7.7.

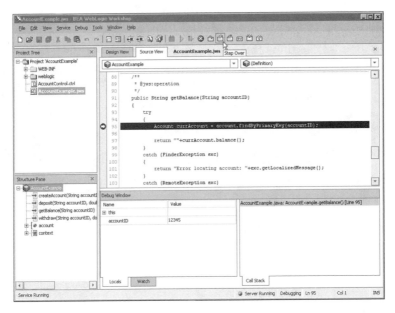

FIGURE 7.7   The Step Over icon executes a line but does not step into any method calls.

Continue

At some point during debugging, you realize that you have seen everything you needed to see and you just want to continue on until the Web service hits another breakpoint, if any. You can select Debug, Continue from the menu or press F5. You can also click the Continue icon, as shown in Figure 7.8.

Variables

Although it can be useful just to trace the execution of your code, most of the time you need to examine the values of variables at a particular point in the code to see why the code is behaving the way it is. For example, if you have a complicated calculation that continually tries to divide by zero, you want to look at the variables in the calculation and see where the zero comes from. You might be debugging an order-processing method and you only want to debug the processing of a specific order. You examine the current order and see if it is the one you want to watch. If not, you just click the Continue button and wait for the service to hit another breakpoint. Workshop lets you examine local variables (variables declared in the current method) and also watch other variables outside the scope of the current method.

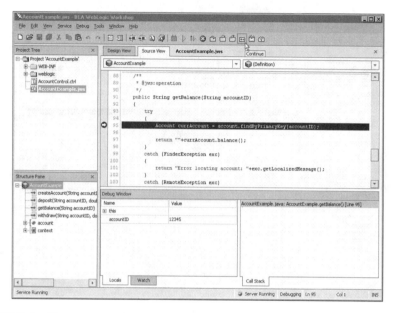

FIGURE 7.8   The Continue button resumes execution of the program.

TIP

You can also view the value of a variable by hovering the mouse pointer on top of the variable name (you don't need to click a button). After a short 1- to 2-second delay, the variable's value appears in a ToolTip next to the mouse pointer.

Locals

The Locals window shows any variables that are local to the current method. For each variable, the window shows both the variable name and its value. For some complex variables that the debug tool is unable to display, it shows "..." for the value. For Java classes, the name portion of the window displays a plus sign, indicating that you can expand it to show the contents of the class. Because the variable this is always local to a non-static method, you can examine the contents of the current class by expanding this.

Figure 7.9 shows the Locals window with some classes expanded.

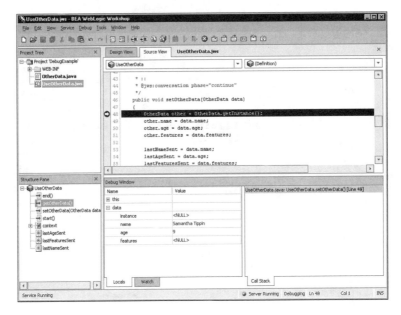

FIGURE 7.9   The Locals window shows the values of all local variables.

Watching Variables

Sometimes you want to examine the values of non-local variables. For example, you can step over methods that modify values in other classes and you want to see those values quickly. The Watch window, located on a tab next to the Locals window, allows you to add watches for different variables.

For example, suppose you want to watch the value of the lastNameSent instance variable in the current class. You can add a watch on this.lastNameSent by entering this.lastNameSent in one of the name fields in the Watch window, as shown in Figure 7.10. The value appears to the right of the field name in the Watch window.

Notice that to watch member variables, you must reference them via the this variable.

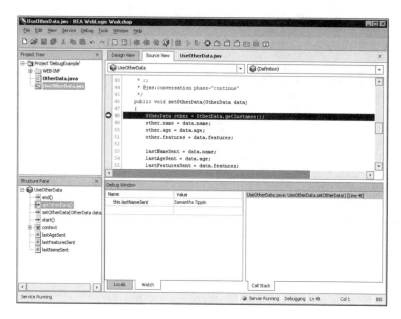

FIGURE 7.10   A watch constantly monitors the value of a variable.

The Call Stack

The Call Stack window shows you the current calling context of the method you are debugging. That is, it shows you which method called the current method (and which method called that one, and so forth). The handy thing about the Call Stack is that you can double-click on a method in the stack and view its source code as well as its local variables. When you double-click on a method, the source for the method appears in the main Source View window, replacing the source code you were previously viewing.

Figure 7.11 shows the call stack for an example of method invocation.

The more you work with WebLogic Workshop and its debugger, the more you realize how great it is to have a debugger that understands Web services. Even more importantly, if you use scripts to preprocess your XML, it is outstanding to have a debugger that can step through these scripts. Sometimes, you might want to just run the debugger and step through your code even if there aren't any bugs. Sometimes you find the code behaving in ways you never expected.

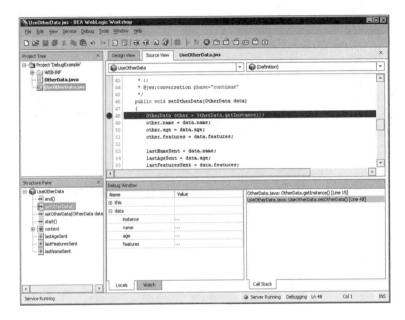

FIGURE 7.11   The Call Stack window lets you see which methods invoked the current method.

PART III

Declaring Maps and
Controls

IN THIS PART

8 Creating a Map

9 Messaging Using JMS

10 Including an EJB Control

11 Accessing Web Services from Java

12 @jws JavaDoc Tags

13 An Online Ordering System

8

Creating a Map

IN THIS CHAPTER

- Customizing XML Content
- Building XML Maps Using Workshop
- XML Map Elements
- Storing Maps in External Files
- Using XMLScript

Sometimes the default XML shape for JWS messages is not quite what your application needs. You might need to interact with another system that expects the data in a particular form, or you might want to return a specific subset of some data (for instance, only certain fields of a Java object). In these cases, you must tell WebLogic Workshop the format of the XML you want to use. You define the XML format using an XML map, which is basically the XML you expect with annotations showing where the incoming data is located or where the outgoing response should be placed.

Customizing XML Content

For example, you might receive data using the FIXML format, which is a standard for exchanging financial information. Because the FIXML format differs from the default format used by Workshop, you must create a map to interpret incoming FIXML data and assign the various data values to parameters for your Web service method.

Building XML Maps Using Workshop

Workshop provides a dialog box for editing maps. Although you can edit the Javadoc comments in the code editor, the Edit Maps and Interface dialog box provides syntax highlighting and other handy editing features.

You access the Edit Maps and Interface dialog box by clicking on the Output XML Map icon, as shown in Figure 8.1.

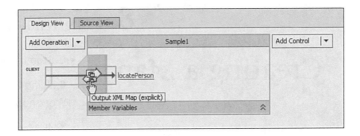

FIGURE 8.1   The Output XML Map icon invokes the Edit Maps and Interface dialog box.

Figure 8.2 shows the Edit Maps and Interface dialog box.

FIGURE 8.2   You can edit both input and output maps from the Edit Maps and Interface dialog box.

The Parameter XML tab lets you edit the map for incoming parameters, whereas the Return XML tab lets you edit the map for return values. When you finish editing the map(s), click the OK button to save your changes.

Input Maps

To define an input map, go to the Parameter XML tab in the Edit Maps and Interface dialog box. The dialog box initially shows the default XML map. To indicate that the text data of an element should be used as a method parameter, insert the parameter name surrounded by curly braces ({}). For example, suppose you have a <name> tag and you want to use its text value as the personName parameter in your method. The <name> portion of your map would look like this:

```
<name>{personName}</name>
```

Figure 8.3 shows the Parameter XML tab from the Edit Maps and Interface dialog box. You can see the default XML map generated by Workshop, along with the Java method signature at the bottom of the dialog box.

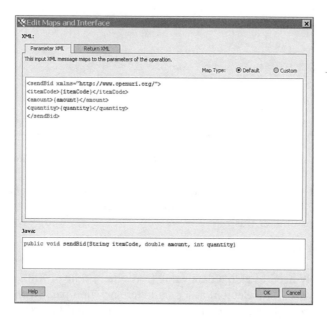

FIGURE 8.3 Workshop generated a default XML map based on the method parameters.

Figure 8.4 shows a modified map that expects different XML tags for the data and a slightly different structure.

CAUTION

The names of the root elements for both an input map and an output map *must* be unique within a single JWS file. That is, two different methods cannot use the same root element name for either the input map or the output map.

FIGURE 8.4   Use the Edit Maps and Interface dialog box to edit the XML map.

One thing that you can't do in an input map is to pick a parameter value out from the middle of XML data. That is, the parameter must come from the entire text. You can't define a parameter this way:

```
<name>Hello, my name is {personName}!</name>
```

If you absolutely need to grab a data value from the middle of XML data, you need to accept the whole data element as a parameter and then parse through the data in your Web service method. In other words, your map would look something like this:

```
<name>{personName}</name>
```

Your service method would then use some of the common Java string routines like indexOf and substring to isolate the part you are interested in.

As an alternative, you can also parse text from the middle of XML data by creating an ECMAScript script, as you will see later in this chapter.

You can also use an attribute value as a parameter. Use the variable name surrounded by {}s in place of the attribute value, just as you do for element text. For example, to use the name attribute in the <person> tag as the personName parameter, use the following declaration:

```
<person name="{personName}">
```

Output Maps

Just as you can define the shape of the incoming XML, you can also define the shape of the outgoing XML. Again, you use the Edit Maps and Interface dialog box, but this time, select the Return XML tab. As with the Parameter XML tab, you use {}s within the XML to indicate where you want to place the return value. Because there is usually only one return value, you just use the name "return" to indicate where to place the return value. You will see an exception to this rule shortly when you learn how to map Java objects to return values.

Figure 8.5 shows the default output map for a simple Web service method. As you can see, Workshop generates a single parameter substitution named {return}.

FIGURE 8.5   Workshop generates a default output map for each method.

Figure 8.6 shows a modification of the map shown in Figure 8.5.

FIGURE 8.6   You can modify the output map to return a custom XML format.

XML Map Elements

When you embed a parameter name inside element text or an attribute, you are actually using shorthand for two different XML elements: `<xm:value>` and `<xm:attribute>`.

`<xm:value>`

The `<xm:value>` indicates that the text value of an element should be used as a parameter for an incoming or outgoing parameter. Use the `<xm:value>` in exactly the same place as you would use the {}s for an element value. Use the `obj` attribute to indicate the name of the parameter. In other words, the value of the `obj` attribute is the same as the name you would enclose in {}s. For example, the following two declarations are equivalent:

```
<name>{personName}</name>
```

```
<name><xm:value obj="personName"/><name>
```

`<xm:attribute>`

Just as the `<xm:value>` element lets you control how element text is evaluated, the `<xm:attribute>` element lets you control how attributes are evaluated. The `id` attribute specifies the name of the attribute containing the value, and the `obj` attribute specifies which parameter the value represents. For example, the following two declarations are equivalent:

```
<person name="{personName}">
```

```
<person><xm:attribute id="name" obj="personName"/></person>
```

Mapping Java Objects

Sometimes you want to pass Java objects to a Web service method, or return a Java object from a Web service method. You can modify the XML map to populate individual fields of a Java object input parameter, or populate XML elements from a Java object return value. Simply use the dot-notation that you usually use to access fields.

For example, suppose you have the Java object shown in Listing 8.1.

LISTING 8.1   Source Code for Person.java

```java
public class Person
{
    protected String _firstName;
    protected String _lastName;
    protected int _age;

    public Person()
    {
    }

    public String getFirstName()
    {
        return _firstName;
    }

    public void setFirstName(String aFirstName)
    {
        _firstName = aFirstName;
    }

    public String getLastName()
    {
```

LISTING 8.1   Continued

```
        return _lastName;
    }

    public void setLastName(String aLastName)
    {
        _lastName = aLastName;
    }

    public int getAge()
    {
        return _age;
    }

    public void setAge(int anAge)
    {
        _age = anAge;
    }
}
```

You can reference the individual fields in the object in both the Parameter XML and Return XML tabs of the Edit Maps and Interface dialog box. Listing 8.2 shows an input map that stores data in a Java object. In this case, the Java method looks like this:

```
public void storePerson(Person person)
```

LISTING 8.2   Sample Java Object Input Map

```
<storePerson xmlns="http://openuri.org/">
    <person>
        <first-name>{person.firstName}</first-name>
        <last-name>{person.lastName}</last-name>
        <age>{person.age}</age>
    </person>
</storePerson>
```

When you create an output map for a Java object, use `return` as the variable name for the object. If you want to access the `firstName` field in the return value, use the name `return.firstName`. Listing 8.3 shows a sample output map that maps values in the `Person` object into XML.

LISTING 8.3   Sample Java Object Output Map

```
<findPerson>
   <person>
      <first-name>{return.firstName}</first-name>
      <last-name>{return.lastName}</last-name>
      <age>{return.age}</age>
   </person>
</findPerson>
```

Declaring Map Variables

You can declare temporary variables within an XML map. For example, sometimes you need to populate many fields in a Java object, and the value names become unwieldy. You might end up with a value name like `employee.personal.address.city` and `employee.personal.address.state`. You can create a variable using the `xm:bind` attribute and then use the variable in future value names. An `xm:bind` variable is only available from within the element in which it is defined.

The format of `<xm:bind>` is

```
<some-element xm:bind="variable-type variable-name is value">
```

The *variable-type* attribute is the Java class name of the object you want to bind, whereas *variable-name* is the name you want to call the variable within the XML map. Finally, the *value* attribute indicates what the variable actually refers to. Remember that the bind really just represents a shortcut. The *value* attribute indicates what the variable is really a shortcut for.

For example, the following map defines a variable called `addr` that takes the place of `employee.personal.address`, and then uses the variable to populate part of the employee parameter:

```
<personal-address xm:bind="Address addr is employee.personal.address">
   <street>{addr.street}</street>
   <city>{addr.city}</city>
   <state>{addr.state}</state>
   <zip>{addr.zip}</zip>
</personal-address>
```

The `addr` variable is only available from inside the `<address>` element because it was defined in the `<address>` tag.

Including Multiple Elements

The `xm:multiple` attribute indicates that values in a repeated element can be used as values for an array parameter. In a `return-xml` map, the `xm:multiple` attribute indicates that an element can be repeated to contain the values returned in an array.

You specify the `xm:multiple` attribute in the element that is repeated. That is, if an `<order>` element can have many `<part>` elements, you specify `xm:multiple` in the `<part>` element. The value of `xm:multiple` is a list of declarations of the form *type-name variable-name* in *parameter-name*. If you have multiple declarations, list them all in one `xm:multiple` attribute separated by commas.

For example, suppose you have the following method:

```
public String[] getResults(Person[] people, int ages[])
```

Furthermore, suppose that you want the incoming request to look like this:

```
<roster>
    <person>
        <first-name>Samantha</first-name>
        <last-name>Tippin</last-name>
        <age>9</age>
    </person>
    <person>
        <first-name>Kaitlynn</first-name>
        <last-name>Tippin</last-name>
        <age>6</age>
    </person>
</roster>
```

You want to store the `<first-name>` and `<last-name>` elements in an array of `Person` objects and store the `<age>` elements in an array of ints. Your `parameter-xml` declaration would look like this:

```
<person xm:multiple="Person person in people, int age in ages">
    <first-name>{person.firstName}</first-name>
    <last-name>{person.lastName}</last-name>
    <age>{age}</age>
</person>
```

Remember that the Java method looks like this:

```
public String[] getResults(Person[] people, int ages[])
```

Because the `getResults` method returns an array, you need to handle multiple values in your output map as well. Your declaration for the array of strings returned by the `getResults` method might look like this:

```
<results xm:multiple="String name in return">
    <result>{name}</result>
</results>
```

The resulting XML output looks like this:

```
<results>
    <result>Atlanta</result>
    <result>Dallas</result>
    <result>Tampa</result>
</results>
```

Storing Maps in External Files

Sometimes you might want to use the same map in different Web services. This is especially true if you have a set of common methods that your entire Web services implement—perhaps for login information, billing, or inquiries. You can store a map in an external file and use the same map in several different Web services.

External XML map files must have the extension `.xmlmap`. The map file must start with the following line:

```
<xm:map-file xmlns:xm="http://bea.com/jws/xmlmap">
```

Within the `<xm:map-file>` element, you create your maps for various methods. Each map begins with an `<xm:xml-map>` element with a `signature` attribute specifying the signature of the method that the map is for. For example:

```
<xm:xml-map signature="getCatalog(String category, int maxItems)">
```

You then describe the XML shape of the map just as you do for incoming parameters:

```
<category>{category}</category>
<max-items>{maxItems}</max-items>
```

Use the `</xm:xml-map>` to close the map element.

If you need to reference Java classes that might not be available within the method that you are mapping (because you reference a superclass, for example), you can use the `<xm:java-import>` element to import a Java class:

```
<xm:java-import class="java.util.HashMap">
```

You can only import single classes, not entire packages.

At the end of your list of <xm:xml-map> elements and optional <xm:java-import> elements, close the map file with the </xm:map-file> tag.

Listing 8.4 shows a complete xmlmap file.

LISTING 8.4   Source Code for Person.xmlmap

```
<xm:map-file xmlns:xm="http://bea.com/jws/xmlmap">

<xm:xml-map signature="findPerson(String firstName, String lastName)">
    <findPerson>
        <first-name>{firstName}</first-name>
        <last-name>{lastName}</last-name>
    </findPerson>
</xm:xml-map>
</xm:map-file>
```

Using XMLScript

Sometimes your XML is so complicated or requires so much preprocessing that the basic XML map provided by Workshop isn't enough. One of the goals of WebLogic Workshop is that you should be able to write your Web service without needing to work directly with XML—your Web service methods should have Java types as parameters and Java types as return values. You can write special scripts to bridge the gap between XML and Java.

Workshop uses ECMAScript (the European Computer Manufacturers Association version of JavaScript) for custom scripts. The ECMAScript interpreter works well with XML data and can also interact with Java objects. In case you haven't seen JavaScript or ECMAScript before, it is similar to Java, but differs in several aspects.

NOTE

You can download the complete ECMAScript specification from http://www.ecma.ch/ecma1/STAND/ECMA-262.HTM. The standard is known as EC-262. Also, because ECMAScript is just a standardized JavaScript, any book or tutorial on JavaScript is also useful. Remember, though, if you're studying JavaScript, that the browser-oriented Document Object Model (DOM) objects like document and window don't apply in the WebLogic Workshop ECMAScript.

ECMAScript Overview

Although ECMAScript has some support for objects, you generally just write functions, not methods. Variables in ECMAScript don't have a type. In Java, you might declare an int or a String with declarations like this:

```
int x = 12345;
String name = "Kaitlynn";
```

In ECMAScript, however, you declare variables with var:

```
var x = 12345;
var name = "Kaitlynn";
```

Also, since variables don't have a type, you don't declare return types on functions. Instead, you just use this form:

```
function functionName(param1, param2, ...)
```

In Java, you might declare a method like this:

```
public String findOrderId(String customer, Date orderDate)
```

In ECMAScript, however, you omit all the type declarations and end up with something like this:

```
function findOrderId(customer, orderDate)
```

Most of the control structures you are familiar with are available in ECMAScript. The if, while, switch, for, continue, and return statements all work the same way. The expression operators like +, -, *, /, and % all work the same way as well. ECMAScript can interpret 0 (zero) and null as being the same thing as the Boolean false. In Java, the following statement is illegal:

```
int i = 0;
if (!i) j = j / i;
```

Because the if statement requires a Boolean value and i is an int, Java reports an error. The equivalent in ECMAScript is legal:

```
var i = 0;
if (!i) j = j / i;
```

ECMAScript supports arrays just like Java. You use [ ]s to access individual array elements. Unlike Java, however, you can insert array values directly into your code surrounded by [ ]s. For example, the following code snippet initializes a variable with an array of three names:

```
var stooges = [ "Moe", "Larry", "Curly" ];
```

There is a lot more to ECMAScript than can be covered in this chapter. When you delve into the deeper aspects of the language, such as the way you can add data and methods to objects on the fly, you see how powerful it really is.

XML Scripts

When you elect to use a script for XML mapping, you must write two different ECMAScript functions—one to process incoming XML and convert it to Java, and the other to process Java return values and convert them to XML. The function to convert XML to Java must be named *yourMethodName*FromXML, and the function to convert Java to XML must be named *yourMethodName*ToXML where *yourMethodName* is the name of the Web service method that the script serves.

Remember that in an XML map, you can't extract values from the middle of element text. You can only use the entire element text. Using ECMAScript, however, you *can* extract values from element text. You can also adapt to more dynamic XML. For example, you might have an XML structure that may contain many nested elements. You don't know the exact structure ahead of time, so it is difficult to create a static XML map. Using ECMAScript, however, you can process the XML and look for specific attributes and elements no matter how the XML document looks.

ECMAScript and XML

Although you might be familiar with JavaScript, WebLogic Workshop's version of ECMAScript contains XML extensions that might look a little unfamiliar. First of all, you can assign raw XML to a variable, as shown in Listing 8.5.

LISTING 8.5   Sample XML Initialization

```
var accounts =
  <accounts>
    <account id="x127">
      <owner>Fred Jones</owner>
      <number>5554321987</number>
      <balance>1234.56</balance>
      <account-type>Checking</account-type>
      <referenced-accounts>
```

LISTING 8.5 Continued

```
            <referenced-account id="x128"/>
            <referenced-account id="x129"/>
        </referenced-accounts>
    </account>
</accounts>;
```

In ECMAScript, XML documents look like objects. That is, you can access nested elements using the dot-notation that you use for accessing the fields of objects. If there are multiple elements, the field acts like an array. For example, if you have an XML structure like the one shown in Listing 8.5, you can process the accounts from Listing 8.5 using the following loop:

```
for (acct in accounts.account)
{
        var jAcct = new Account();
        jAcct.setId(acct.@id);
        jAcct.setAccountNumber(acct.number);
        jAcct.setName(acct.owner);
        jAcct.setBalance(acct.balance);

        accountList.add(jAcct);
}
```

You can use .. to reference an element at any level. For example, to loop through the balance elements anywhere underneath accounts, use the following loop:

```
for (balance in accounts..balance)
{
   // do something here
}
```

You can also use curly braces ({}) to access a specific element by its index. For example:

```
for (i=0; i < accounts.account.length; i++)
{
   var acct = accounts.account[i];
   // do something with acct here
}
```

To access an attribute, use .@ followed by the attribute name. For example:

```
var id = acct.@id; // Fetch the id attribute
```

When you embed XML directly within ECMAScript, as you saw in Listing 8.5, you can use the {} notation to insert ECMAScript values into the XML.

For example, suppose you have the following assignments:

```
var firstName = "Samantha";
var lastName = "Tippin";
var person =
    <person>
        <name>{firstName} {lastName}</name>
    </person>;
```

The XML structure stored in the person variable would be:

```
<person>
    <name>Samantha Tippin</name>
</person>
```

You can also search for specific elements using a special query operator. Use the .() operator to perform a search, putting a search predicate inside the parentheses. For example, to search for an account with an account number of 8787878787:

```
var acct87 = accounts.account.(number=="8787878787");
```

You can search for accounts with balances > 10000 this way:

```
var bigAccounts = accounts.account.(balance > 10000);
```

To include attributes in a search, you must use a special keyword called thisXML that refers to the current XML element. For example, to search for an account with id x129, use the following statement:

```
var x129 = accounts.account.(thisXML.@id == "x129");
```

The WebLogic Workshop extensions to ECMAScript also include a number of functions for manipulating XML, shown in Table 8.1.

TABLE 8.1   Functions for Manipulating XML

Function	Description
add(element)	Adds an element to a list of elements
appendChild(child)	Adds an element as a child of another element
attribute(attributeName)	Returns the value of an attribute
Attributes()	Returns a list of all an element's attributes
childIndex()	Returns the index of this element within its parent's list of elements (that is, a value of 2 means the current element has an index of 2 in its parent's element list)

TABLE 8.1 Continued

Function	Description
Children	Returns a list of the element's children
copy()	Returns a deep copy of the element
innerXML(newXML)	Replaces the XML content of the element with the new XML content
length()	Returns the length of a list of elements
parent()	Returns the parent of the element
prependChild(child)	Inserts a child element as the first child of the element (before any existing children)
Remove	Removes the element
removeChild(child)	Removes a child element from the element's list of children
tagName	Returns the element's tag name
toArray	Returns the element's content as an array
toString	Returns the element's content as a string
xpath(xpathExpression)	Evaluate the element's content using Xpath notation

If you need to import a Java class into ECMAScript, use the `importClass` function:

```
importClass("java.util.ArrayList);
importClass("mypackage.Person");
```

The final step in using an ECMAScript script is to include the script in the `parameter-xml` and `return-xml` Javadoc comments. The <xm:use> tag lets you specify an ECMAScript script. The format is

```
<xm:use call="scriptFileName.functionName(parameters)"/>
```

The `scriptFileName` parameter is the name of the `.jsx` file containing your ECMAScript (without the `.jsx` extension). If your `.jsx` file is stored in a package, put the package name before the filename. The `functionName` parameter is the name of the ECMAScript function to call. Remember that the actual function names in the ECMAScript file will be *functionName*ToXML and *functionName*FromXML.

Extracting Parameters from XML Data

You can use ECMAScript to extract parameters embedded within XML data. Typically, this is only an issue when you don't want the entire data. For example, you might have an XML element like this:

```
<greeting>Hello, my name is Inigo Montoya!</greeting>
```

If you just want the name from this greeting, you need to extract it yourself. This is just the kind of thing that ECMAScript is good for. Listing 8.6 shows an ECMAScript that parses this kind of greeting.

LISTING 8.6   Source Code for Extractor.jsx

```
/**********************************************************
 * This function parses a greeting of the form:
 * <greeting>Hello, my name is: xxxxx yyyyy!</greeting>
 **********************************************************/
function extractNameFromXML(xml)
{
    // Locate the greeting in the XML
    var greetingString = xml..greeting;

    // Convert the greeting to a string
    greetingString = greetingString.toString();

    // The greeting should start with "Hello, my name is ", so look
    // for "name is "
    var nameIsPos = greetingString.indexOf("name is ", 0);

    // Find the ! after the name
    var bangPos = greetingString.indexOf("!", 0);

    // if there is no !, take the rest of the string
    if (bangPos < 0) bangPos = greetingString.length();

    // Grab the portion of the string after "name is " and before the !
    var name = greetingString.substring(nameIsPos+8, bangPos);

    // Return an array containing just the name
    return [ name ];
}
```

Mapping XML into Java with ECMAScript

Listing 8.7 shows a Web service that uses an ECMAScript script to map the incoming XML to an `ArrayList` of Account objects. The incoming XML uses the format shown in Listing 8.6.

LISTING 8.7   Source Code for Accounting.jws

```
import java.util.ArrayList;
import java.util.Iterator;

public class Accounting
{
    /** @jws:context */
    weblogic.jws.control.JwsContext context;

    /**
     * @jws:operation
     * @jws:parameter-xml xml-map::
     *       <processAccounts xmlns="http://openuri.org/">
     *       <xm:use call=
"AccountFilterScript.processAccounts(ArrayList accounts)"/>
     *       </processAccounts>

     * ::
     * @jws:return-xml xml-map::
     *       <processAccountsResponse xmlns="http://openuri.org/">
     *       <xm:use call="AccountFilterScript.processAccounts(String[] return)"/>
     *       </processAccountsResponse>

     * ::
     */
    public String[] processAccounts(ArrayList accounts)
    {
        String[] summary = new String[accounts.size()+1];
        Iterator iter = accounts.iterator();

        int i = 0;
        double balance = 0;

        while (iter.hasNext())
        {
            Account acct = (Account) iter.next();
```

LISTING 8.7   Continued

```
            summary[i] = acct.getName()+":"+acct.getBalance();
            balance += acct.getBalance();
            i++;
        }
        summary[i] = "Total:"+balance;

        return summary;
    }
}
```

Listing 8.8 shows the Account class that holds the account information used by the Web service in Listing 8.7.

LISTING 8.8   Source Code for Account.java

```
import java.util.Vector;

public class Account
{
    protected String _name;
    protected String _accountNumber;
    protected String _id;
    protected double _balance;
    protected Vector _references;

    public Account()
    {
    }

    public String getName()
    {
        return _name;
    }

    public void setName(String aName)
    {
        _name = aName;
    }

    public String getAccountNumber()
    {
        return _accountNumber;
```

LISTING 8.8   Continued

```
    }

    public void setAccountNumber(String anAccountNumber)
    {
        _accountNumber = anAccountNumber;
    }

    public String getId()
    {
        return _id;
    }

    public void setId(String anId)
    {
        _id = anId;
    }

    public double getBalance()
    {
        return _balance;
    }

    public void setBalance(double aBalance)
    {
        _balance = aBalance;
    }

    public Account[] getReferences()
    {
        if (_references == null) return new Account[0];

        Account[] refs = new Account[_references.size()];
        _references.copyInto(refs);

        return refs;
    }

    public void addReference(Object account)
    {
        if (!(account instanceof Account)) return;
```

LISTING 8.8   Continued

```
            if (_references == null)
            {
                _references = new Vector();
            }
            _references.addElement(account);
        }

        public void removeReference(Object account)
        {
            if (!(account instanceof Account)) return;

            if (_references != null)
            {
                _references.remove(account);
            }
        }
    }
}
```

Finally, Listing 8.9 shows the ECMAScript script that maps the XML to Java. The incoming XML can contain a list of referenced accounts. The script keeps a table of all accounts that it processes, and after it sweeps through the XML, it goes back again and resolves all the account references using the accountMap object to look up referenced accounts.

LISTING 8.9   Source Code for AccountFilterScript.jsx

```
importClass("Account");
importClass("java.util.ArrayList");


/**************************************************************************
 * processAccountsFromXML is called to map from the XML schema to Java objects.
 * It is passed the XML input and returns an array containing the
 * mapped Java objects.
 **************************************************************************/
function processAccountsFromXML(xml)
{
    var accountList = new ArrayList();
    var accountMap = {};

// Create the initial list of accounts
    for (account in xml..account)
```

LISTING 8.9   Continued

```
    {
        var jAcct = new Account();
        jAcct.setId(account.@id);
        jAcct.setAccountNumber(account.number);
        jAcct.setName(account.owner);
        jAcct.setBalance(account.balance);

        accountList.add(jAcct);

// Create a temporary map to resolve account references
        accountMap[account.@id] = jAcct;
    }


// Loop through the accounts again and resolve the account references
    for (account in xml..account)
    {
        var jAcct = accountMap[account.@id];

        for (ref in account..referenced-account)
        {
// Look for the referenced account in the map
            var refAcct = accountMap[ref.@id];

// If the referenced account exists, add it as a reference
            if (refAcct)
            {
                jAcct.addReference(refAcct);
            }
        }
    }


// Return an array of parameters to pass to the Web Service
    return [ accountList ];
}


/*************************************************************************
 * processAccountsToXML is called to map from Java objects to the XML schema.
 * It is passed Java objects as arguments and returns the mapped
 * XML object.
 *************************************************************************/
function processAccountsToXML(obj)
```

LISTING 8.9   Continued

```
{
// obj is an array of strings, loop through them

    var results = <results></results>;

    for (line in obj)
    {
        results.appendChild(<result>{obj[line]}</result>);
    }

    return results;
}
```

As you can see, WebLogic Workshop gives you several levels of flexibility in mapping XML to Java. The automatic mapping works well if you don't mind letting Workshop determine the shape of your XML. For simple, custom XML shapes, a simple custom map is easy to make and reasonably flexible. For the ultimate in flexibility, you can use ECMAScript.

9

Messaging Using JMS

IN THIS CHAPTER

- Using the JMS Control
- JMS JavaDoc Options
- Sending XML Messages

The Java Message Service (JMS) provides APIs for point-to-point and publish-subscribe messaging. In point-to-point messaging, each message has a single consumer. The message queue is the heart of point-to-point messaging—producers place messages on a queue and the queue's consumer retrieves messages. Although there may be multiple consumers retrieving messages from the queue, each message has only a single consumer.

In publish-subscribe messaging, multiple producers broadcast messages to multiple consumers. A topic is the publish-subscribe equivalent of a message queue. Consumers listen on a particular topic and producers send messages to a topic. A single message may have many consumers.

Point-to-point messaging is most useful for invoking certain procedures within a system. In fact, it is generally used for the same kinds of things that Web services are. That is, you use point-to-point messages for submitting orders, changing the status of an item, or transferring data to a specific recipient.

Because of its broadcast nature, publish-subscribe messaging is most useful for sending notification events. For example, in a trading system, when the current bid for an item changes, you publish an event with the updated price. Any program that is interested in that item receives the updated price.

One of the advantages of publish-subscribe messaging is that you can add new functionality to a system easily without affecting the other parts. You just add new consumers for the published messages. For example, suppose you work for an airline and you have a system that publishes the location of each flight in the air.

At some point, you want to write a program that graphically displays the flights on a large screen. You don't change anything in the program that publishes the location events, nor do you change any of the other programs that consume the events. You just run your new program and it subscribes to the events just like the other programs.

Point-to-point messaging gives you similar advantages, although to a lesser extent. For example, after you write a consumer that processes incoming orders, you can add new programs that receive the orders in different ways and publish them on the order queue. You might add a Java Web service that receives orders and publishes them on the queue.

Connections and Connection Factories

A connection represents a logical connection to a JMS implementation. The connection may be in the form of a socket connection to some JMS server, but it may also just represent a local instance of a JMS implementation. In many ways, a JMS connection is similar to a JDBC connection.

To create a connection, you need a connection factory, which is simply a class used to create connections. There are four types of connection factories:

- `QueueConnectionFactory` creates connections for sending and receiving point-to-point messages.

- `TopicConnectionFactory` creates connections for sending and receiving publish-subscribe messages.

- `XAQueueConnectionFactory` creates connections for sending and receiving point-to-point messages as part of a transaction.

- `XATopicConnectionFactory` creates connections for sending and receiving publish-subscribe messages as part of a transaction.

As you can see, you can send and receive messages as part of a transaction. That is, you can tie the sending or receipt of a message to the execution of other operations. For example, suppose you have a message queue containing orders, and a consumer that receives the orders and inserts them in a database. If a consumer reads an order from the queue and then has an error trying to insert the order into the database, the order may be lost. If the receipt of the order is part of the same transaction as the insertion of the order and the insertion fails, the order stays on the queue. That way, you never lose an order because of an insertion error. Because transactions may take significantly longer to execute, however, you should only use the XA connection factories when you absolutely need to.

Although the JMS API provides connection factories for transacted connections, you can create transacted connections from either QueueConnectionFactory or XAQueueConnectionFactory. That is, you can use QueueConnectionFactory to create a transacted connection. The real difference is that connections default to being trans-acted in the XA versions of the connection factories.

To obtain a connection factory, you use JNDI to locate the factory by a specific name, which you specify when you first create the factory. The WebLogic server comes with a built-in connection factory named weblogic.jws.jms. QueueConnectionFactory that can be used for both queue connections (point-to-point) and topic connections (publish-subscribe).

Sessions

A session represents a single-threaded session with the JMS implementation; similar to the way a JDBC session represents a single database session. A session is basically a conversation between two objects. If a session is single-threaded, it can only perform one operation at a time. Java supports multiple threads of execution—performing several operations simultaneously. In general, WebLogic Workshop handles any thread issues for you, so you don't need to worry about them. A QueueSession lets you create QueueSender and QueueReceiver objects for sending and receiving queue messages. A TopicSession lets you create TopicPublisher and TopicSubscriber objects for publishing and subscribing to topics.

Sending and Receiving

You send and receive JMS messages via the Message class. There are several different subclasses of Message that handle the various ways you might want to encode data. For simple text data, use TextMessage. For name-value pairs, use MapMessage. To send/receive serializable objects, use ObjectMessage. The StreamMessage and BytesMessage objects let you store and retrieve various Java data types, similar to the way DataInputStream and DataOutputStream work.

Using the JMS Control

WebLogic Workshop makes it easy to send and receive JMS messages. It handles all the low-level JMS API calls, letting you send messages with a single method call. You simply include a JMS control in your JWS file and then use the various methods in JMSControl to send and receive messages.

To add a JMS control to your JWS file, select Service, Add Control, Add JMS Control from the Workshop menu. As with other controls, you must supply a variable name for the control (that is, what name you want to give the control) and also decide whether to create a new control or use an existing one.

If you create a new control, you must also specify whether the control uses queues or topics, and specify the JNDI name of the queue/topic used for sending messages and/or the JNDI name of the queue/topic used for receiving messages. You must also specify the name of the connection factory that the control will use.

You must also specify the kind of messages you want to send and receive. The four choices are

- Text—You send/receive simple string messages.

- XML Map—You can create custom send methods in the JMS control that take various parameters just as you do in your Web service. The JMS control then maps these parameters into XML (you can specify the shape of the message, just as with a JWS method).

- Object—You can send/receive Java objects.

- JMS message—You can send/receive any of the built-in JMS message objects.

If you need to change any of these items after you create the new control, you can change them from the Design View screen by simply clicking the control and then editing its properties.

Sending Queue Messages

The name of the send method you use depends on the message type you specify when you create the JMS control. Table 9.1 shows the message types and their corresponding send methods.

TABLE 9.1   JMS Control Message Types and Their Corresponding Method Names

Message Type	Send Method Name
Text	sendTextMessage
XML Map	sendMessage by default, but you can define your own methods
Object	sendObjectMessage
JMS message	sendJMSMessage

Listing 9.1 shows a simple JWS file that uses a JMSControl object to send messages. The corresponding JMS control uses a message type of Text, a send-jndi-name of jms.SimpleJMSQ, and a connection-factory-jndi-name of weblogic.jws.jms. QueueConnectionFactory. Because the example uses a message type of Text, the example uses the sendTextMessage method to send a message on a queue.

LISTING 9.1   Source Code for QueueSender.jws

```
import weblogic.jws.control.JwsContext;

public class QueueSender
{

    /**
     * @jws:control
     */
    private QueueControl queueControl;
    /** @jws:context */
    JwsContext context;

    /**
     * @jws:operation
     */
    public void sendMessage(String message)
    {
        queueControl.sendTextMessage(message);
    }
}
```

Receiving Queue Messages

You can receive messages from a JMSControl just as easily as you send them. The one necessity for handling incoming messages is that you create a callback method for handling the message event from the JMS control.

A callback method is not the same thing as a Web service callback—it is simply a method in your JWS file that the JMS control invokes when it receives an incoming message. To add a JMS control callback, go to the Design view for your JWS file, and then right-click your JMS control and select Add Callback. You supply the name of the callback just as you do for Web service callbacks. You will also notice that in the Design view, your callback is a hyperlink. When you click the link, it creates a callback method in your JWS file with a name of the form *jmsControl_callbackName* where *jmsControl* is the variable name of the JMS control and *callbackName* is the name of the callback.

The easiest way to add a callback is to click the "receiveTextMessage" link for the JMSControl in the Design view, which automatically adds a callback method to handle an incoming text message. The difficulty with receiving JMS messages is that they happen in the background. That is, a Web service may receive messages even while no users are using the service. Presumably, you want to do some processing of the messages, which you can do within your callback method. If you need to keep the messages until a user invokes a Web service method, you can store them in a Java container like an ArrayList.

Listing 9.2 shows a Web service that uses a JMSControl to receive text messages. It stores the messages in an `ArrayList` until a user invokes the `receiveMessages` method, at which point the service returns any accumulated messages. After it displays the messages, it clears the `ArrayList` so that the next call to `receiveMessages` shows only messages received since the last call. You can use this service to receive messages sent by the Web service in Listing 9.1.

LISTING 9.2   Source Code for QueueReceiver.jws

```
import weblogic.jws.control.JwsContext;

public class QueueReceiver
{

    /**
     * @jws:control
     */
    private QueueControl2Control queueControl;

    private java.util.ArrayList messages = new java.util.ArrayList();


    /** @jws:context */
    JwsContext context;

    /**
     * @jws:operation
     */
    public String[] receiveMessages()
    {
        String[] retval = (String[]) messages.toArray(new String
➥[messages.size()]);
        messages.clear();
        return retval;
    }

    private void queueControl_receiveTextMessage(String payload)
    {
        messages.add(payload);
    }
}
```

Sending Topic Messages

The JMS control can send to either a queue or topic. You use the same procedure to send to a queue or a topic. That is, you add a JMS control to your JWS file using Service, Add Control, Add JMS Control, and then configure the settings for your control. You must specify the same items for the JMS control that you do when you want to use queues—that is, you still specify the JNDI name of the topic you want to send to and/or the topic you want to receive from, and the connection factory. Listing 9.3 shows a JWS file that sends messages to a topic. The corresponding JMS control specifies a message type of "Text", a send-jndi-name of `jws.SimpleJMSTopic`, and a connection-factory-jndi-name of "weblogic.jws.jms.QueueConnectionFactory" (remember, although the name says QueueConnectionFactory, WebLogic doesn't distinguish between queue and topic connection factories).

LISTING 9.3   Source Code for TopicExample.jws

```
import weblogic.jws.control.JwsContext;

public class TopicSender
{

    /**
     * @jws:control
     */
    private Topic1Control topicControl;
    /** @jws:context */
    JwsContext context;

    /**
     * @jws:operation
     */
    public void sendMessage(String message)
    {
        topicControl.sendTextMessage(message);
    }
}
```

Before you can run the `TopicExample` Web service, you must set up your environment the same way you did for the `ExampleQueueReceiver` program. Before you run the program, you must create the topic. Although WebLogic Workshop comes with a preconfigured queue, it doesn't have a preconfigured topic. To create a topic, take the following steps:

1. Bring up the WebLogic console by pointing your Web browser to
   `http://yourhostname:7001/console`. The WebLogic server must be running
   before you do this, so you may need to select Tools, Start WebLogic Server in
   Workshop first.

2. Log in. The default username and password is "installadministrator".

3. From the tree on the left, click Workshop, Services, JMS, Servers, cgJMSServer,
   Destinations.

4. Click Configure a New JMSTopic.

5. Choose a name for the topic (the default is MyJMSTopic). The name doesn't
   matter; it is just the name that shows in the WebLogic console.

6. Enter the JNDI name for the topic—the examples in this chapter use a topic
   name of jms.SimpleJMSTopic.

7. Click the Create button.

Figure 9.1 shows the console screen for creating `jws.queue`.

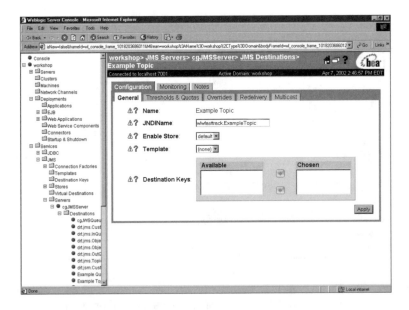

FIGURE 9.1   You must create a topic before you can use it.

Receiving Topic Messages

You can receive incoming topic messages from the JMSControl. As with queue messages, you must create a callback to handle the topic messages. To create the callback, simply click the "receiveTextMessage" link in the JMSControl's Design view, or add the callback manually.

Listing 9.4 shows a Web service that receives messages sent to a topic. It saves incoming messages in an ArrayList just like the QueueReceiver service in Listing 9.2.

LISTING 9.4   Source Code for TopicReceiver.jws

```
import weblogic.jws.control.JwsContext;

public class TopicReceiver
{
    java.util.ArrayList messages = new java.util.ArrayList();

    /**
     * @jws:control
     */
    private TopicControl topicControl;
    /** @jws:context */
    JwsContext context;

    /**
     * @jws:operation
     */
    public String[] receiveMessages()
    {
        String[] retval = (String[]) messages.toArray(new String
➥[messages.size()]);
        messages.clear();
        return retval;
    }

    private void topicControl_receiveTextMessage(String payload)
    {
        messages.add(payload);
    }
}
```

JMS JavaDoc Options

The `@jws:jms` JavaDoc tag configures a `JMSControl`. Within this one tag, you must specify the names of the queues you want to use, as well as the name of the connection factory. You can also specify the JMS property names to use for correlating messages.

Table 9.2 shows the attributes available for the `@jws:jms` tag.

TABLE 9.2   Attributes of the `@jws:jms` Tag

Attribute	Description
`Type`	Either "queue" or "topic" to indicate whether to send/receive on a queue or a topic
`Send-jndi-name`	Name of the topic or queue to send messages on
`receive-jndi-name`	Name of the topic or queue to receive messages from
`Connection-factory-jndi-name`	Name of the connection factory to use
`Send-correlation-property`	Name of the message property to use for sending a correlation id (defaults to `JMSCorrelationID`)
`receive-correlation-property`	Name of the message property to use for retrieving a correlation id (defaults to `JMSCorrelationID`)
`receive-selector`	Selector string used to select specific messages to receive

Sending XML Messages

Currently, JMS doesn't have built-in support for XML. That is, JMS doesn't have any methods for sending and receiving XML. You can send XML as a text message, and parse XML from incoming text messages. Workshop, however, can send XML as a JMS text message. You can create custom JMS control methods that take a list of parameters and format them into XML, similar to the way you map return values to a custom XML shape.

To create a JMS control that maps parameters into XML, simply select Service, Add Control, Add JMS Control, and then fill in the values in the dialog box. The key part of this operation is that you select a message type of XML Map. Figure 9.2 shows sample settings for the dialog box.

After you add the custom control, you can edit it. From the Design view, you can add new methods and callbacks by right-clicking the control and selecting either Add Method or Add Callback. To customize the XML for a method or callback, click the arrow to the right of the method name, to bring up the Properties window for that method/callback. This procedure is identical to the procedure you use for customizing the XML for a JWS method. Listing 9.5 shows an example of a custom control.

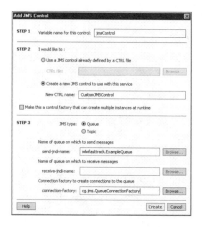

FIGURE 9.2   The Add JMS Control dialog box adds a custom JMS control.

LISTING 9.5   Source Code for CustomJMSControlControl.ctrl

```
import weblogic.jws.control.JMSControl;
import java.io.Serializable;

/**
 *    @jws:jms type="queue" send-jndi-name="wlwfasttrack.ExampleQueue"
 *    connection-factory-jndi-name="cg.jms.QueueConnectionFactory"
 */
public interface CustomJMSControlControl extends JMSControl
{
    /**
     * If you would like to use XML maps to give the body of the outgoing
     * message a specific XML shape, you may define a method in this file and
     * annotate it with an XML map. For example, if you want the payload
     * to look like this:
     *
     * <YourOuterTag>
     *   <SampleParameter1>Param1</SampleParameter1>
     *   <SampleParameter2>Param2</SampleParameter2>
     * </YourOuterTag>
     *
     * Then define a "sendMessage" method as follows:
     *
     * @jws:jms-message xml-map::
     * <Person>
```

LISTING 9.5   Continued

```
 *     <name>{name}</name>
 *     <age>{age}</age>
 * </Person>::
 */
public void sendPerson(String name, int age);


/*
 * NOTE: if you do not want to use XML map to shape the outgoing message
➥you
 * do not need to define any "publishing" methods here. In your JWS, simply
 * use one of the methods defined in JMSControl. For example,
➥publishText(String)
 */


/**
 * If your control specifies receive-jndi-name, that is your JWS expects to
➥ receive messages
 * from this control, you will need to implement callback handlers.
 * There are 2 ways to do this.
 * If the incoming message is in the form of XML, and you would like to use
➥ XML maps
 * to extract values from it, you need to define a Callback interface in
➥this file as
 * follows.
 */
interface Callback extends JMSControl.Callback
{
    /**
     * Define only 1 callback method here.
     *
     * For example, if your incoming message looks like
     * <YourOuterTag>
     *     <SampleParameter1>Param1</SampleParameter1>
     *     <SampleParameter2>Param2</SampleParameter2>
     * </YourOuterTag>
     *
     * Then define the method like this:
     *
     * @jws:jms-message xml-map::
     * <YourOuterTag>
     *     <SampleParameter1>{param1}</SampleParameter1>
```

LISTING 9.5   Continued

```
      *    <SampleParameter2>{param2}</SampleParameter2>
      * </YourOuterTag>
      * ::
      */
      public void receiveMessage(String param1, String param2);
  }

  /*
   * NOTE: if you do not need to use XML maps to parse the values from the
➥ incoming
   * message, then you dont need to define any Callback interface in this
➥file.
   * In this case, in your JWS file, implement a handler for one callback
➥from
   * JMSControl.Callback. You may only implement one handler; this handler
➥will be called
   * for all incoming methods.
   */
}
```

JMS gives you flexibility in designing your applications. You can use JMS to exchange messages with existing JMS-based Java applications, or to communicate with new servers that may not support Web services.

10

Including an EJB Control

IN THIS CHAPTER

- EJB Overview

- Including an EJB in Your Workshop Project

- An EJB Control Example

- EJB JavaDoc Options

A typical business application has three main parts— presentation, business logic, and data. The presentation portion can be a Web page, or a GUI application, or even a printed document—it is some kind of representation of information from the application. An application can have more than one kind of presentation. For example, an airline reservation system might have a Web interface, a custom GUI application running on a PC, and a text-based interface on a green-screen terminal. You could also consider the printing of tickets and boarding passes to be part of the presentation as well.

Business logic is where all the decision making takes place and where business rules are applied. For instance, a business can choose not to accept orders from companies who are more than 60 days past due on payments for previous orders. The code that implements this decision is part of the business logic. In addition to these decisions, business logic also includes data validation, which ensures that all the data items are in their proper format and proper ranges.

The data portion of the application stores all the "things" that an application keeps track of. It can store orders, customers, reservations, tickets, catalog information, personnel, and so on. Typically, the data portion of an application is the database itself—that is, you don't actu- ally write the data portion of the application; you use some off-the-shelf components.

EJB Overview

Although an application can have these three parts, they can be intermingled. For example, many applications just consist of a GUI or Web interface and a database. The code that executes the business logic is intermingled with the presentation code. The problem with this approach is that it becomes difficult to change the business logic—especially when several applications implement the same business rules. It is usually better, although more time-consuming, to move the business logic to a set of Java objects that are separate from the presentation code. If you have multiple applications, they can all use the same business logic objects, and if you need to change the business logic, you only need to change it in one place.

You can think of these parts as layers. The presentation layer is the part that is closest to the user. The business logic layer sits between the presentation and the data, and the data layer is furthest away from the user. Figure 10.1 shows this layering.

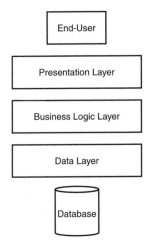

FIGURE 10.1   You can separate presentation, business logic, and data into different layers.

For these parts to truly be layers, a layer must only interact with an adjacent layer. The presentation layer interacts with the business layer, and the business layer interacts with the data layer. Generally, the interaction is one-way. The presentation layer can invoke methods in the business layer, but the business layer typically doesn't know anything about the presentation layer and doesn't invoke its methods. Similarly, the business layer can invoke methods in the data layer, but the data layer doesn't invoke methods in the business layer.

The implementation of the business logic and data layers has been a particularly interesting task for developers. Many projects have implemented their own toolkits and frameworks to help develop these layers. The business logic layer often includes objects that represent items that are stored in the database. That is, you often see orders, customers, and similar items as objects in the business logic layer. The data layer then contains code that stores these objects in the database and retrieves them.

So many developers have implemented this type of architecture that Sun created a standard Java framework to make this architecture available to all developers.

Enterprise JavaBeans (EJB) provide a framework for implementing business logic in an application server. A JavaBean is simply a Java object consisting of properties, methods, and events. A bean method is the same thing as a Java method. A bean property represents a data item in a bean and is accessed via special get and set methods (usually called "accessor" methods). In a regular Java object, you might expose data items as fields, like this:

```
public class Person
{
    public String firstName;
    public String lastName;
}
```

In a JavaBean, however, you make these items available via accessor methods. The get and set methods define the name of a property. To make a property called firstName, you create methods called getFirstName and setFirstName (even though FirstName is capitalized in the get/set methods, the property name is still considered to start with a lowercase letter). For example, the JavaBean version of the Person is shown in Listing 10.1.

LISTING 10.1   The Person Class

```
public class Person implements java.io.Serializable
{
    protected String firstName;
    protected String lastName;

    public Person()
    {
    }

    public String getFirstName() { return firstName; }
    public void setFirstName(String aName)
    {
        firstName = aName;
    }

    public String getLastName() { return lastName; }
    public void setLastName(String aName)
    {
        lastName = aName;
    }
}
```

Listing 10.2 throws in a pair of additional JavaBean requirements. First, the bean must implement the `java.io.Serializable` interface (the interface has no methods; you just need to include `implements java.io.Serializable` after the class name). Second, the bean must include a default constructor (that is, a constructor that takes no parameters). You don't need to do anything else to make a JavaBean. That is, almost any Java class can be a bean, and you can use beans just like any other class.

The third feature of beans, events, aren't really applicable to Enterprise JavaBeans. An *event* is a callback mechanism that allows a bean to send information out to other objects. For example, you might want to know when an Order bean has shipped, so the Order bean can define a "has shipped" event that fires when the order ships. Because Enterprise JavaBeans don't really use events, however, you don't need to worry about events for now.

Enterprise JavaBeans (EJBs) are a special kind of JavaBeans that implement the business logic portion of an application. There are three types of EJBs—session beans, entity beans, and message-driven beans.

An *entity bean* represents items that are typically stored in a database. For example, an entity bean might represent an order, a product, an employee, or an account. Entity beans know how to retrieve and store entity data in a persistent store (like a database). An EJB container (the object that manages the beans) can also manage the retrieval and storage of the data, making development of the bean much easier. If the entity bean handles its own persistence, it is said to be using Bean-Managed Persistence (BMP). If the EJB container manages the persistence for an entity bean, that bean is using Container-Managed Persistence (CMP). CMP is particularly attractive to some developers because it frees them from the burden of writing database code. For some situations, whether because of performance constraints or a complex data model, BMP might be the better choice. You can choose between CMP and BMP for each individual bean. That is, one bean can use CMP while another uses BMP.

A *session bean* represents a conversation between a client and the EJB container. Typically, a session bean represents business processes and usually provides the sole means of manipulating entity beans. That is, clients don't normally operate on entity beans directly; they use session beans instead. Session beans might or might not contain data of their own. If a session bean contains data about its current client (perhaps a customer ID or a current order), the session bean is a stateful bean. That is, the session preserves its state between method calls. A stateless session bean doesn't keep client-specific information between method calls. Unlike an entity bean, a session bean's data is not normally stored in the database. The session bean can elect to store the data by interacting with the database directly, of course. In general, however, the EJB view of things is that the entity beans contain the data that should be stored in the database.

A ***message-driven bean*** doesn't interact directly with clients. Instead, it responds only to JMS messages. To interact with a message-driven bean from a Web service, you use the `JMSControl` object you saw in the previous chapter. A message-driven bean can interact with other beans. It can, for example, use a session bean to perform a particular sequence of actions, or it can use entity beans directly to update various data items. It can also send messages to other message-driven beans, but cannot invoke methods in other message-driven beans directly. A message-driven bean can contain its own data elements, but like the session beans, this data is not normally stored in the database. Again, the message-driven bean can store data manually, but usually these beans make use of entity beans to store data.

Clients access session and entity beans via Remote Method Invocation (RMI). RMI is a mechanism that allows a Java object to invoke a method in another Java object that can reside in a different Java Virtual Machine, possibly on another computer somewhere else on the network. An EJB has two different interfaces, a remote interface and a home interface. A remote interface defines the business-related methods that manipulate a session or entity bean. For example, a session bean's remote interface might include methods like `getShippingTotal` or `addItemToOrder`. A home interface implements basic lifecycle methods, managing the creation, deletion, and finding of beans. A home interface has methods like `create`, `remove`, and `findAll`. An entity bean's remote interface usually includes methods to update the various fields in the bean, like `setFirstName` or `getDepartment`. A home interface, for either a session bean or an entity bean, has methods like `create`, `remove`, and `findAll`.

Message-driven beans are rather peculiar in this case because they have neither home nor remote interfaces. You don't access these beans via RMI, so there is no need for these interfaces. You simply send messages to these beans via the Java Message Service (JMS).

To access an entity bean or a session bean, you first use Java Naming and Directory Interface (JNDI) to locate the bean's factory. Then, you use either the `create` method or one of the `find` methods to either create or locate the bean. From that point on, you interact with the bean's remote interface.

Including an EJB in Your Workshop Project

Before you can use an EJB in a Workshop project, you need the EJB client jar file generated by your EJB deployment tool. Although different EJB servers have different deployment tools, almost all of them can create a client jar file. The client jar file contains the home and remote interfaces for a bean as well as any additional code required to access the bean. It does not, however, contain the bean itself.

To add the client jar to your workshop project, simply copy the jar to the `WEB-INF\lib` directory for your Workshop project. For example, if your project is called

EJBTest and WebLogic is installed in `c:\bea`, the path for `WEB-INF\lib` is `c:\bea\weblogic700\samples\workshop\applications\EJBTest\WEB-INF\lib`. Although the WEB-INF directory should always be present, you might need to create the `lib` directory yourself.

After you add the jar file to the `WEB-INF\lib` directory, you can add an EJB control to your project. Simply select the Service, Add Control, Add EJB Control menu option to bring up the Add EJB Control dialog box, as shown in Figure 10.2.

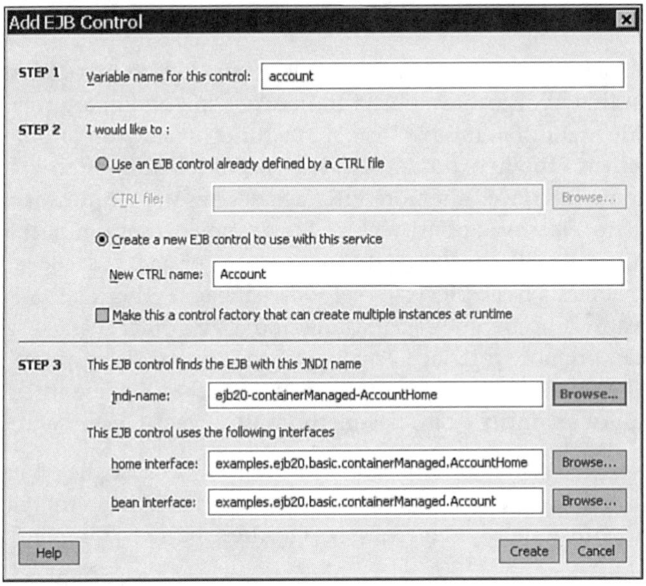

FIGURE 10.2   The Add EJB Control dialog box.

To create a new control, enter the variable name for the control (the name your Web service will use to access the control) and the control name.

Next, enter the JNDI name of the EJB's home interface. The JNDI name is not part of the EJB client jar file, because an EJB can be deployed on many different servers under different names while still having the same client jar file. The Add EJB Control dialog box can search for any EJBs already deployed on your server, so if the bean you want to use has been deployed on your server, you should be able to select it from a list of choices. Otherwise, you need to ask your server administrator what JNDI name the EJB has been deployed under.

Finally, enter the fully qualified class names of the EJB's home and remote interfaces (called "bean interface" in the Add EJB Control dialog box). If you don't know the names, use the Browse button. Workshop automatically looks at jar files in the `WEB-INF\lib` directory and will show you the choices available.

After you add an EJB control, it shows up in the Web service Design view along with the various methods it supports, as shown in Figure 10.3.

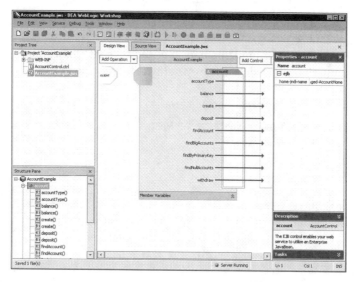

FIGURE 10.3   An EJB control shows its available methods in the Design view.

Now that you have added the control, you can call any of the EJB's methods from your Web service methods. The EJB control contains both the home and remote methods for the EJB, which might seem a little odd because they come from two separate interfaces. The odd thing about it is that the home interface is used to locate specific beans, whereas the remote interface is used to manipulate a particular bean.

An EJB Control Example

The default Workshop server comes with several built-in EJBs, including the AccountEJB bean. You can use this bean to try out the EJB control. Listing 10.2 shows the remote interface for the AccountEJB bean. These are the methods that you can invoke on a specific bean. The source code for this method is in *bea-install-dir*\weblogic700\samples\server\src\examples\ejb20\basic\containerManaged.

The AccountEJB bean is an entity bean that represents a bank account. It has methods to deposit money, withdraw money, and retrieve a balance. An account is uniquely identified by a combination of an account ID and an account type. The account ID is a string and can contain any combination of characters (it isn't limited to numbers like a standard bank account number). The account type is also a string and is usually something like "checking" or "savings," although there is no restriction on what account types you can use. The `AccountEJB` bean uses container-managed persistence (CMP), so you won't see any database code in the bean—the EJB container knows how to store and retrieve `AccountEJB` beans.

As you can see in Listing 10.2, the remote interface simply defines the methods to withdraw, deposit, check the balance, and retrieve the account type. This chapter doesn't include the actual implementation of the `AccountEJB` bean, just the home and remote interfaces that define how you interact with the bean.

LISTING 10.2   Source Code for Account.java

```
package examples.ejb20.basic.containerManaged;
import java.rmi.RemoteException;
import javax.ejb.*;

/**
 * The methods in this interface are the public face of AccountBean.
 * The signatures of the methods are identical to those of the bean,
 * except that these methods throw a java.rmi.RemoteException.
 * Note that the EJBean does not implement this interface.
 * The corresponding code-generated EJBObject implements this interface
 * and delegates to the EJBean.
 *
 * @author Copyright (c) 1998-2002 by BEA Systems, Inc. All Rights Reserved.
 */
public interface Account extends EJBObject {

  /**
   * Deposits an amount.
   *
   * @param amount         double Amount to deposit
   * @return               double Account Balance
   * @exception            java.rmi.RemoteException if there is
   *                       a communications or systems failure
   */
  public double deposit(double amount)
    throws RemoteException;

  /**
   * Withdraws an amount.
   *
   * @param amount         double Amount to withdraw
   * @return               double Account Balance
   * @exception
➥examples.ejb20.basic.containerManaged.ProcessingErrorException
```

LISTING 10.2   Continued

```
 *                          if there is an error while depositing
 * @exception               java.rmi.RemoteException if there is
 *                          a communications or systems failure
 */
public double withdraw(double amount)
  throws ProcessingErrorException, RemoteException;

/**
 * Balance in account.
 *
 * @return                  double Account Balance
 * @exception               java.rmi.RemoteException if there is
 *                          a communications or systems failure
 */
public double balance()
  throws RemoteException;

/**
 * Type of account.
 *
 * @return                  String account Type
 * @exception               java.rmi.RemoteException if there is
 *                          a communications or systems failure
 */
public String accountType()
  throws RemoteException;


}
```

Listing 10.3 shows the home interface for AccountEJB. The home methods let you create, delete, and locate accounts. They do not modify individual accounts, however. Remember, the home interface doesn't manipulate individual beans—that's the job of the remote interface. Again, the home interface in Listing 10.3 just defines methods; it doesn't contain any logic. The EJB container automatically generates the implementation code when the bean is deployed.

LISTING 10.3   Source Code for AccountHome.java

```
package examples.ejb20.basic.containerManaged;
import javax.ejb.CreateException;
import javax.ejb.EJBHome;
import javax.ejb.FinderException;
import java.rmi.RemoteException;
```

LISTING 10.3   Continued

```java
import java.util.Collection;

/**
 * This interface is the home interface for the EJBean AccountBean. A home
 * interface may support one or more create methods,
 * which must correspond to methods named "ejbCreate" in the EJBean.
 *
 * @author Copyright (c) 1998-2002 by BEA Systems, Inc. All Rights Reserved.
 */
public interface AccountHome extends EJBHome {

  /**
   * This method corresponds to the ejbCreate method in the bean
   * "AccountBean.java".
   * The parameter sets of the two methods are identical.  When the client calls
   * <code>AccountHome.create()</code>, the container (which in WebLogic EJB is
   * also the factory) allocates an instance of the bean and
   * calls <code>AccountBean.ejbCreate()</code>
   *
   * For container-managed persistence, <code>ejbCreate()</code>
   * returns a null, unlike the case of bean-managed
   * persistence, where it returns a primary key. See section 9.4.2
   *
   * @param accountID        String Account ID
   * @param initialBalance   double Initial balance
   * @param type             String Account type
   * @return                 Account
   * @exception              javax.ejb.CreateException
   *                         if there is an error creating the bean
   * @exception              java.rmi.RemoteException if there is
   *                         a communications or systems failure
   * @see                    examples.ejb20.basic.containerManaged.AccountBean
   */
  public Account create(String accountId, double initialBalance, String type)
    throws CreateException, RemoteException;

  /**
   * Given a Primary Key, refreshes the EJBean from
   * the persistent storage.
   *
   * @param primaryKey       Primary Key
   * @return                 Account
```

LISTING 10.3   Continued

```
 *  @exception            javax.ejb.FinderException
 *                        if there is an error finding the bean
 *  @exception            java.rmi.RemoteException if there is
 *                        a communications or systems failure
 *  @see                  examples.ejb20.basic.containerManaged.AccountBean
 */
public Account findByPrimaryKey(String primaryKey)
  throws FinderException, RemoteException;

/**
 * Finds an EJBean with a balance equal to a given amount.
 * Returns a single EJBean Account.
 *
 * @param balanceEqual        double Test Amount
 * @return                    Account
 * @exception                 javax.ejb.FinderException
 *                            if an error occurs while accessing
 *                            the persistent storage
 * @exception                 java.rmi.RemoteException if there is
 *                            a communications or systems failure
 * @see                       examples.ejb20.basic.containerManaged.AccountBean
 */
public Account findAccount(double balanceEqual)
  throws FinderException, RemoteException;

/**
 * Finds all EJBeans with a balance greater than a given amount.
 * Returns a Collection of found EJBean Accounts.
 *
 * @param balanceGreaterThan double Test Amount
 * @return                    Collection of Account
 * @exception                 javax.ejb.FinderException
 *                            if an error occurs while accessing
 *                            the persistent storage
 * @exception                 java.rmi.RemoteException if there is
 *                            a communications or systems failure
 * @see                       examples.ejb20.basic.containerManaged.AccountBean
 */
public Collection findBigAccounts(double balanceGreaterThan)
  throws FinderException, RemoteException;

/**
```

LISTING 10.3   Continued

```
 * Finds all EJBeans with a type of 'null'.
 *
 * @return                Collection of Account
 * @exception             javax.ejb.FinderException
 *                        if an error occurs while accessing
 *                        the persistent storage
 * @exception             java.rmi.RemoteException if there is
 *                        a communications or systems failure
 * @see                   examples.ejb20.basic.containerManaged.AccountBean
 */
public Collection findNullAccounts()
   throws FinderException, RemoteException;


}
```

Create a new Java Web service within Workshop. After you create the project, you need to add the AccountEJB client jar file. Because the bean has already been deployed, the client jar has already been created. Workshop ships with a sample Web service that also uses AccountEJB, so you can copy the client jar from the other service.

The client jar is in *bea-install-dir*\weblogic700\samples\workshop\application\ samples\WEB-INF\lib\AccountEJB.jar. Copy this file to the WEB-INF\lib directory for your own project.

Next, select Service, Add Control, Add EJB Control from the menu and add the control. For the JNDI name, use ejb20-containerManaged-AccountHome. To choose the home and remote interfaces, just click on Browse and select the interface shown in the list box. Figure 10.4 shows the completed dialog box.

When you create a new account using AccountEJB, you must supply an account ID (used as a key to locate the account in the future) as well as an initial balance and an account type. The account type can be anything, like "checking" or "savings."

EJB methods can throw several kinds of exceptions, but you can't throw exceptions back to your Web Service client. You must be sure to catch any exceptions thrown by the EJB control. For example, Listing 10.4 shows a Web service method that creates a new account, returning a string indicating the success or failure of the operation. The create method is part of AccountEJB's home interface and is used to create new entity beans. The code in Listing 10.4 simply invokes the create method and returns a message indicating whether the creation was successful.

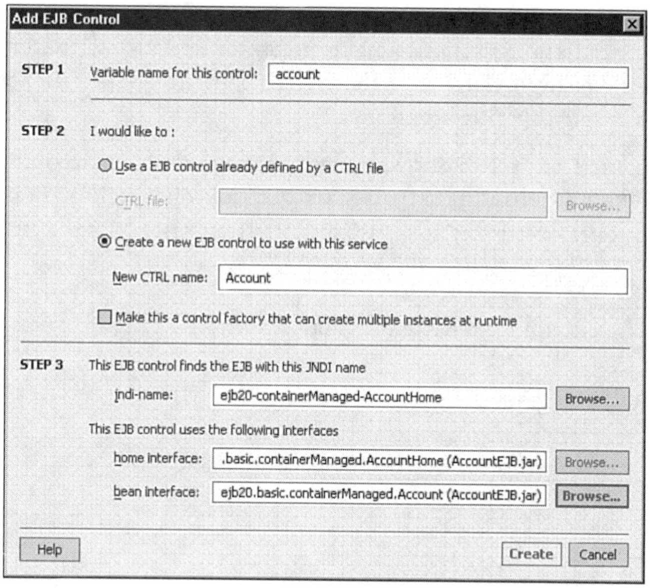

FIGURE 10.4   Fill in the values for accessing the AccountEJB bean.

LISTING 10.4   Excerpt from AccountExample.jws

```
/**
 * @jws:operation
 */
public String createAccount(String accountID, double initialBalance,
    String accountType)
{
    try
    {
        account.create(accountID, initialBalance, accountType);
        return "Account created.";
    }
    catch (CreateException exc)
    {
        return "Error creating account: "+exc.getLocalizedMessage();
    }
    catch (RemoteException exc)
    {
        return "Error creating account: "+exc.getLocalizedMessage();
    }
}
```

To access any of the remote methods, you must locate the EJB using one of the `find` methods. Every EJB home interface has a `findByPrimaryKey` method that lets you locate a specific bean. Because the `accountID` is the primary key for `AccountEJB`, you can use it to locate a specific account.

For example, the Listing 10.5 shows a method that locates an account and then deposits an amount into it. It uses the `findByPrimaryKey` method (a home interface method) to locate a particular account, and then uses the remote interface method `deposit` to deposit money into the account.

LISTING 10.5   Excerpt from AccountExample.jws

```
/**
 * @jws:operation
 */
public String deposit(String accountID, double amount)
{
    try
    {
        Account currAccount = account.findByPrimaryKey(accountID);
        currAccount.deposit(amount);
        return "Deposit complete.";
    }
    catch (FinderException exc)
    {
        return "Error locating account: "+exc.getLocalizedMessage();
    }
    catch (RemoteException exc)
    {
        return "Error locating account: "+exc.getLocalizedMessage();
    }
}
```

You can perform other operations on the account as well. For example, you can add methods to withdraw funds and retrieve a balance. Listing 10.6 shows a complete Web service that can deposit, withdraw, and retrieve balances. Notice the `import` statements at the top. You typically need to import exceptions from `javax.ejb` as well as `java.rmi.RemoteException`. For this example, you must also import the bean's remote interface and exceptions from `examples.ejb20.basic.containerManaged`.

As you can see in Listing 10.6, the Web service doesn't really need to do much. The `AccountEJB` entity bean is doing most of the work. The `createAccount` Web service method simply calls the `create` method in the bean's home interface (via the `AccountControl` EJB control). The `deposit`, `withdraw`, and `getBalance` methods use the findByPrimaryKey method to locate a specific account, and they invoke the appropriate remote method (either deposit, withdraw, or getBalance). This example shows the real power of EJB. In this short, simple Web service, you are loading objects from a database, interacting with them and saving them again, and you interact with these objects just as if they are typical Java objects.

LISTING 10.6   Source Code for AccountExample.jws

```
import weblogic.jws.control.JwsContext;
import javax.ejb.*;
import java.rmi.RemoteException;
import examples.ejb20.basic.containerManaged.*;

public class AccountExample
{

    /**
     * @jws:control
     */
    private AccountControl account;
    /** @jws:context */
    JwsContext context;

    /**
     * @jws:operation
     */
    public String createAccount(String accountID, double initialBalance,
        String accountType)
    {
        try
        {
            account.create(accountID, initialBalance, accountType);
            return "Account created.";
        }
        catch (CreateException exc)
        {
            return "Error creating account: "+exc.getLocalizedMessage();
        }
        catch (RemoteException exc)
        {
            return "Error creating account: "+exc.getLocalizedMessage();
        }
    }
```

LISTING 10.6   Continued

```java
/**
 * @jws:operation
 */
public String deposit(String accountID, double amount)
{
    try
    {
        Account currAccount = account.findByPrimaryKey(accountID);
        currAccount.deposit(amount);
        return "Deposit complete.";
    }
    catch (FinderException exc)
    {
        return "Error locating account: "+exc.getLocalizedMessage();
    }
    catch (RemoteException exc)
    {
        return "Error depositing to account: "+exc.getLocalizedMessage();
    }
}

/**
 * @jws:operation
 */
public String withdraw(String accountID, double amount)
{
    try
    {
        Account currAccount = account.findByPrimaryKey(accountID);
        currAccount.withdraw(amount);
        return "Withdrawal complete.";
    }
    catch (ProcessingErrorException exc)
    {
        // This happens if you try to withdraw more than is in the account
        return "Processing error: "+exc.getLocalizedMessage();
    }
    catch (FinderException exc)
    {
        return "Error locating account: "+exc.getLocalizedMessage();
    }
    catch (RemoteException exc)
```

LISTING 10.6   Continued

```
        {
            return "Error withdrawing from account: "+
                exc.getLocalizedMessage();
        }
    }

    /**
     * @jws:operation
     */
    public String getBalance(String accountID)
    {
        try
        {
            Account currAccount = account.findByPrimaryKey(accountID);
            return ""+currAccount.balance();
        }
        catch (FinderException exc)
        {
            return "Error locating account: "+exc.getLocalizedMessage();
        }
        catch (RemoteException exc)
        {
            return "Error retrieving account balance: "+
                exc.getLocalizedMessage();
        }
    }
}
```

EJB JavaDoc Options

The @jws:ejb JavaDoc tag lets you configure the JNDI name for an EJB control. The only attribute available for the JavaDoc tag is home-jndi-name, which specifies the JNDI name for the EJB's home interface. No other JavaDoc tags or attributes are required to use the EJB control.

The EJB control allows you to provide Web service access to business logic contained in Enterprise Java Beans. It forms an integral part of an enterprise application.

11

Accessing Web Services from Java

IN THIS CHAPTER

- The Client Side of Web Services
- Java Proxy Details
- JavaServer Pages and the Java Proxy
- Using the Proxy Outside the WebLogic Environment
- Changing the Web Service Location

So far, you have seen how to create Web services and invoke them from a browser. You have also seen how to use a control for accessing other Web services from your Web service. Sooner or later, you will need to access a Web service from a Java program or from a JavaServer page.

The Client Side of Web Services

Because Web services use standard protocols like XML, HTTP, and SOAP, you can use existing libraries to access the services. If you're using Java, however, WebLogic Workshop provides libraries for accessing a Web service. For each Web service, Workshop generates a special client jar file containing classes for accessing the service. This special jar file is referred to as a Java proxy.

The Java proxy handles all the underlying SOAP communication for you. It makes a Web service's methods available through a local Java class, so you can invoke Web services just as easily as you invoke regular Java methods. WebLogic Workshop automatically generates a Java proxy for each Web service you create. You simply create an instance of this proxy in your Java program and invoke its methods. Figure 11.1 shows the relationship between the proxy, a Web service, and a program that uses the proxy.

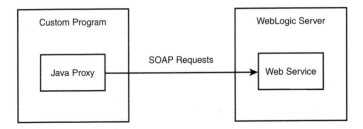

FIGURE 11.1   The Java proxy makes it easy for programs to access Web services.

The Java proxy for a particular Web service is available from the service's Overview page. Figure 11.2 shows the Overview page, with the link to the Java proxy in the section labeled "Web Service Clients."

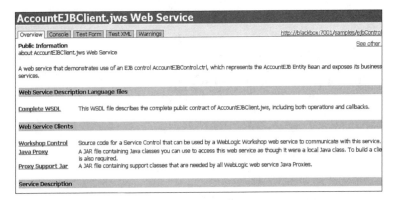

FIGURE 11.2   You can download the Java proxy from the WebLogic server.

NOTE

When you click on the link to download the proxy jar, your browser will probably give you a choice of what to call the jar file. The default is usually the name of the Web service followed by ".jar"; it doesn't matter what you call the file as long as it ends with the ".jar" suffix.

Java Proxy Details

A Java proxy jar file for a Web service contains many Java classes, including a class with the same name as the Web service. This Java class isn't the actual proxy; it just contains a method for accessing the actual proxy. The proxy has a name of the form *serviceName*Soap where *serviceName* is the name of the Web service. You obtain a copy of the proxy by calling a method named get*ServiceName*Soap.

All of the WebLogic proxy classes belong to the `weblogic.jws.proxies` package, so you must remember to import the package at the beginning of any program that uses one or more proxies.

For example, WebLogic Workshop comes with a sample Web service named AccountEJBClient, which uses Enterprise Java Beans to maintain bank accounts. The proxy jar file includes classes named `AccountEJBClient` and `AccountEJBClientSoap`. You would access the proxy this way:

```
AccountEJBClient client = new AccountEJBClient();
AccountEJBClientSoap proxy = client.getAccountEJBClientSoap();
```

The proxy class contains the same methods as those defined in the Web service. For example, the `AccountEJBClient` Web service contains methods like these:

```
public String createNewAccount(String key, double openingBalance, String type)
public double balance(String accountKey)
public double deposit(String accountKey, double depositAmount)
```

Likewise, the `AccountEJBClientSoap` class contains similar methods, with the same parameter types and return types.

JavaServer Pages and the Java Proxy

You might often find that you need to access Web services from a JavaServer page. For example, you might have a Web application that uses several of your existing Web services to store and retrieve data. Because the WebLogic server is a complete Java 2 Enterprise Edition container, it supports JavaServer pages.

Listing 11.1 shows a simple JavaServer page that uses the `AccountClientEJB` proxy.

LISTING 11.1　　Source Code for Account.jsp

```
<%@ page import="weblogic.jws.proxies.*" %>
<html>
<body>
<%
// Locate the server
    AccountEJBClient client = new AccountEJBClient();

// Get the proxy
    AccountEJBClientSoap proxy = client.getAccountEJBClientSoap();

%>
```

LISTING 11.1   Continued

```
Current balance: <%= proxy.balance("123321") %><p>
After depositing $400.0: <%= proxy.deposit("123321", 400.0) %><p>
</body>
</html>
```

In order to run this example, you must deploy both Account.jsp and the proxy jar file as a Web application. You can actually piggyback the application onto an existing Web application. For example, the WebLogic server comes with a DefaultWebApp application, located at

installdir\bea\weblogic700\samples\workshop\applications\DefaultWebApp

To run Account.jsp as part of the default Web application, copy Account.jsp to the DefaultWebApp directory.

Because Account.jsp also uses the proxy jar file, you must install the jar as part of the default Web application. Underneath the DefaultWebApp directory is another directory called WEB-INF. Under the WEB-INF directory, create another directory called lib (if one doesn't already exist) and copy the proxy jar file into this lib directory.

You should now be able to run Account.jsp with the URL http://*yourhostname*:7001/Account.jsp. The :7001 part of the URL comes from the default port number of the WebLogic server. If you change the default port number to something other than 7001, make sure you update the URL accordingly.

Using the Proxy Outside the WebLogic Environment

The proxy jar understands a specific Web service, but it relies on other classes that are part of the WebLogic server. If you need to use the proxy jar outside of the WebLogic server, you can download a jar file containing the support files from the same overview page where you download the proxy jar, under the link "Proxy Support jar."

If you're writing a standalone Java application, you just need to make sure that both the proxy jar and the proxy support jar appear in your class path. If you are writing a Web application, it's best to place the jar files in the WEB-INF\lib directory, but you can also place them in your Web server's class path.

Changing the Web Service Location

By default, the proxy jar accesses the Web service on the host where you generated the jar. If you deploy the Web service on a different server, you *can* use the same jar file, but you must specify where to locate the service.

Remember that you use two different classes when you use the proxy jar. The first class you instantiate, the one with the same name as the Web service, is the one you use to specify an alternate Web service location. For example, if you use a proxy to access the `AccountEJBClient` Web service, you specify the alternate server location when you create the `AccountEJBClient` class.

When you specify an alternate URL, you actually specify the URL for the WSDL file that describes the service. The WebLogic server lets you access the WSDL file for any Web service installed on the server. When you run a Web service and WebLogic Workshop launches a browser, you'll see the root URL for the Web service in the browser's address bar. For example, on a machine named "blackbox," the URL for AccountEJBClient might be

```
http://blackbox:7001/samples/ejbControl/AccountEJBClient.jws
```

To access the WSDL file for this service, add "?:WSDL" to the end of this URL, like this:

```
http://blackbox:7001/samples/ejbControl/AccountEJBClient.jws?WSDL
```

You don't need to do anything ahead of time to create this WSDL file; WebLogic Workshop generates it automatically.

12

@jws JavaDoc Tags

IN THIS CHAPTER

- Method Tags
- Control Tags
- Defining Filewide Enhancements

WebLogic Workshop uses JavaDoc tags to specify many Web service attributes within a Java file without requiring an additional configuration file. These JavaDoc tags all begin with a prefix of @jws, indicating that it is a Java Web service parameter.

Method Tags

Several of the JavaDoc tags used by WebLogic Workshop define items related to a single method. These tags typically control the shape of the incoming and outgoing XML and the method's relation to a conversation.

@jws:conversation—**Define Conversation Boundaries**

When a Web service must remember information between successive requests from a single client, the Web service must define a conversation. Each method has a conversation phase, which indicates how the method relates to the conversation. The four phases are as follows:

- none—This method does not participate in a conversation.

- start—Invoking this method starts a new conversation.

- continue—This method participates in a conversation, but does not begin a new conversation nor end an existing conversation.

- finish—This method terminates a conversation.

The general format of the @jws:conversation tag is

```
/**
 * @jws:conversation phase="which-phase"
 */
```

where *which-phase* is none, start, continue, or finish.

@jws:operation—**Label a Method as a Web Service Method**

The @jws:operation tag marks a method as being a Web service method—that is, it allows the method to be called using one of the supported Web service protocols (HTTP form, SOAP, JMS). There are no attributes associated with the @jws:operation tag. For example:

```
/*
 * jws:operation
 */
public String getCurrentTime();
```

@jws:parameter-xml—**Define Incoming XML Format**

WebLogic Workshop can handle incoming XML in many different formats. If you do not specify a format, it uses its own custom format based on the method parameters. To specify your own XML format, use the @jws:parameter-xml tag.

You specify the XML format with the xml-map attribute, which uses opening and closing :: pairs instead of quotes. For example:

```
/**
 * @jws:parameter-xml xml-map::
 *     <locatePerson xmlns="http://openuri.org/">
 *     <person age="{age}">
 *     <first-name>{firstName}</first-name>
 *     <last-name>{lastName}</last-name>
 *     </person>
 *     </locatePerson>
 *  ::
 */
```

If you need to map incoming values to specific types, you can use the include-java-types attribute, listing the various classes you intend to use:

```
include-java-types="SpecialAddress ZipCode"
```

If you use an XML schema and want to include the definitions for various schema elements, use the schema-elements attribute, listing the various elements:

```
schema-elements="xsd:string xsd:integer"
```

For example:

```
/**
 * @jws:parameter-xml include-java-types="SpecialAddress ZipCode"
 *      schema-elements="xsd:string xsd:integer"
 *      xml-map::
 *      <SpecialAddress>
 *          <street>{street}</street>
 *          <city>{city}</city>
 *          <ZipCode>{zip}</ZipCode>
 *      </SpecialAddress>
 */
```

@jws:return-xml—Define Outgoing XML Format

The @jws:return-xml tag defines the shape of an outgoing XML message in the same way that @jws:parameter-xml defines the shape of the incoming XML. The format of @jws:return-xml is identical to @jws:parameter-xml, including all three attributes—xml-map, include-java-types, and schema-elements.

@jws:sql—Define SQL Statement

The @jws:sql tag defines a SQL statement to be used in a database control. You can substitute parameters in the statement using the familiar {} notation. The statement attribute specifies the actual SQL statement and may either be of the form statement="*your SQL statement*" or

```
statement::
    Your SQL statement
::
```

For database control methods that return a Java iterator, the iterator-element-type attribute indicates the Java type of each element contained in the iterator.

The array-max-length attribute limits the maximum number of elements returned in an array. The value may either be an integer or the keyword all. By default, a database control will return up to 1,024 elements in an array. There is no fixed limit on the maximum number of elements that may be returned if you specify all. It is only limited by the amount of memory available to Java.

@jws:target-namespace—**Specify Namespace for Outgoing Messages**

If you need to specify an XML namespace for your outgoing XML, use the @jws:target-namespace tag. The single attribute for this tag is namespace, which specifies the namespace. For example:

```
/**
 * @jws:target-namespace namespace="http://mycom.com/xml/Namespace"
 */
```

Control Tags

Many @jws tags configure various settings for the different controls that may be included in a Web service.

@jws:connection—**Define a Database Connection**

The @jws:connection tag specifies the Java Naming and Directory Interface (JNDI) name of a data source to be used in a database control. The only attribute for this tag is data-source-jndi-name. For example:

```
/**
 * @jws:connection data-source-jndi-name="prodDataSource"
 */
```

@jws:ejb—**Specify an EJB Home Interface**

The @jws:ejb tag specifies the JNDI name of an EJB's Home interface (Enterprise JavaBeans). The only attribute for this tag is home-jndi-name. For example:

```
/**
 * @jws:ejb home-jndi-name="OrderEJBHome"
 */
```

@jws:jms—**Configure a JMS Control**

The @jws:jms JavaDoc tag configures the various settings for a JMSControl. Table 12.1 shows the attributes available for the @jws:jms tag.

TABLE 12.1   JMS Tag Attributes

Attribute	Description
Type	Either "queue" or "topic" to indicate whether to send/receive on a queue or a topic
send-jndi-name	Name of the topic or queue to send messages on
receive-jndi-name	Name of the topic or queue to receive messages from
connection-factory-jndi-name	Name of the connection factory to use
send-correlation-property	Name of the message property to use for sending a correlation id (defaults to JMSCorrelationID)
receive-correlation-property	Name of the message property to use for retrieving a correlation id (defaults to JMSCorrelationID)
receive-selector	Selector string used to select specific messages to receive

@jws:jms-header—Specify the Format of a JMS Header

The @jws:jms-header tag specifies the XML format used for JMS message headers. The only attribute for this tag is xml-map, which is in the same format as in the @jws:parameter-xml and @jws:return-xml tags.

@jws:jms-message—Specify the Format of a JMS Message

The @jws:jms-message tag specifies the XML format used for the JMS message body. The only attribute for this tag is xml-map, which is in the same format as it is in @jms:jms-header, as well as @jws:parameter-xml and @jws:return-xml.

@jws:jms-property—Specify JMS Message Properties

The @jws:jms-property tag specifies the XML format used for the JMS message properties. The only attribute for this tag is xml-map, which is in the same format as @jms:jms-header, as well as @jws:parameter-xml and @jws:return-xml.

@jws:timer—Configure a Timer Control

The @jws:timer tag configures a timer control, setting the timeout length and the repeat count. The timeout attribute sets the length of the timeout. It may consist of years, months, days, hours, minutes, and seconds. You can list a number of units in a single timeout, like: "1 year, 5 months, 7 days". You can abbreviate the various values all the way down to a single character. Since months and minutes have the same single-letter abbreviation, use longer abbreviations to eliminate any ambiguity, like "mo" for months and "mi" for minutes.

If a timeout value begins with P or p, the value must contain all six time values in the order y m d h m s. For example: "P1y5m7d11h57m23s".

The `repeats-every` attribute indicates when a timer repeats. By default, the value is 0 seconds, which means that the timer fires only once. For non-zero repeat values, use the same time notation as in the `timeout` attribute.

The `coalesce-events` attribute determines whether undelivered timer events are lumped into a single event delivery. If the timer is unable to deliver an event before the next one fires, you have the option to have it coalesce the two events into a single firing. By default, `coalesce-events` is `false`, meaning that you will always get an event for each time interval that has passed. If `coalesce-events` is `true`, you may receive fewer events if the system becomes bogged down.

Defining Filewide Enhancements

Many of the options you have seen for Java Web services have been for individual methods, for example, defining the incoming or outgoing XML maps for a specific method. Other options refer to specific controls, like the EJB control or the JMS control. Workshop includes several options that operate over the entire JWS file.

@jws:conversation-lifetime

You can control the maximum length of a Web service conversation. This can become an issue if your service is very busy; you want the server to dispose of idle conversations fairly quickly to conserve memory. The `@jws:conversation-lifetime` tag allows you to specify the maximum idle time (the amount of time that can elapse without receiving a message before closing the conversation) and the maximum age of the conversation (the total elapsed time of the conversation regardless of idle time).

The `maxIdleTime` attribute specifies the maximum idle time, whereas the `maxAge` attribute specifies the absolute maximum time limit on a conversation. For both of these attributes, use the time notation used by the `@jws:timer` JavaDoc tag. For example, to specify a maximum idle time of 30 minutes and a maximum age of 12 hours:

```
/**
 * @jws:conversation-lifetime
 *    maxIdleTime="30 min" maxAge="12 h"
 */
```

@jws:define—Create Inline Files

If your Web service references an external file, like a WSDL file or an XML schema, you can choose to embed the file within your JWS file instead of referencing an external file. This technique can make it easier to maintain your application because you only have a single file to edit. If the file must be shared by multiple Web services, you should keep it in a separate file instead of embedding it.

The `@jws:define` JavaDoc tag embeds data in a JWS file that would otherwise be stored in a file. The two attributes required for this tag are `name` and `value`.

The `name` attribute specifies the name that other tags must use when referencing this data. For example, if you specify `name="mywsdl"` to embed a WSDL file, you use the filename `#mywsdl` in the `@jws:wsdl` tag that includes your embedded file.

The `value` attribute specifies the contents of the embedded file. As with several other JavaDoc tags, you use `::` to surround the value data instead of quotes. For example, the following `@jws:define` tag specifies an XML schema:

```
/**
 * @jws:define name="personschema"" *      value::
 * <?xml version="1.0"?>
 * <xsd:schema xmlns:xsd="http://www.w3.org/2001/XMLSchema">
 * <!-- Define an element called "person" that is of type PersonType -->
 * <xsd:element name="person" type="PersonType">
 * <!-- Define what PersonType means -->
 * <xsd:complexType name="PersonType">
 * <!-- A person has a sequence of elements -->
 *     <xsd:sequence>
 *        <xsd:element name="first-name" type="xsd:string"/>
 *        <xsd:element name="middle-name" type="xsd:string"/>
 *        <xsd:element name="last-name" type="xsd:string"/>
 *        <xsd:element name="age" type="xsd:positiveInteger"/>
 *        <xsd:element name="born" type="xsd:date"/>
 *        <xsd:element name="children" type="listOfPersonType"/>
 *     </xsd:sequence>
 * </xsd:complexType>
 * <!-- Define listOfPerson as a list of person elements -->
 * <xsd:simpleType name="listOfPersonType">
 *     <xsd:list itemType="PersonType"/>
 * </xsd:simpleType>
 * </xsd:schema>
 * ::
 */
```

`@jws:protocol`—Specify Web Service Protocols

The `@jws:protocol` JavaDoc tag specifies what types of protocols your Web service can accept. The allowable types are as follows:

- `form-get`—Allows a simple HTML form sent using an HTTP GET request

- `form-post`—Allows a simple HTML form sent using an HTTP POST request

- `http-soap`—Allows a SOAP request sent over HTTP

- `http-xml`—Allows an XML message sent over HTTP, but cannot be used in conversations or callbacks

- `jms-soap`—Allows a SOAP request sent using the Java Message Service (JMS)

- `jms-xml`—Allows an XML message sent over JMS, but cannot be used in conversations or callbacks

For each of these protocol options, you specify either `true` or `false` in the `@jws:protocol` tag. For example, to allow only `http-soap` and `jms-soap` requests, use the following declaration:

```
/**
 * @jws:protocol form-get="false" form-post="false"
 *     http-soap="true" http-xml="false" jms-soap="true"
 *     jms-xml="false"
 */
```

Each protocol has a default value if you do not specify one. The `form-get`, `form-post`, and `http-soap` protocols default to true, while the `http-xml`, `jms-soap`, and `jms-xml` protocols default to false.

You can also specify the style of SOAP messages used by your Web service. The `soap-style` attribute has two possible values—`"document"` and `"rpc"`. The default value is `"document"` and indicates the document literal form of SOAP request. The `"rpc"` value specifies the SOAP RPC form of SOAP messaging.

`@jws:schema`—**Use an XML Schema**

An XML schema defines the data types and formats used by an XML document. You can use these data types when specifying an XML mapping for a Web service method, but you must first import the schema. The `@jws:schema` JavaDoc tag imports an XML schema. The only attribute allowed in the `@jws:schema` tag is `import`, which specifies the name of the file to import. For example, to import a file called `defs.xsd`, use the declaration:

```
/**
 * @jws:schema import="defs.xsd"
 */
```

If you import an embedded schema defined by a `@jws:define`, the import filename should be a # followed by the name of the embedded definition. For example, if the `@jws:define` tag specifies `name="schemadefs.xsd"`, the `@jws:schema` tag should be `@jws:schema import="#schemadefs.xsd"`.

@jws:wsdl—Use a WSDL File

If your Web service implements methods defined in a WSDL file, you can specify the WSDL file using the @jws:wsdl tag. The only attribute allowed for the @jws:wsdl tag is file, which specifies the name of the WSDL file. For example, to include service.wsdl, use the following declaration:

```
/**
 * @jws:wsdl file="service.wsdl"
 */
```

If you import an embedded WSDL definition defined by a @jws:define tag, make sure you put a # in front of the definition name.

@jws:xmlns—Specify an XML Namespace

The @jws:xmlns JavaDoc tag lets you specify an XML namespace used within the JWS file. You can include multiple namespaces if necessary by simply including multiple @jws:xmlns tags. The two attributes required for the @jws:xmlns tag are prefix and namespace.

The prefix attribute specifies the namespace prefix that appears at the beginning of tags from this namespace. For example, if the prefix is mycom, the product tag in the mycom namespace looks like <mycom:product>.

The namespace attribute specifies the URI of the namespace and is often an HTTP URL.

To use a namespace called mycom that is defined by the URL http://www.mycom.com/xml/mycom, and another namespace called sec from http://www.mycom.com/xml/security, use the following declaration:

```
/**
 * @jws:xmlns prefix="mycom" namespace="http://www.mycom.com/xml/mycom"
 * @jws:xmlns prefix="sec" namespace="http://www.mycom.cm/xml/security"
 */
```

13

An Online Ordering System

IN THIS CHAPTER

- Designing an Ordering System
- Working with the Database
- Creating the `OrderEntry` Service
- Creating the `OrderTracking` Service

One of the most common uses for Web services is in the area of online ordering. The difference between online ordering with a Web browser and online ordering with a Web service is that a Web service makes it easier to automate a process. As companies streamline their operations, they can place orders with vendors automatically as inventory gets low. A Web service also allows you to create different user interfaces and still use the same server. For example, you might create a browser-based ordering site that uses a Web service to place the orders. The end result is that a user can place orders via a Web browser, but you have now separated the actual ordering process from the user interface. You can then add ordering capability to an existing GUI application just by invoking the same Web service.

In this chapter, you'll see how to create a simple online ordering system that allows users to retrieve a product catalog, place orders for multiple items, and check the status of their orders.

Designing an Ordering System

A typical ordering system needs a catalog of products in order to validate each order. A simple catalog includes the price for each item, although a more complicated system might require more dynamic pricing. For example, some companies might offer a volume discount or charge different prices for different customers. Sometimes a company might offer a discount on a particular combination of items, such as Amazon offering a special deal on pairs of books. For this example, the catalog of products includes the prices. It includes a product I.D. number, a description, and a price.

When it comes to storing the order, one of the things you must consider is whether you need to keep track of customers separately from their orders. For example, if a typical customer places more than one order, you probably want to save the customer's data for later use. This is especially useful in interactive applications because it saves the customer from re-entering his or her address and other information. You will almost always find that you will eventually need to keep customer data separate from the orders, so you should go ahead and separate them from the beginning. One company's order entry application decided to keep customer data together with the orders, which seemed fine at first. When they made the application available over the Internet, however, they found that it was difficult to locate information for a particular customer. There were millions of orders in the database, and they needed to search each one to see if they came from the same customer. Sometimes the names on the orders didn't quite match, so the system had to adopt a loose name-matching policy, which also meant that it could display orders for a different customer. Had they stored the customer data separately, the search for a particular customer would have been far quicker and more accurate.

If you need to associate several addresses with a customer (shipping address, billing address, and so on), you might consider keeping addresses in a separate database table. For this example, however, the customer address is stored in the customer table along with the other customer data.

Because an order can contain multiple products, the order information is split between an order table and an order item table. The order item table contains the individual products and quantities for each item in the order, whereas the order table contains information about the customer who placed the order. The order item table also contains the order ID, which associates the item with a particular order. Likewise, the order table contains a customer ID, which associates the order with a particular customer.

You will need Web service methods for ordering and tracking. You can either offer these methods in separate services or the same service. You should try to keep related methods in the same service, and keep dissimilar methods in different services. For example, if you offer stock quotes as a service and also offer book ordering, you should put them in separate services with names that indicate the kind of service performed (like StockQuote and BookOrdering). If you put the methods in the same service, what would you name it? There is no technical reason why you couldn't group these methods together, but it makes it easier to describe a service when all the methods perform similar functions.

In the case of the ordering system, you could split order entry and order tracking into separate services, or you could keep them together. They are similar enough that grouping them into a service called Ordering would still make sense, but different enough that it would also make sense to split them into OrderEntry and OrderTracking. In this example, they are split into two different services.

Order tracking usually requires some kind of authentication (username/password, digital certificates) because you don't want someone to be able to check on someone else's order. You can also use authentication on the order entry if you want to restrict the set of customers allowed to use the system. For example, you might make the Web service available only to certain high-volume customers. You might also choose to make the service available to all customers, but add a customer registration service to allow new customers to register. You could also make the registration service an internal administration service for your own employees to enter customer data.

The methods in the Ordering service are

```
public Product[] getProductCatalog();
public OrderStatus placeOrder(String custLogin, String custPassword,
    OrderItem orderItems[]);
```

The methods in the OrderTracking service are

```
public OrderStatus[] getAllOrderStatus(String custLogin, String custPassword);
public OrderStatus getOrderStatus(String custLogin, String custPassword,
    int orderNumber);
public Order getOrder(String custLogin, String custPassword,
    int orderNumber);
public OrderStatus cancelOrder(String custLogin, String custPassword,
    int orderNumber);
```

Notice that the Ordering service requires the customer login and password for every method. As an alternative to this technique, you might consider creating a login method that starts a Web service conversation. The login method verifies the login and password one time, and the other methods execute as part of the conversation. A conversation involves additional memory overhead, however, and in this case, a customer usually just invokes one of these methods. If the customer needs multiple methods to perform a task, you should consider starting a conversation. Not only does a conversation involve extra overhead, it also increases the number of service methods that a client must invoke. If a user typically invokes several methods when using a service, a conversation is usually the best technique. If the customer typically invokes just a single method within a reasonable period of time (15 minutes or more, perhaps), it might be better to authenticate each time. That way, the user only needs to send one request instead of three (login, request, logout). This system assumes that the customer interaction is infrequent, so it authenticates each time.

Working with the Database

The database control provided by WebLogic Workshop handles much of the database work that you would otherwise need to write. It isn't always that convenient to use, because you can only execute a single SQL statement from a single database control method, but for this example, it does the job. One thing to keep in mind with the database control is that even though you are limited to one SQL statement per method, multiple methods execute within a single transaction, so you can still execute several statements as part of one transaction.

For a more complicated database model, you will probably need to resort to using JDBC to supplement the capabilities of the database control. You can use the database control to handle the simple operations and only use JDBC for the complex operations.

Creating the Database Tables

WebLogic Workshop comes with a built-in database called PointBase that is already configured for use. You simply create a database control and make it use the cgSampleDataSource data source. When you create your database tables, you usually create scripts and execute them from an SQL tool of some sort. Sometimes, you don't even create the tables yourself—you let a database administrator do it for you. For this example, however, you just create the tables from the database control. Listing 13.1 shows the database control methods that create the tables.

LISTING 13.1   Excerpt from DBControl.ctrl

```
/**
    * @jws:sql statement::
    *    CREATE TABLE CUSTOMER (
    *        ID INTEGER constraint pk_customer PRIMARY KEY,
    *        LOGIN VARCHAR(32),
    *        PASSWORD VARCHAR(32),
    *        NAME VARCHAR(128),
    *        ADDRESS1 VARCHAR(128),
    *        ADDRESS2 VARCHAR(128),
    *        ADDRESS3 VARCHAR(128),
    *        CITY VARCHAR(50),
    *        STATE VARCHAR(2),
    *        ZIP VARCHAR(10))
    * ::
    */
public void createCustomerTable();

/**
    * @jws:sql statement::
    *    CREATE TABLE PRODUCT (
    *        ID INTEGER constraint pk_product PRIMARY KEY,
```

LISTING 13.1   Continued

```
 *          DESCRIPTION VARCHAR(128),
 *          PRICE DECIMAL(12,2))
 * ::
 */
public void createProductTable();

/**
 * @jws:sql statement::
 *     CREATE TABLE ORDERS (
 *         ID INTEGER constraint pk_orders PRIMARY KEY,
 *         CUSTOMERID INTEGER FOREIGN KEY REFERENCES CUSTOMER(ID),
 *         PRICE DECIMAL(12,2),
 *         STATUS VARCHAR(128))
 * ::
 */
public void createOrdersTable();

/**
 * @jws:sql statement::
 *     CREATE TABLE ORDERITEMS (
 *         ID INTEGER constraint pk_orderitems PRIMARY KEY,
 *         ORDERID INTEGER FOREIGN KEY REFERENCES ORDERS(ID),
 *         PRODUCTID INTEGER FOREIGN KEY REFERENCES PRODUCT(ID),
 *         QUANTITY INTEGER,
 *         PRICE DECIMAL(12,2))
 * ::
 */
public void createOrderItemsTable();
```

As you can see, the methods simply execute CREATE TABLE statements.

Creating the Database Control

When you use the database control to retrieve data, it is often useful to store the data in a Java object. If the field names in the Java object match the column names in the database, the database control will automatically copy the column values into the Java object. The end result is that you don't have to do much work to retrieve objects from the database (although you still do some work to insert them).

Listing 13.2 shows the Product class, which represents the data stored in the database.

LISTING 13.2   Source Code for Product.java

```java
public class Product
{
    int id;                // The primary key of the product
    String description;    // The product description
    double price;          // The product price

/** Create a new, empty product */
    public Product()
    {
    }

/** Create a new product and initialize it with specific values */
    public Product(int anId, String aDescription, double aPrice)
    {
        id = anId;
        description = aDescription;
        price = aPrice;
    }

/** Return the primary key value */
    public int getId() { return id; }
/** Change the primary key value */
    public void setId(int anId) { id = anId; }

/** Return the product description */
    public String getDescription() { return description; }
/** Change the product description */
    public void setDescription(String desc) { description = desc; }

/** Return the product price */
    public double getPrice() { return price; }
/** Change the product price */
    public void setPrice(double aPrice) { price = aPrice; }
}
```

The Product class is little more than a data holder. The various get/set methods are
necessary to let the database control populate the product values automatically.
When copying a database row into a Java object, the database control looks for set
methods in the object that match the column names. This get/set pattern is so
common that many Java development environments can automate the creation of
these methods (WebLogic Workshop is not one of them, unfortunately).

Listing 13.3 shows the Customer class.

LISTING 13.3   Source Code for Customer.java

```java
public class Customer
{
    int id;             // The primary key of the customer
    String login;       // The customer's login username
    String password;    // The customer's password
    String name;        // The customer's name
    String address1;    // The first line of the customer's address
    String address2;    // The second line of the customer's address
    String address3;    // The third line of the customer's address
    String city;        // The customer's city
    String state;       // The customer's state
    String zip;         // The customer's zip code

/** Create a new, empty Customer */
    public Customer()
    {
    }

/** Create a new Customer and initialize its fields */
    public Customer(int id, String name, String login, String password,
        String address1, String address2, String address3, String city,
        String state, String zip)
    {
        this.id = id;
        this.login = login;
        this.password = password;
        this.name = name;
        this.address1 = address1;
        this.address2 = address2;
        this.address3 = address3;
        this.city = city;
        this.state = state;
        this.zip = zip;
    }

/** Return the primary key value */
    public int getId() { return id; }
/** Change the primary key value */
    public void setId(int anId) { id = anId; }
```

LISTING 13.3   Continued

```
/** Return the login name (username) */
    public String getLogin() { return login; }
/** Change the login name */
    public void setLogin(String aLogin) { login = aLogin; }

/** Return the password */
    public String getPassword() { return password; }
/** Change the password */
    public void setPassword(String aPassword) { password = aPassword; }

/** Return the name */
    public String getName() { return name; }
/** Change the name */
    public void setName(String aName) { name = aName; }

/** Return the first address line */
    public String getAddress1() { return address1; }
/** Change the first address line */
    public void setAddress1(String anAddress1) { address1 = anAddress1; }

/** Return the second address line */
    public String getAddress2() { return address2; }
/** Change the second address line */
    public void setAddress2(String anAddress2) { address2 = anAddress2; }

/** Return the third address line */
    public String getAddress3() { return address3; }
/** Change the third address line */
    public void setAddress3(String anAddress3) { address3 = anAddress3; }

/** Return the city */
    public String getCity() { return city; }
/** Change the city */
    public void setCity(String aCity) { city = aCity; }

/** Return the state */
    public String getState() { return state; }
/** Change the state */
    public void setState(String aState) { state = aState; }
```

LISTING 13.3   Continued

```
/** Return the zip code */
    public String getZip() { return zip; }
/** Change the zip code */
    public void setZip(String aZip) { zip = aZip; }
}
```

As with the Product class, the Customer class contains get/set methods that make it easier to work with the database control. Beyond these methods, the class is simply a data holder.

Listing 13.4 shows the Order class. Notice that the Order class includes the order items. The database control can't retrieve the items when it retrieves the orders—you have to do that yourself with a second database method. The items are there so that the OrderTracking service can show a customer the entire order.

LISTING 13.4   Source Code for Order.java

```
public class Order
{
    int id;              // The Order's primary key
    int customerId;      // The id of the customer placing the order
    double price;        // The total order price
    String status;       // The order status
    OrderItem[] items;   // The line items in the order

/** Create a new, empty order */
    public Order()
    {
    }

/** Create a new order and initialize it with the specified values */
    public Order(int id, int customerId, double price, String status)
    {
        this.id = id;
        this.customerId = customerId;
        this.price = price;
        this.status = status;
    }

/** Return the primary key */
    public int getId() { return id; }
```

LISTING 13.4   Continued

```java
/** Change the primary key */
    public void setId(int anId) { id = anId; }

/** Return the customer id (primary key of the customer */
    public int getCustomerId() { return customerId; }
/** Change the customer id */
    public void setCustomerId(int aCustomerId) { customerId = aCustomerId; }

/** Return the price */
    public double getPrice() { return price; }
/** Change the price */
    public void setPrice(double aPrice) { price = aPrice; }

/** Return the status */
    public String getStatus() { return status; }
/** Change the status */
    public void setStatus(String aStatus) { status = aStatus; }

/** Return the order items */
    public OrderItem[] getItems() { return items; }
/** Change the order items */
    public void setItems(OrderItem[] theItems) { items = theItems; }
}
```

The `Order` class is a data holder just like `Product` and `Customer`.

Finally, Listing 13.5 shows the `OrderItem` class.

LISTING 13.5   Source Code for OrderItem.java

```java
public class OrderItem
{
    public int id;          // The primary key of the Order Item
    public int orderId;     // The id (primary key) of the order
    public int productId;   // The id (primary key) of the product
    public int quantity;    // The quantity for this item
    public double price;    // The total price of this item

/** Create a new, empty order item */
    public OrderItem()
    {
    }
```

LISTING 13.5   Continued

```java
/** Create a new order item and initialize it with the specified values */
    public OrderItem(int id, int orderId, int productId, int quantity, double
price)
    {
        this.id = id;
        this.orderId = orderId;
        this.productId = productId;
        this.quantity = quantity;
        this.price = price;
    }

/** Return the primary key */
    public int getId() { return id; }
/** Change the primary key */
    public void setId(int anId) { id = anId; }

/** Return the order id (primary key of the order this item belongs to) */
    public int getOrderId() { return orderId; }
/** Change the order id */
    public void setOrderId(int anOrderId) { orderId = anOrderId; }

/** Return the product id (primary key of the product being ordered) */
    public int getProductId() { return productId; }
/** Change the product id */
    public void setProductId(int aProductId) { productId = aProductId; }

/** Return the quantity */
    public int getQuantity() { return quantity; }
/** Change the quantity */
    public void setQuantity(int aQuantity) { quantity = aQuantity; }

/** Return the price */
    public double getPrice() { return price; }
/** Change the price */
    public void setPrice(double aPrice) { price = aPrice; }
}
```

The `OrderItem` class is also a data holder.

Now that you have created the data objects, you simply add methods to the database control to insert and retrieve the objects. When a customer logs in, you need to locate a customer by his login (user name), so you need a method to do this in the database control. When a customer places an order, you need a method to insert the order and the order items. You also need a method to retrieve products by product ID so that you can verify the products before you try to add the order (that is, make sure that the product ID refers to a valid product). To check order status, you need to be able to retrieve an order by its order ID. You should also allow customers to view all their orders, so you need a way to retrieve all orders by customer ID. Finally, you need a method to retrieve all products, so the customer can see the complete product catalog.

Many database tables make use of automatically generated primary key values, usually from some kind of sequential number generator. The difficulty with these keys is that it is difficult to get the key value after you insert a new row in the database, and you often need the key value in order to associate the new item with another item. For example, after you insert a new order, you need the order's primary key in order to create the order items. Different databases have different ways to do this, and the database control doesn't always work with them. This example uses a simple solution—instead of using automatically generated primary key values, it looks for the highest key value for a particular table and adds 1 to it in order to determine what the next ID should be. Although this isn't a very efficient solution, it allows you to continue to use the database control rather than resorting to hand-coded SQL. For example, the `getNextProductId` method in the database control executes the following statement:

```
SELECT MAX(id)+1 FROM PRODUCT
```

The other methods for retrieving ID values perform a similar statement.

Listing 13.6 shows the complete database control, including the methods to add and retrieve customer and order information.

LISTING 13.6   Source Code for DBControl.ctrl

```
import weblogic.jws.*;
import weblogic.jws.control.*;
import java.sql.SQLException;

/**
 * Defines a new database control.
 *
 * The @jws:connection tag indicates which WebLogic data source will be used by
 * this database control. Please change this to suit your needs. You can see a
```

LISTING 13.6 Continued

```
 * list of available data sources by going to the WebLogic console in a browser
 * (typically http://localhost:7001/console) and clicking Services, JDBC,
 * Data Sources.
 *
 * @jws:connection data-source-jndi-name="cgSampleDataSource"
 */
public interface DBControl extends DatabaseControl
{

// Create the customer table
    /**
     * @jws:sql statement::
     *     CREATE TABLE CUSTOMER (
     *         ID INTEGER constraint pk_customer PRIMARY KEY,
     *         LOGIN VARCHAR(32),
     *         PASSWORD VARCHAR(32),
     *         NAME VARCHAR(128),
     *         ADDRESS1 VARCHAR(128),
     *         ADDRESS2 VARCHAR(128),
     *         ADDRESS3 VARCHAR(128),
     *         CITY VARCHAR(50),
     *         STATE VARCHAR(2),
     *         ZIP VARCHAR(10))
     * ::
     */
    public void createCustomerTable();

// Create the product table
    /**
     * @jws:sql statement::
     *     CREATE TABLE PRODUCT (
     *         ID INTEGER constraint pk_product PRIMARY KEY,
     *         DESCRIPTION VARCHAR(128),
     *         PRICE DECIMAL(12,2))
     * ::
     */
    public void createProductTable();

// Create the order table
    /**
     * @jws:sql statement::
```

LISTING 13.6   Continued

```
 *       CREATE TABLE ORDERS (
 *            ID INTEGER constraint pk_orders PRIMARY KEY,
 *            CUSTOMERID INTEGER FOREIGN KEY REFERENCES CUSTOMER(ID),
 *            PRICE DECIMAL(12,2),
 *            STATUS VARCHAR(128))
 * ::
 */
public void createOrdersTable();

// Create the orderitems table
/**
 * @jws:sql statement::
 *       CREATE TABLE ORDERITEMS (
 *            ID INTEGER constraint pk_orderitems PRIMARY KEY,
 *            ORDERID INTEGER FOREIGN KEY REFERENCES ORDERS(ID),
 *            PRODUCTID INTEGER FOREIGN KEY REFERENCES PRODUCT(ID),
 *            QUANTITY INTEGER,
 *            PRICE DECIMAL(12,2))
 * ::
 */
public void createOrderItemsTable();

// Insert a new product into the product table
/**
 * @jws:sql statement::
 *       INSERT INTO PRODUCT (ID, DESCRIPTION, PRICE)
 *       VALUES ({product.id}, {product.description}, {product.price})
 * ::
 */
public void addProduct(Product product);

// Compute the next available product primary key
/**
 * @jws:sql statement::
 *       SELECT MAX(ID)+1 FROM PRODUCT
 * ::
 */
public int getNextProductId();

// Compute the next available customer primary key
/**
```

LISTING 13.6   Continued

```
 * @jws:sql statement::
 *      SELECT MAX(ID)+1 FROM CUSTOMER
 * ::
 */
public int getNextCustomerId();

// Insert a new customer into the customer table
/**
 * @jws:sql statement::
 *      INSERT INTO CUSTOMER (ID, LOGIN, PASSWORD, NAME,
 *      ADDRESS1, ADDRESS2, ADDRESS3, CITY, STATE, ZIP)
 *      values ({cust.id}, {cust.login}, {cust.password},
 *      {cust.name}, {cust.address1}, {cust.address2},
 *      {cust.address3}, {cust.city}, {cust.state}, {cust.zip})
 * ::
 */
public void addCustomer(Customer cust);

// Compute the next available order primary key
/**
 * @jws:sql statement::
 *      SELECT MAX(ID)+1 FROM ORDERS
 * ::
 */
public int getNextOrderId();

// Compute the next avaiable order item primary key
/**
 * @jws:sql statement::
 *      SELECT MAX(ID)+1 FROM ORDERITEMS
 * ::
 */
public int getNextOrderItemId();

// Insert an order into the orders table
/**
 * @jws:sql statement::
 *      INSERT INTO ORDERS (ID, CUSTOMERID, PRICE, STATUS) values
 *      ({order.id}, {order.customerId}, {order.price}, {order.status})
```

LISTING 13.6   Continued

```
 *  ::
 */
public void addOrder(Order order);

// Insert an order item into the orderitems table
 /**
  * @jws:sql statement::
  *      INSERT INTO ORDERITEMS (ID, ORDERID, PRODUCTID,
  *      QUANTITY, PRICE) values
  *      ({item.id}, {item.orderId}, {item.productId}, {item.quantity},
  *      {item.price})
  * ::
  */
public void addOrderItem(OrderItem item);

// Return an array of all available products
 /**
  * @jws:sql statement::
  *      select * from PRODUCT where id <> 0
  * ::
  */
public Product[] getAllProducts();

// Return the product with the specified primary key
 /**
  * @jws:sql statement::
  *      SELECT * FROM PRODUCT WHERE ID={productId}
  * ::
  */
public Product getProduct(int productId);

// Return the customer with the specified primary key
 /**
  * @jws:sql statement::
  *      SELECT * FROM CUSTOMER WHERE ID={customerId}
  * ::
  */
public Customer getCustomer(int customerId);

// Return the customer with the specified login (username)
 /**
```

LISTING 13.6   Continued

```
     * @jws:sql statement::
     *     select * from CUSTOMER where login={login}
     * ::
     */
    public Customer getCustomerByLogin(String login);

// Return the order with the specified primary key
    /**
     * @jws:sql statement::
     *     select * from orders where id={orderId}
     * ::
     */
    public Order getOrder(int orderId);

// Return the order items associated with the specified order
    /**
     * @jws:sql statement::
     *     select * from ORDERITEMS where orderid={orderId}
     *     order by id
     * ::
     */
    public OrderItem[] getOrderItems(int orderId);

// Delete the product table
    /**
     * @jws:sql statement::
     *     drop table product
     * ::
     */
    public void dropProductTable();

// Delete the customer table
    /**
     * @jws:sql statement::
     *     drop table customer
     * ::
     */
    public void dropCustomerTable();

// Delete the order table
    /**
```

LISTING 13.6   Continued

```
    * @jws:sql statement::
    *       drop table orders
    * ::
    */
    public void dropOrderTable();

// Delete the orderitems table
    /**
    * @jws:sql statement::
    *       drop table orderitems
    * ::
    */
    public void dropOrderItemsTable();

// Return all orders belonging to the specified customer
    /**
    * @jws:sql statement::
    *       select * from orders where customerid = {customerId}
    * ::
    */
    public Order[] getOrdersByCustomer(int customerId);

// Change the status of the specified order
    /**
    * @jws:sql statement::
    *       update orders set status={status} where id={orderId}
    * ::
    */
    public void setOrderStatus(int orderId, String status);
}
```

You have already seen fragments of the database control, so Listing 13.6 should look somewhat familiar. Basically, it contains some of the administration methods like create*XXXX*Table and drop*XXXX*Table. It also contains the methods to compute the next primary key for each table, because the database control can't use automatically generated primary keys (with this database, at least). It also contains methods to insert new rows in the table (addProduct, addCustomer, and so on) and to retrieve specific items by their primary key (getCustomer, getOrder).

There are also several query methods that search for multiple items (getAllProducts, getOrdersByCustomer, and getOrderItems). All of these methods simply execute a single SQL statement.

In order to perform the administration functions of DBControl, you need an administration service. Listing 13.7 shows the DBAdmin service, which lets you create the set of tables, drop the tables, and insert test data into the database.

LISTING 13.7   Source Code for DBAdmin.jws

```
import weblogic.jws.control.JwsContext;

public class DBAdmin
{

    /**
     * @jws:control
     */
    private DBControl dbAdmin;
    /** @jws:context */
    JwsContext context;

// Create all the database tables used in this application
    /**
     * @jws:operation
     */
    public void createDatabase()
    {
        dbAdmin.createCustomerTable();
        dbAdmin.createProductTable();
        dbAdmin.createOrdersTable();
        dbAdmin.createOrderItemsTable();
    }

// Delete all the database tables used in this application
    /**
     * @jws:operation
     */
    public void dropDatabase()
    {
        dbAdmin.dropOrderItemsTable();
        dbAdmin.dropOrderTable();
        dbAdmin.dropProductTable();
        dbAdmin.dropCustomerTable();
    }
```

LISTING 13.7   Continued

```
// Create an initial set of data items
    /**
     * @jws:operation
     */
    public void addData()
    {
// Create a dummy product so the primary key computation works
        dbAdmin.addProduct(new Product(0, "null", 0.0));

// Create some new products and add them to the database
        dbAdmin.addProduct(
            new Product(dbAdmin.getNextProductId(),
                "A random assortment of used chess pieces", 1.35));
        dbAdmin.addProduct(
            new Product(dbAdmin.getNextProductId(),
                "Mark's golf balls, some water damage/embedded tree bark",
                3.00));
        dbAdmin.addProduct(
            new Product(dbAdmin.getNextProductId(),
                "Big Book of Incorrectly-Solved Crossword Puzzles", 5.25));
        dbAdmin.addProduct(
            new Product(dbAdmin.getNextProductId(),
                "Slightly-balding Goodyear tire (with comb-over)", 10.00));
        dbAdmin.addProduct(
            new Product(dbAdmin.getNextProductId(),
                "Peanut", 0.01));
        dbAdmin.addProduct(
            new Product(dbAdmin.getNextProductId(),
                "Shoddy bomb casing full of used pinball machine parts",
                99.00));

// Create a dummy customer so the primary key computation works
        dbAdmin.addCustomer(new Customer(0, "null", null, null, null, null,
            null, null, null, null));

// Create a dummy order so the primary key computation works
        dbAdmin.addOrder(new Order(0, 0, 0.0, null));

// Create a dummy order item so the primary key computation works
        dbAdmin.addOrderItem(new OrderItem(0, 0, 0, 0, 0.0));
```

LISTING 13.7   Continued

```
// Create a new customer and add it to the database
        dbAdmin.addCustomer(
            new Customer(dbAdmin.getNextCustomerId(),
                "Samantha's Import Company",
                "samco", "barbie", "123 Main St.", null, null,
                "Drawington", "AK", "12345"));

// Create another new customer and add it to the database
        dbAdmin.addCustomer(
            new Customer(dbAdmin.getNextCustomerId(),
                "Kaitlynn's Export Company",
                "katco", "sayam", "125 Main St.", null, null,
                "Drawington", "AK", "12345"));
    }

    /**
     * @jws:operation
     */
    public Product[] getProducts()
    {
        return dbAdmin.getAllProducts();
    }
}
```

The DBAdmin Web service is a utility that lets you create the database tables and data items you need in order to run the main order entry service. You must execute the createDatabase method to create the database tables, and then the addData method to add data to the tables, before you can run the order entry or order tracking services. These methods use the database control to perform their various operations. Also, notice that the DBAdmin service can initialize the new data items when it creates them—each data object contains a constructor that initializes all its values.

Creating the OrderEntry Service

The bulk of the work in creating the ordering system has already been done. The DBControl database control performs most of the important database operations. The only thing left is to create a Web service that takes XML input and invokes the proper database methods. Now, you must create the service that performs the order entry operations.

Listing 13.8 shows the OrderEntry service.

LISTING 13.8   Source Code for OrderEntry.jws

```java
import weblogic.jws.control.JwsContext;

public class OrderEntry
{

    /**
     * @jws:control
     */
    private DBControl dbControl;
    /** @jws:context */
    JwsContext context;

// Return a list of all available products
    /**
     * @jws:operation
     */
    public Product[] getProductCatalog()
    {
        return dbControl.getAllProducts();
    }

// Verify a customer's login and password, returning null
// if the login or password is invalid
    Customer getCustomer(String login, String password)
    {
        Customer cust = dbControl.getCustomerByLogin(login);

        if (cust == null) return null;
        if (!password.equals(cust.password)) return null;
        return cust;
    }

// Place a new order given a login, password, and an array of
// order items. This is the method that customers use to place
// orders.
    /**
     * @jws:operation
     */
    public OrderStatus placeOrder(String login, String password,
        OrderItem items[])
    {
```

LISTING 13.8   Continued

```java
// Make sure the customer is valid
        Customer cust = getCustomer(login, password);
        if (cust == null) return new OrderStatus(-1, "Invalid login");

// Create a variable to hold the list of invalid product codes
        String badProductList = null;

// The total order price starts at 0
        double totalPrice = 0.0;

        // Check the product ids to make sure they are valid
        for (int i=0; i < items.length; i++)
        {
            // Locate the product
            Product prod = dbControl.getProduct(items[i].productId);

            // If the product doesn't exist, make a note of it
            // and check the rest
            if (prod == null) {
                if (badProductList == null) {
                    badProductList = ""+items[i].productId;
                }
                else {
                    badProductList = badProductList+","+items[i].productId;
                }
            }
            else {
// If the product is valid, compute the item price (quantity * product price)
// and then add the item price to the total for the order
                items[i].price = prod.price * items[i].quantity;
                totalPrice = totalPrice + items[i].price;
            }
        }

// If there were invalid products in the order, return the list of bad products
// instead of placing the order.
        if (badProductList != null) {
            return new OrderStatus(-1, "Invalid product(s): "+badProductList);
        }

// Create a new order
```

LISTING 13.8 Continued

```
        Order order = new Order(dbControl.getNextOrderId(), cust.id,
            totalPrice, "Order Placed");

// Add it to the database
        dbControl.addOrder(order);

// Add the order items to the database
        for (int i=0; i < items.length; i++) {
            OrderItem item = new OrderItem(dbControl.getNextOrderItemId(),
                order.id, items[i].productId, items[i].quantity,
                items[i].price);
            dbControl.addOrderItem(item);
        }

// Tell the customer about the new order
        return new OrderStatus(order.id, "Order Placed");
    }
}
```

The first thing you will notice is the `getCustomer` method, which locates a customer by login name and checks the password. This method is also in the `OrderTracking` service and is used more heavily there.

The `placeOrder` method is the key part of the `OrderEntry` service because it takes an order and stores it in the database. For convenience, the `placeOrder` method takes an array of `OrderItem` objects, but it ignores some of the incoming fields, like `price` and `id`. It really only cares about `productId` and `quantity`. The method verifies that each ordered product exists and calculates a price for each item. It then creates a new order and adds order items to the order. Finally, it returns an order status indicating that the order was successful.

Creating the `OrderTracking` Service

The order tracking part of the application is easy to write because the database control already handles most of the difficult parts. The only thing the tracking service needs to do is fetch orders in various ways, and then allow users to cancel an order.

Listing 13.9 shows the `OrderTracking` service.

LISTING 13.9   Source Code for OrderTracking.jws

```
import weblogic.jws.control.JwsContext;

public class OrderTracking
{

    /**
     * @jws:control
     */
    private DBControl dbControl;
    /** @jws:context */
    JwsContext context;

// Verify a customer's login and password, returning null
// if the login or password is invalid
    Customer getCustomer(String login, String password)
    {
        Customer cust = dbControl.getCustomerByLogin(login);

        if (cust == null) return null;
        if (!password.equals(cust.password)) return null;
        return cust;
    }

// Return the statuses of all a customer's orders
    /**
     * @jws:operation
     */
    public OrderStatus[] getAllOrderStatus(String custLogin, String custPassword)
    {
// Make sure the customer is valid
        Customer cust = getCustomer(custLogin, custPassword);

        if (cust == null) {
            return new OrderStatus[] { new OrderStatus(-1, "Invalid login") };
        }

// Locate all the customer's orders
        Order[] orders = dbControl.getOrdersByCustomer(cust.id);

// Create an array to hold the status of each order
        OrderStatus[] statuses = new OrderStatus[orders.length];
```

LISTING 13.9   Continued

```java
// Loop through the orders and create an OrderStatus object for each one
      for (int i=0; i < orders.length; i++) {
           statuses[i] = new OrderStatus(orders[i].id, orders[i].status);
      }

// Return the statuses for the orders
      return statuses;
   }

// Returns the status for a particular order
   /**
    * @jws:operation
    */
   public OrderStatus getOrderStatus(String custLogin, String custPassword,
      int orderNumber)
   {
// Make sure the customer is valid
      Customer cust = getCustomer(custLogin, custPassword);

      if (cust == null) {
         return new OrderStatus(-1, "Invalid login");
      }

// Locate the order
      Order order = dbControl.getOrder(orderNumber);

// If the order doesn't exist or doesn't belong to this customer,
// tell the user that the order is invalid
      if ((order == null) || (order.customerId != cust.id)) {
           return new OrderStatus(-1, "Invalid order");
      }

// Return the order status
      return new OrderStatus(order.id, order.status);
   }

// Returns the contents of a particular order
   /**
    * @jws:operation
    */
   public Order getOrder(String custLogin, String custPassword,
```

LISTING 13.9   Continued

```
        int orderNumber)
    {
// Make sure the customer is valid
        Customer cust = getCustomer(custLogin, custPassword);

        if (cust == null) {
            return null;
        }

// Locate the order
        Order order = dbControl.getOrder(orderNumber);

// If the order doesn't exist or doesn't belong to this customer,
// Tell the user that the order is invalid
        if ((order == null) || (order.customerId != cust.id)) {
            return null;
        }

// Get the order items that belong to the order and store them
// in the Order object
        order.items = dbControl.getOrderItems(order.id);

// Return the order object
        return order;
    }

// Cancels an existing order
    /**
     * @jws:operation
     */
    public OrderStatus cancelOrder(String custLogin, String custPassword,
        int orderNumber)
    {
// Make sure the customer is valid
        Customer cust = getCustomer(custLogin, custPassword);

        if (cust == null) {
            return new OrderStatus(-1, "Invalid login");
        }
```

LISTING 13.9   Continued

```
// Locate the order
      Order order = dbControl.getOrder(orderNumber);

// If the order doesn't exist or doesn't belong to this customer,
// tell the user that the order is invalid
      if ((order == null) || (order.customerId != cust.id)) {
          return new OrderStatus(-1, "Invalid order");
      }

// Set the order status to deleted, but don't delete the order
      dbControl.setOrderStatus(order.id, "Order deleted");

// Tell the user that the order has been deleted
      return new OrderStatus(order.id, "Order deleted");
    }
}
```

Like the OrderEntry service, the OrderTracking service uses the getCustomer method to perform the login name lookup to verify the user's password.

Also, notice that any time the service locates an order, it verifies that the customer numbers match. You can either do this in the database control or in the application itself. It is probably safer to do it in the database control (by adding a WHERE clause to the SELECT statement), because you only have to add the code in one place. If you perform the check within the application, you must be careful to perform it in every method. The disadvantage of performing the check in the database control is that you limit the capabilities of the database control. You can no longer use it to search for any order, only one for a specific customer. If you know the order ID and not the customer ID, you can't locate the order. This example takes the slightly riskier approach of performing the check within the application.

As you can see, it is pretty easy to make a database-powered Web service with WebLogic Workshop. Although the database control has some limitations, its ease of use and flexibility make up for these limitations. The database control and the other Workshop controls make it relatively easy to add a Web service interface to an existing database or application.

PART IV

Appendixes

IN THIS PART

A Java Essentials

B XML

C Web Service Description Language (WSDL)

D SOAP

A

Java Essentials

IN THIS APPENDIX

- Your First Java Program
- Declaring Variables
- Operators
- Conversions
- Classes and Objects
- Control Flow
- Exceptions
- Interfaces
- Packages
- Common Java Packages
- Where to Go from Here

Most of the time, when you learn a new language, you start with simple data types—numbers, strings, and so on. Only after you learn how to declare simple variables, and maybe even write a few if/for/while statements, do you venture into the world of objects. If you want to learn Java, however, you need to learn how to create a Java class right away.

Your First Java Program

You can't write a Java program without creating a class. A *class* is a grouping of data items and code. A class definition may consist of only code, only data items, or both. A class is actually a blueprint of an object. That is, an object is really the thing that contains data and code. The class merely defines what a particular type of object can contain. You usually say that an object is an "instance of" a particular class. For example, you may have the blueprint for a car—the blueprint is like the car's class. It shows all the features the car has and maybe even describes what the car can do, but you can't drive a blueprint. The car itself is like an object. It is an instance of the class defined by the blueprint.

The items contained in a class are referred to as *members*. Data items are usually referred to as either member variables or fields. A function contained in a class is called a *method*.

Listing A.1 shows the ever-popular "Hello World" program in Java. Notice that it contains a class definition.

LISTING A.1   Source Code for HelloWorld.java

```
public class HelloWorld
{
    public static void main(String[] args)
    {
        System.out.println("Hello World!");
    }
}
```

> **TIP**
>
> If you come from a Windows background, you might not be picky about capitalization, but Java is. Make sure you use the name HelloWorld.java with the H and W capitalized. In Java, the filename must always match the class name exactly (with .java added onto the end).

To compile and run the HelloWorld.java program, you need to install the Java Development Kit (JDK), which is available from http://java.sun.com. One of the things that often confuses Java newcomers is that there is a JDK and also a JRE (Java Runtime Environment). The JDK includes everything necessary to run Java programs, and also includes the compiler that translates source code into byte codes. The JRE just includes everything necessary to run Java programs—it doesn't let you compile them.

WebLogic Workshop comes with a JDK, so if you have already installed WLW, you don't need to download the JDK. If you plan on compiling programs outside of WLW, however, you need to make sure that the JDK's bin and jre/bin directories are in your system path. For example, if your WLW has JDK 1.3.1 and you have installed WLW in c:\bea, you can set your path using the following command:

```
set PATH=c:\bea\jdk131\bin;c:\bea\jdk131\jre\bin;%PATH%
```

If you have your path set correctly, you should be able to compile your program using the javac command. Try entering the command from a command prompt:

```
javac HelloWorld.java
```

> **TIP**
>
> If you are uncomfortable working from a command prompt and manually compiling your program, you should investigate one of the many Java IDEs available. There are two very good, free IDEs—Forte (available from http://www.sun.com/forte, look for the Community Edition) and Eclipse (http://www.eclipse.org).

If you get the response "'javac' is not recognized as an internal or external command, operable program or batch file" or something similar, you still don't have your path set up correctly. If everything is working and you don't have any typos in HelloWorld.java, the system should just come back with another prompt.

Assuming everything compiles successfully, you can now run the program with the following command:

```
java HelloWorld.java
```

If everything works well, you should see a response similar to the one shown in Figure A.1.

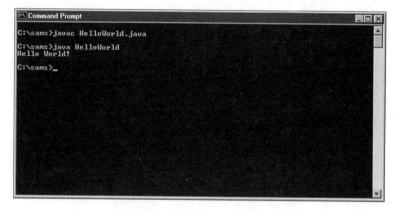

FIGURE A.1 The HelloWorld class simply prints out "Hello World!"

Now that you see how to create a simple Java class, you can experiment with the basic parts of Java. For future experiments, you can use a template like this:

```
public class YourClassNameHere
{
    public static void main(String[] args)
    {
        Your Java Code goes here
    }
}
```

The first line of the template declares the name of your class and makes the class public, meaning anyone can use it. The contents of the class must be surrounded by {}s, which are on the second and last lines of the template.

The line `public static void main(String[] args)` declares a method (a Java function) that has no return value (void) and takes an array of strings as a parameter (`String[] args`). The `main` method is special in Java. When you type "`java SomeClassName`", Java looks for a public static void method called `main` in the class that takes an array of strings as parameters. If it finds one, it executes that method. In other words, the `main` method is the startup method for a Java program.

Don't forget to make the class name and filename match. The class `MyClass` should be stored in a file called MyClass.java.

Declaring Variables

Java has two basic kinds of data types—primitive types and objects. A primitive type is almost always a number (the only exceptions are the `char` type, which represents characters, and the `boolean` type, which can either be `true` or `false`. Table A.1 shows the primitive Java types.

TABLE A.1   Primitive Java Types

Primitive Type	Size	Range
byte	8 bits	-128 to 127
short	16 bits	-32768 to 32767
int	32 bits	-2147483648 to 2147483647
long	64 bits	-9223372036854775808 to 9223372036854775807
float	32 bits	Approx. +/- 10^{38} (7 digits of precision)
double	64 bits	Approx. +/- 10^{308} (15 digits of precision)
char	16 bits	-32768 to 32767 although normally used for alphabetic characters (like 'A' or '@')
boolean	N/A	false, true

To declare a variable, use the following:

```
type-name variable-name;
```

For example:

```
int totalDays;
short age;
boolean isFinished;
long johnSilver;
```

You can also initialize a variable when you declare it:

```
double pi = 3.1415926536;
```

In fact, you can assign a value to a variable at any time, like this:

```
double pi;
pi = 3.1415926536;
```

Values

There are several different ways to represent values (numbers, characters, Booleans) in Java. For numbers, you can always use a series of digits, like 12345 or 3.14159. There are also some special numeric notations for certain other number bases and for certain types of floating-point numbers.

NOTE

Values are often referred to as "literals."

A number with a leading 0 is assumed to be an octal number (base 8). For instance, the literal 077 is the same as 63 in decimal.

A number with a leading 0x or 0X is assumed to be hexadecimal (base 16). For instance, the value 0x3f is the same as 077 in octal or 63 in decimal.

A number followed by L or l (Sun recommends using L because the lowercase letter l looks too much like the number 1) indicates a long value. If you need to write a literal larger than around 2 billion, don't forget the L at the end!

A number followed by F or f is a floating-point number. A number followed by D or d is a double-precision floating-point number. For example, 1.0 is the same as 1F or 1f. Also, you can use scientific notation in a floating-point number. For example, 3.65E3 is the same as 365.0.

A Boolean value can be either `true` or `false`.

A character value can be a single character enclosed in single quotes, like 'A' or 'g'. You can also specify a character by its octal value. The letter A in octal is 101. The octal character representation for 'A' is '\101'. You can also specify characters using their four-digit hexadecimal Unicode value. For example, the Unicode value for 'A' is 0041. The Unicode representation for 'A' is '\u0041'. A Unicode constant must always have four digits. The Unicode and octal representations of a character are equivalent to the character itself. In other words, 'A', '\101', and '\u0041' are all identical.

Java also recognizes several special characters, as shown in Table A.2.

TABLE A.2   Special Characters in Java

Character	Meaning
\b	Backspace (\0008)
\f	Form Feed (\000c)
\n	New line (\000a)
\r	Carriage return (\000d)
\t	Tab (\0009)

For example:

```
char newline='\n';
```

Finally, for certain characters like ' and \, you need to insert a \ before the character. As in C and several other languages, the \ is a special escape character. It tells the compiler to interpret the character following the \ as-is (except in the case of the special characters like \n). To represent a ' in a character literal, use '\''. To represent a \ in a character literal, use '\\'.

A string literal is a series of characters enclosed in double quotes, like "Hello World". You can also use the special character literal forms in a string, like "Hello M\u0041rk" (Hello Mark). If you need to represent a " in a string, put a \ in front of it, like this "My \"quoted\" text" (My "quoted" text).

Object References

A variable can also refer to an object. One thing you may have heard about Java is that it doesn't have pointers (variables that refer to specific memory locations). Java doesn't have the kind of pointers that C and C++ have, where you can access raw memory, but it does have references, which behave like pointers to objects. That is, you use a reference to access an object. Unlike C++ where you must explicitly manage memory, Java has automatic memory management. When there are no more references pointing to an object, that object is destroyed and its memory reclaimed using a process called garbage collection. You don't need to do anything to make garbage collection happen; Java does it automatically.

You can declare a reference to an object just as you declare other variables. You use the class name of the object as the variable's type. For example, a string in Java is an object and its class name is String. To declare a string variable, you use a declaration like this:

```
String name;
```

You can also initialize a string like this:

```
String name = "Ceal";
```

One important point to remember about Java strings is that they are immutable—you can't change the value of a string. Instead, you always create new strings. For example, suppose you have the following declarations:

```
String name = "Samantha";
String name2 = name;
```

At this point, name and name2 refer to the same object—the string "Samantha". Now you want to add a last name to the string. You can just add an additional string like this:

```
name = name + " Tippin";
```

Java doesn't modify the existing "Samantha" string, it just creates a new string whose value is "Samantha Tippin". If you print out name and name2, you see that name is now "Samantha Tippin" while name2 is still "Samantha".

When you reassign a string to a variable, the old string is eventually destroyed by the garbage collector, assuming no more references to it exist.

There is one literal value for an object reference—null. A value of null means that a reference doesn't refer to an object at the moment. You can assign null as the value of a reference:

```
String x = null;
```

In this case, x can refer to a String object, but at the moment, it doesn't refer to anything.

Operators

Variables don't do much good unless you have a way to manipulate them. Java supports most of the operators you are familiar with. In general, Java operators work like C and C++ operators. Table A.3 shows the common Java operators.

TABLE A.3   Java Operators

Expression	Result
A+B	Add A to B.
A-B	Subtract B from A.
A*B	Multiply A by B.
A/B	Divide A by B.
A%B	The remainder when A is divided by B.
A<<B	Bitwise shift A to the left by B bits, fills rightmost B bits with 0.
A>>B	Arithmetic shift A to the right by B bits; if leftmost bit is 1, fills the leftmost B bits with 1.

TABLE A.3   Continued

Expression	Result
A>>>B	Logical shift of A to the right by B bits, filling the leftmost B bits with 0.
A&B	Bitwise AND of A and B.
A|B	Bitwise OR of A and B.
A^B	Bitwise exclusive-OR of A and B.
~A	Bitwise complement of A (1's become 0, 0's become 1).
A++	Result is A, but then A is incremented by 1. If A=1 and you print A++, you'll print 1, but then A's value will be set to 2.
++A	A is incremented by 1 and the result is the new A. If A=1 and you print ++A, you'll print 2 and A's value will be 2.
A--	Result is A, but then A is decremented by 1.
--A	A is decremented by 1 and the result is A.
A == B	True if A is equal to B.
A != B	True if A is not equal to B.
A > B	True if A is greater than B.
A >= B	True if A is greater than or equal to B.
A < B	True if A is less than B.
A <= B	True if A is less than or equal to B
A && B	Logical AND of A and B (A and B must be Boolean).
A || B	Logical OR of A and B (A and B must be Boolean).
!A	Logical complement of A (true is false, false is true). A must be Boolean.
A instanceof B	True if variable A refers to an object that is an instance of class B.

NOTE

To compare strings and other objects, do not use the == operator—it only indicates whether two object references refer to exactly the same object. Instead, use the equals method, like A.equals(B). The equals method returns true if two objects are equivalent (for strings, if they match character for character). To compare two strings regardless of case, use A.equalsIgnoreCase(B).

Java also has some shorthand operators. If you would normally do an expression like A=A+B or A=A-B, Java lets you replace these expressions with A+=B and A-=B. Table A.4 lists the shorthand assignment operators.

TABLE A.4   Assignment Operators

Operator	Result
A+=B	A=A+B
A-=B	A=A-B
A*=B	A=A*B

TABLE A.4   Continued

Operator	Result
A/=B	A=A/B
A%=B	A=A%B
A>>=B	A=A>>B
A>>>=B	A=A>>>B
A<<=B	A=A<<B
A&=B	A=A&B
A|=B	A=A|B
A^=B	A=A^B

Java has one other shorthand operator that may look strange to you if you have never used C. The ?: operator has the form: *expression ? A : B* where *expression* is a Boolean expression like true or a>5. If *expression* is true, the result of the ?: operator is *A* (that is, the first result). If *expression* is false, the result of the operator is *B*. The ?: operator is functionally equivalent to the following statement:

```
If (expression)
{
    A
}
else
{
    B
}
```

For example, suppose you have the following two statements:

```
System.out.println( 4 > 2 ? "Four is bigger" : "Four is smaller");
System.out.println( 2 > 4 ? "Two is bigger" : "Two is smaller");
```

The resulting output of these two lines would be

```
Four is bigger
Two is smaller
```

If the syntax of the ?: operator bothers you, don't use it. Even old C programmers have to look twice at some ?: expressions. They often make the code look more complicated and only save a few keystrokes. You usually spend more time reading the code than writing it, so why not make it more readable?

When evaluating Boolean expressions, Java uses a short-circuit evaluation. That is, it stops evaluating the expression as soon as it knows the outcome for sure.

For example, suppose you have the following expression:

```
if ((5 > 4) && (4 > 6) && (9 > 8))
{
    // Do something here
}
```

As soon as Java sees the (4 > 6), it knows that the whole expression must be false, because in a series of && statements, one false makes the entire expression false. Likewise, in a chain of || expressions, Java stops evaluating at the first true value. One common use of short-circuiting is when you need to check for a null object reference before trying to use the object. Normally, if you try to use a null reference to do something, Java gives you an error called a `NullPointerException`. The following statement avoids the possibility of this exception:

```
if ((myObj != null) && (myObj.age > 10))
```

If `myObj` is null, Java stops evaluating the statement, so it never tries to access `myObj.age`, which would yield a `NullPointerException` when `myObj` is null.

Conversions

You might also need to convert from one type to another. For that, you use the cast operator. To cast a value to a different type, put the new type in parentheses in front of the value you want to cast. For example, suppose you have a variable that is a double and you want to treat it like an int. Just apply the cast operator:

```
double x = 12.34;

int y = (int) x;
```

At this point, y has the value 12 (Java always rounds down when converting from floating point to integer). You don't need to have a variable to do a cast. For example, the following statement prints 12:

```
System.out.println((int)12.34);
```

Classes and Objects

Java really revolves around objects and their corresponding classes. Again, a class is basically a grouping of data items (primitive types and object references) and code. A class is really more like a blueprint and an object is a realization of that blueprint.

You must create at least one class to make a Java program, and typically you create many classes. The basic syntax for a class definition is

```
class ClassName
{
    class declarations
}
```

> **NOTE**
>
> Although Java doesn't require it, the common convention is to begin class names with a capital letter and class members (data items and methods) with lowercase letters. Typically, you also capitalize subsequent words in class or member names. For instance, firstName would be a member variable, whereas OrderForm is usually a class.

Typically, you declare a class as public, meaning any other class can use it:

```
public class ClassName
```

A class can contain *fields* (variables) and *methods* (functions). Both fields and methods may have access modifiers that determine who can use them. The three access modifiers are: public, protected, and private.

- A public field or method is accessible from any class in any package.

- A protected field or method is only accessible from any subclass of the current class, or any class in the same package as the class (you'll learn about packages later in this chapter in the section "Packages").

- A private field or method is only accessible from the current class. Subclasses may not access the private variables of their superclass.

There is actually a fourth form of access modifier, called the package modifier. If you don't specify an access modifier, the default is package scope. A field or method with package scope is accessible by any class within the same package as the current class, regardless of whether it is a subclass or not.

To access a field in an object (an instance of a class) you specify a variable name, then a period, and the field. For example, suppose you define a Person class like this:

```
public class Person
{
    public String firstName;
    public String lastName;
}
```

If you have a variable called `person1`, you can access the first name as `person1.firstName`.

You already know how to declare fields—they use the syntax you saw in the section on declaring variables. You can even assign a value to a field when you declare it. The syntax for a method declaration is as follows:

```
access-modifier return-type method-name(parameters)
{
    method body
}
```

For example:

```
public String setNameInformation(String aFirstName,
    String aLastName)
{
    firstName = aFirstName;
    lastName = aLastName;
}
```

The return type of a method may be any Java primitive type or any Java class. If a method doesn't return a value, the return type should be `void`.

You can have multiple methods with the same name, as long as they have different parameters. Specifically, they must differ either by the number of parameters or by the types of parameters.

You often need to initialize a class instance when you first create it. A class can have any number of initializer methods, called constructors. A constructor is a method that has no declared return type and has the same name as the class. For example, a `Person` class might have a constructor like this:

```
public Person(String aFirstName, String aLastName)
{
    firstName = aFirstName;
    lastName = aLastName;
}
```

A constructor with no parameters is referred to as the "default constructor." If you create a subclass and you don't explicitly call the superclass's constructor, Java will invoke the superclass's default constructor (if it has one). For example, suppose you have a class `Person`:

```
public class Person
{
    public String name;
```

```
    public Person()
    {
        name = null;
    }

    public Person(String aName)
    {
        name = aName;
    }
}
```

Control Flow

Java has most of the control flow structures that you find in other languages. One difference is that any of the structures that involve a test (such as `if-else` and `while`) require a Boolean expression. Many other languages allow integer expressions where zero means false and non-zero means true. Java does not—the expression must be Boolean.

if-else

The short syntax for `if-else` is

```
if (boolean expression)
    statement
else
    statement
```

If you want to execute multiple statements as part of an `if` or any other control flow structure, enclose the statements in {}s. For example:

```
if (a > b)
{
    System.out.println("A is greater than b");
    b = a;
}
```

The `else` portion of an `if` statement is optional. You can also chain `else` and `if` together like this:

```
if (a == 1)
{
    System.out.println("A is 1");
}
```

```
else if (a == 2)
{
    System.out.println("A is 2");
}
else
{
    System.out.println("A is neither 1 nor 2");
}
```

while

A while loop executes while a Boolean expression is true:

```
while (boolean expression)
    statement
```

For example:

```
int x = 5;
while (x < 10)
{
    System.out.println(x);
    x = x + 1;
}
```

You can also perform a while loop that evaluates the expression after executing the statement:

```
do
    statement
while (boolean expression);
```

For example:

```
int x = 5;
do
{
    System.out.println(x);
    x = x + 1;
}
while (x < 10);
```

for

A `for` loop is really just a special kind of `while` loop. As usual, Java follows the C/C++ method of doing `for` loops as opposed to the Basic/Pascal method. The general form is

```
for (initialization; boolean expression; increment)
    statement
```

The initialization part of a `for` loop usually initializes the looping variable. The Boolean expression tests the looping variable and while the variable is true, continues the loop. The increment usually increments the looping variable.

One of the nice things in Java is that when you declare a variable within the initialization section of a `for` loop, the variable only exists until the end of the loop. You can redeclare the same variable in another `for` loop.

Here is a `for` loop that counts from 1 to 10:

```
for (int i=1; i <= 10; i++)
{
    System.out.println(i);
}
```

Here is a loop that counts from 10 down to 1:

```
for (int i=10; i >= 1; i--)
{
    System.out.println(i);
}
```

switch

A `switch` statement is the equivalent of a `case` statement in Pascal or Basic. It lets you choose between several different values. The general format is

```
switch (expression)
{
    case value:
        statement(s)
    case value:
        statement(s)
    default:
        statement(s)
}
```

CAUTION

By default, a switch statement starts at the first matching case option and then executes all statements afterward, including those in subsequent case options. If you want to break out of the switch statement before hitting the next case option, include a break statement as the last statement in the option.

You can execute multiple statements after each case without wrapping them in {}s. Remember to use break statements to break out of an option if you don't want to fall through into the next option. Here is an example:

```
switch (x)
{
    case 1:
        System.out.println("x = 1");
        break;
    case 2:
        System.out.println("x = 2");
        break;
    default:
        System.out.println("x = "+x);
}
```

continue **and** break

Sometimes you want to leave a for or while loop immediately, rather than waiting for the Boolean expression to change. You can use the break statement to break out of the loop. The syntax is just

```
break;
```

For example, to break out of a loop when a variable is greater than a particular value, use this syntax:

```
int sum = 0;
for (int i=0; i < 100; i++)
{
    sum = sum + i;
    if (sum > 50) break;   // Quit when sum > 50
}
```

Likewise, the continue statement jumps back to the top of a for or while loop. In a for loop, it executes the increment, so you aren't really repeating the loop; you're jumping to the next iteration. The syntax is

```
continue;
```

For example, when doing one loop inside another, you often want to skip the case where the two loop variables are the same:

```
for (int j=0; j < 100; j++)
{
    for (int k=0; k < 100; k++)
    {
        if (j == k) continue;  // Go on to the next k
    }
}
```

return

The return statement returns a value from a method. The syntax is

```
return value;
```

For example:

```
public double getPI()
{
    return 3.1415926536;
}
```

Exceptions

Java supports an exception handling mechanism that makes it easy to report errors. When an error occurs in a method call, the method can "throw" an exception. When you throw an exception (using the throw keyword), Java looks for code to catch the exception. Basically, to catch an exception, you use a try-catch block. You "try" to execute some methods, and if one of them throws an exception, Java executes the catch block. When you execute a method that can throw an exception, you can surround it with a try-catch block, like this:

```
try
{
    a.doSomething();
}
catch (NumberFormatException exc)
{
    exc.printStackTrace();
}
```

The gist of a try block is that you execute some statements, and if any of those statements throw an exception, you immediately abandon the rest of the try block and look for a `catch` statement that handles the exception. In the previous example, the `catch` block handles only a `NumberFormatException`; if any other exception occurs, the exception "bubbles up" to the first `catch` block that handles the exception. When you catch `Exception`, you catch all possible exceptions. In other words, the following `catch` block catches all possible exceptions:

```
catch (Exception exc)
{
    // do something here
}
```

You might wrap the previous `try`-`catch` block with another block:

```
try
{
    try
    {
        a.doSomething();
    }
    catch (NumberFormatException exc)
    {
        exc.printStackTrace();
    }
}
catch (Exception exc)
{
    System.out.println("I handle any exception.");
    exc.printStackTrace();
}
```

Now, if `a.doSomething` throws an exception other than `NumberFormatException`, the code still handles it because the outer `try`-`catch` block catches `Exception`. If an exception occurs within a method and the method doesn't handle the exception, Java jumps back to where the method was called and searches for a `catch` block. If that method doesn't catch the exception, Java jumps back up and keeps going until it finds a handler. If Java gets back to the main method and the exception still isn't handled, the program exits.

You can also add a `finally` block that executes whether or not an exception has been thrown. Typically, you use a `finally` block to close files or database connections—you want to make sure you close them whether an exception occurs or not. Here is an example:

```
DBConnection conn = getDBConnection();
try
```

```
{
    conn.doSomeDatabaseOperation();
}
catch (DatabaseException exc)
{
    exc.printStackTrace();
}
finally
{
    conn.close();
}
```

The `conn.close()` statement always executes, whether the `catch` block executes or not.

If you have a method that throws an exception, or doesn't handle an exception that may be thrown by one of the methods it calls, you must declare that the method can throw the exception. Java has strict exception checking and requires you to specify what exceptions a method can throw. To declare that a method can throw an exception, use the `throws` keyword immediately after the method declaration, like this:

```
public void myMethod()
    throws IOException, DatabaseException
{
```

Although Java is strict about declaring exceptions, there is a special type of exception called a `RuntimeException` that you do not need to declare. Among the runtime exceptions, the most common one is `NullPointerException`, which occurs when you try to access a field or method from an object reference that is null. You don't need to declare that your method can throw `NullPointerException`.

Interfaces

An interface is nothing more than a set of methods that have some kind of behavior in common. For example, an interface might define a set of methods related to driving a car, or manipulating a stock trade. Interfaces can be confusing to people who have never seen them before. The idea behind an interface is that you define a set of methods that some objects should perform. Then, an object that has those methods can declare that it implements that interface.

An interface looks like an object—you can declare variables of the interface's type, you can assign objects to them, and you can pass them to methods and return them as values from methods. An interface isn't an object, though, it is more like a view of an object. Paraphrasing Dan Rather's famous "if it walks like a duck, acts like a duck, quacks like a duck, then you got a duck," an interface lets you define the characteristics of a duck. For example:

```
public interface Duck
{
    public void quack();
    public void waddle();
    public void sayAflac();
}
```

You can now declare variables of type Duck:

```
Duck donald, daisy, daffy;
```

Still, there is no such thing as a Duck object. You can't do this:

```
iWantA = new Duck();
```

You can, however, create a class that implements the Duck interface. That is, you can create a class that has the methods declared in the Duck interface:

```
public class Elephant implements Duck
{
    public Elephant() {}
    public void eatPeanuts() { System.out.println("Yum!"); }
    public void quack() { System.out.println("Quack!"); }
    public void waddle() { System.out.println("Thud thud thud"); }
    public void sayAflac() { System.out.println("Aflac!"); }
}
```

Now, an Elephant walks like a Duck, quacks like a Duck, and acts like a Duck, so it is legal to say:

```
Duck daffy = new Elephant();
```

Interfaces allow you to treat many different types of objects as being essentially the same without requiring the objects to have a common base class.

Packages

With all the Java libraries that are floating around, it is inevitable that two people will choose the same name for a class. Ordinarily, this would be a problem because the class names must be unique. Fortunately, Java solves this problem by organizing classes into packages.

A package isn't really a "thing"; you can't create a package from a program. It's just like an extra name that gets stuck onto the front of your class name. For example, the Object class, which is the superclass of all other objects, is in a package called java.lang. The full class name of Object, then, is java.lang.Object.

A class can only belong to a single package, and you declare the package at the beginning of your source file. The naming convention for packages is that they start with your Internet domain name in reverse order. Classes from ibm.com are usually in packages that start with com.bea, while classes defined by omg.org are in packages that start with org.omg.

To declare that your class belongs to the com.mycompany.utils package, put the following statement at the top of your source file:

```
package com.mycompany.utils;
```

When it comes to organizing your source code, you usually create separate directories for each package. For com.mycompany.utils, you would have a com directory that contains a mycompany directory, which in turn contains a utils directory. The utils directory would then contain any source files for classes in the com.mycompany.utils package. Some development environments, like WebLogic Workshop, enforce this package structure.

Now, if a package means that a class name actually includes the package name, how do you keep from having to type in package names? After all, you'd go nuts if you had to type java.lang.String every time you wanted to declare a string.

Java has an import keyword that tells the compiler to look for classes in specific packages. By default, the compiler already knows about the java.lang package. It doesn't know, however, about the java.io package, which includes classes for reading and writing files. If you didn't import the java.io package, you'd be writing things like java.io.FileReader and java.io.IOException. You can omit the java.io. from the beginning of class names by just including the following line at the top of your program (below a package statement but before the class or interface statement):

```
import java.io.*;
```

Rather than importing an entire package with *, you can import individual classes, like this:

```
import java.io.FileReader;
import java.io.IOException;
```

By explicitly importing classes, you reduce the chances of having name collisions. For example, the java.util and java.sql packages both include a class called Date. If you just import java.util.* and java.sql.*, the compiler won't know which

Date you want. You have to either qualify it with a package name every time, or explicitly include the Date you want, like this:

```
import java.util.Date;
```

Java locates packages and classes using an environment variable called CLASSPATH. The class path contains a list of directories where Java should look for packages and classes. Because the packages are organized into directories, the class path only needs to point to the location of the base package directory. That is, if the package com.mycompany.utils is located in c:\javastuff\com\mycompany\utils, the class path only needs to refer to c:\javastuff. You can also include "." in the class path to include the current directory. Under Windows, the class path directories are separated by ";", whereas under Unix they are separated by ":". For example, under Windows, you might set the class path this way:

```
set CLASSPATH=.;c:\javastuff;c:\javalibs
```

Under Unix, you might set it this way:

```
CLASSPATH=.:/home/mark/javastuff:/home/mark/javalibs
```

You don't need to worry about the class path when using WebLogic Workshop, however.

Common Java Packages

One of Java's strengths is its rich class library. You can find most of the features you need to write powerful applications in Java's standard set of libraries. These libraries are all part of the standard Java runtime (included with the Java SDK and also the Java Runtime Environment).

java.lang

The java.lang package includes several core parts of Java including the Object class, the System class (from which you get System.out for printing to the screen), and wrapper classes that represent the various primitive types. Because primitive types aren't objects themselves, if you need one to behave like an object, you create a wrapper class.

java.io

The java.io package includes classes to read and write files (FileReader and FileWriter). It also includes a set of stream filters that let you process data easily. For example, you can open a FileInputStream and then wrap it with an ObjectInputStream to read Java objects directly from a file.

java.util

The `java.util` package includes various collection classes (lists, queues, hash tables) and also classes for working with dates and for generating random numbers.

java.net

The `java.net` package contains classes for accessing Internet URLs (downloading the contents of Web pages, posting data to URLs). The package also contains socket classes for doing TCP data streams and UDP datagrams.

java.sql

The `java.sql` package contains classes for accessing SQL databases. The package is designed to be database-independent, so you can often switch from one database to another without changing your Java code.

Where to Go from Here

This appendix barely scratches the surface of Java. You can download the Java language specification and other documentation from `http://java.sun.com`. You should also download the JDK documentation, which includes a nice HTML API reference (Java has a built-in mechanism called Javadoc for generating API documentation). Browse through the API documentation to see what other features Java has—you'll be surprised.

B

XML

IN THIS APPENDIX

- What Is XML?
- XML Basics
- XML Schema
- Related XML Specifications

What Is XML?

The Extensible Markup Language (XML) is a standard format for representing structured data in text form. It is an integral part of Web Services, and therefore an integral part of WebLogic Workshop. Web Services use a protocol called SOAP (Simple Object Access Protocol), which uses XML to represent requests.

If you have ever stored data in a Java properties file or in other simple configuration files, you might have discovered that it isn't easy to store structured data in a flat format. For example, you might have a configuration file that looks like this:

```
service.name=MyService
service.maxClients=500
service.class=com.mycompany.MyServiceImpl
```

Although this format works well for a single item, when you add similar items, you usually need a numbering scheme, like this:

```
service1.name=MyService
service1.maxClients=500
service1.class=com.mycompany.MyServiceImpl
service2.name=OtherService
service2.maxClients=100
service2.class=com.mycompany.OtherServiceImpl
```

XML solves this problem because it lets you structure the configuration data like this:

```
<?xml version="1.0"?>
<config>
   <service>
```

```
    <name>MyService</name>
    <maxClients>500</maxClients>
    <class>com.myCompany.MyServiceImpl</class>
  </service>
  <service>
    <name>OtherService</name>
    <maxClients>100</maxClients>
    <class>com.myCompany.OtherServiceImpl</class>
  </service>
</config>
```

As you can see, XML uses a tag structure similar to that found in HTML. Just as with HTML, a tag of the form `</tagname>` ends a tag that starts with `<tagname>`. Tags define XML elements, which are the building blocks of XML. An element can contain other elements—the `<service>` tag contains elements called `<name>`, `<maxClients>`, and `<class>` in the preceding example. An element can also contain text data—the first `<name>` tag contains the data `"MyService"`. XML data is stored in an XML document, which can be a data file or just dynamically generated information. An XML document consists of a prolog and then a single element. In the preceding XML document, the prolog is just the following line:

```
<?xml version="1.0"?>
```

This line must be present in any XML document. There are also other tags that can appear in the prolog, but this is the only one that is absolutely required. The main element in the preceding example is `<config>`.

You can find the full specification for XML online at
`http://www.w3.org/TR/2000/REC-xml-20001006`.

Why Use XML?

You might be wondering why you should even use XML. After all, with all those tags, it certainly isn't a compact format. In fact, for many XML documents, the tags take up more space than the actual data.

Although it is not very efficient in size, XML still has several things going for it. First, it is human-readable. You don't need a special program to edit an XML file as you do for more compact binary formats. Second, XML can represent fairly complex data structures. Many data file formats can't handle data items within other data items. Third, although it can handle complex data, XML is still fairly easy to parse. You can find XML parsers written in almost every common programming language. Finally, XML is platform- and language-independent. You can write out an XML file using Visual Basic in Windows and read the file using Perl on a Unix machine.

XML Basics

Although XML can represent a wide range of data structures, the core of the language is quite simple. A minimal XML file consists of the <?xml?> processing instruction (which makes up the prolog) and a pair of tags that defines the main element. A tag is simply a name surrounded by < and >. A processing instruction is a special tag that starts with <? and ends with ?>. For example:

```
<?xml version="1.0"?>
<MyRootTag>This is an XML file</MyRootTag>
```

Notice that the <MyRootTag> tag has a closing </MyRootTag> tag. In this case, <MyRootTag> is called a start tag and its corresponding </MyRootTag> is the end tag. These tags denote XML *elements*—MyRootTag is an XML element in this example.

Every start tag must either have a corresponding end tag, or it must have the format <tagname/>, which is referred to as an "empty element" because it can't contain other tags or text data. For example:

```
<DatabaseConnection/>
```

Although this form of XML tag might look somewhat useless because it can't contain other elements or text data, it can contain attributes, which you will learn about shortly.

Elements

An XML document can contain many elements nested within each other, but it must have only one root element. For example, the following file contains several Item elements contained within a single Basket root element:

```
<?xml version="1.0"?>
<Basket>
    <Item>apple</Item>
    <Item>orange</Item>
    <Item>banana</Item>
</Basket>
```

If you try to omit the <Basket> element and just make a list of <Item> elements, however, you create an invalid XML file:

```
<?xml version="1.0"?>
<item>apple<item>
<item>orange<item>
<item>banana<item>
```

Because this example has more than one element following the <?xml?> processing instruction, it is invalid.

With the exception of the root element, all other elements must be completely nested within other elements. That is, an element's start and end tags must both be contained within the start and end tags of another element. You can't have a start tag within one element and the corresponding end tag outside the element. In other words, the following tag structure is invalid:

```
<Basket>
    <Item>
</Basket>
    </Item>
```

Attributes

So far, you have seen elements that contain data between the tags, like <Item>apple</Item>. XML attributes allow you to specify data within an element tag. An attribute is simply a name=value pair within the element itself. For example:

```
<Item type="apple"/>
```

The attribute name is "type" and the attribute value is "apple". Without attributes, the single < /> tag wouldn't be very useful because it has no closing tag to enclose any data. If you are familiar with HTML, you might have developed the bad habit of omitting quotes in your attributes. For example, you might think nothing of a tag like <body bgcolor=#ffffff>, but in XML, the XML parser will flag an error because you must always enclose the attribute's value in quotes (that is, bgcolor="#ffffff"). You can use single or double quotes.

Sometimes it is difficult to decide whether to represent a data item using an element or an attribute. In other words, would you do this:

```
<database><url>jdbc:mysql:mydb</url></database>
```

or this

```
<database url="jdbc:mysql:mydb"/>
```

One of the obvious factors is whether or not the data item can contain nested data. An attribute can't contain any XML tags—it represents a single data value. If a data item can contain complex data, it should be represented as an XML element. When you do have a single value, it's really a matter of choice whether to use an element or an attribute. Which to choose, however, is a matter of great debate among XML experts.

Comments

You can insert comments anywhere in an XML document. A comment begins with `<!--` and ends with `-->` and cannot contain two consecutive dashes (`--`). For example:

```
<!-- This is an XML comment - it isn't an element or data -->
```

The following comment, however, is illegal because it contains two consecutive dashes:

```
<!-- This is a bad comment -- it has two dashes -->
```

Data

In an XML document, anything that isn't markup—that is, anything that isn't an element, a processing instruction, or a comment—is data. When you indent tags, the blank space before the tags is also data.

Sometimes, you want to put special characters like < and > in your data. XML doesn't normally allow these characters to be contained in text data. You can, however, use one of two alternate text representations for these characters.

You can represent a character either numerically or by special named constants. To represent a number numerically, use `&#nn;` where *nn* is the numeric value of the character. For instance, < has a value of 60, so you can represent a < with `&#60;`. You can also use `&#xnn;` to specify a character value in hexadecimal. For example, 3c in hex is the same as 60 in decimal, so `&#x3c;` is the same as `&#60;`. Although the values for the characters can vary according to the character encoding you are using, most XML documents use an encoding that uses the ASCII encoding for letters and numbers. That is, A–Z are represented as 65-90, a–z by 97-122, and 0–9 by 48-57.

XML supports five named constants for special characters:

- `&amp;` Ampersand (&)
- `&apos;` Apostrophe (')
- `&gt;` Greater than (>)
- `&lt;` Less than (<)
- `&quot;` Quotation mark (")

In addition to these special characters, you can also add blocks of data containing special characters. The `<![CDATA[` tag begins a block of characters and the `]]>` tag ends the block. The nice thing about the `CDATA` tag is that it can contain an entire XML file (or HTML or whatever) and still be valid XML. For example:

```
<?xml version="1.0">
<DataFile>
```

```
<![CDATA[
   <?xml version="1.0">
   <Basket>
      <Item>apple</Item>
   </Basket>
]]>
</DataFile>
```

In the preceding example, there is only one XML element—<DataFile>. The XML you see inside the tag isn't really XML—it is just character data. The XML parser doesn't try to interpret the enclosed <?xml?> tag or <Basket>. Without the <![CDATA[tag, you'd have to encode the data this way:

```
<?xml version="1.0">
<DataFile>
   &lt;?xml version=&quot;1.0&quot;&gt;
   &lt;Basket%gt;
      &lt;Item&gt;apple&lt;/Item&gt;
   &lt;/Basket&gt;
</DataFile>
```

The only character sequence not allowed in a CDATA section is]].

Document Type Definitions

Although XML allows you to use any tag anywhere (assuming you follow the formatting guidelines), you sometimes need to impose a little extra order on your XML files. You might want to ensure that only certain tags appear, or that one tag can appear only within another specific tag. This is especially true when you start sharing XML data with other companies.

A Document Type Definition (DTD) allows you to specify which tags and attributes can appear in a document, and also which tags can contain which other tags. This definition of which tags and attributes can appear is typically called an "XML grammar."

A DTD typically contains a mixture of <!ELEMENT> and <!ATTLIST> tags. The <!ELEMENT> tag defines an element, whereas the <!ATTLIST> tag defines the allowable attributes for a specific element.

The format for the <!ELEMENT> tag is <!ELEMENT *tag content-type*>. The content type can be EMPTY, ANY, or a list of elements including a special #PCDATA type that represents text data. When you specify a list of elements, you can use vertical bars (|) to indicate a choice of different elements, or a comma (,) to indicate a list of elements.

For example, the following declaration allows the `<Basket>` element to contain exactly one of three different items:

```
<!ELEMENT Basket (ItemType1|ItemType2|ItemType3)>
```

Similarly, this declaration specifies that `<Basket>` must contain a sequence of three items:

```
<!ELEMENT Basket (ItemType1,ItemType2,ItemType3)>
```

A question mark (?) after an item in a list indicates that there may be 0 or 1 occurrences of the item. A plus sign (+) indicates 1 or more occurrences, and an asterisk (*) indicates 0 or more. For example, `Basket` would most likely contain 0 or more items, so you would declare it as follows:

```
<!ELEMENT Basket (Item*)>
```

If an element contains only data, use `(#PCDATA)`:

```
<!ELEMENT Name (#PCDATA)>
```

You must include parentheses around `#PCDATA`.

The `<!ATTLIST>` tag lets you declare what attributes a given element can have. The general format for `<!ATTLIST>` is

```
<!ATTLIST attribute-name type default-value>
```

The type of an attribute is usually either `CDATA` or a list of values of the form (`value1|value2|value3|...`). For example, you might declare a `Person` element to have a sex attribute like this:

```
<!ATTLIST Person sex (male|female) #REQUIRED>
```

The default value parameter for an attribute can be either `#REQUIRED`, `#IMPLIED`, `#FIXED`, or a string constant. If the default value is a string constant and you don't specify the attribute value in your XML file, the XML parser should substitute the default value. That is, when you read the XML file using an XML parser, the parser will automatically substitute the default value if there is no value for the attribute. If the default is `#REQUIRED`, the attribute must be present (it never needs a default value because it must always be specified). If the default value is `#IMPLIED`, the attribute isn't required, and if it isn't present, there is no default value. Finally, if the default value is `#FIXED`, you must also specify a string constant as the default fixed value. If a fixed attribute is present, its value *must* be the value specified after the `#FIXED` parameter, but the attribute is not required. For example, you might require that the sex attribute for the `Man` element be male, like this:

```
<!ATTLIST Man sex #FIXED "male">
```

According to this declaration, if you specify a sex attribute in the Man element, its value must *always* be male.

You can specify multiple attributes in the <!ATTLIST> tag. You can just list multiple `attribute-name type default-value`s one after another. Typically, you see the attributes appear on different lines in the DTD, but that isn't required. You might declare the attributes for Person this way:

```
<!ATTLIST Person sex (male|female) #REQUIRED
    age CDATA #IMPLIED
    classification CDATA #FIXED "homo sapiens">
```

To include a DTD in an XML file, use the <!DOCTYPE> tag before your root XML element. The simplest form of <!DOCTYPE> is

```
<!DOCTYPE DTD-name SYSTEM "DTD-URL">
```

The `DTD-URL` can be a typical URL reference like "http://mycom.com/dtd/mydtd.dtd" or a file like "/home/mark/dtd/mydtd.dtd".

Here is a sample XML file that includes a DTD:

```
<?xml version="1.0"?>
<!DOCTYPE person SYSTEM "http://localhost/person.dtd">
<person age="6">
    <name>Kaitlynn Tippin</name>
</person>
```

You can also embed a DTD directly in an XML file, using the following form:

```
<!DOCTYPE DTD-name [
    dtd definitions
]>
```

For example:

```
<?xml version="1.0"?>
<!DOCTYPE person [
<!ELEMENT Name (#PCDATA)>
<!ELEMENT Person (Name)>
<!ATTLIST Person sex (male|female) #REQUIRED
    age CDATA #IMPLIED
    classification CDATA #FIXED "homo sapiens">
]>
<person age="6"sex="female">
    <name>Kaitlynn Tippin</name>
</person>
```

XML Schema

As you saw earlier, XML Schema is an alternative to DTDs that lets you specify data types more accurately. Because WebLogic Workshop lets you reference schema definitions from within your Web Services, you might need to know a little more about XML Schema.

XML Schema Basics

Like many XML formats, XML Schema is pretty easy to read. The basic format of a schema is

```
<?xml version="1.0"?>
<xsd:schema xmlns:xsd="http://www.w3.org/2001/XMLSchema">
    schema definitions
</xsd:schema>
```

You can get a pretty good idea of how it works just by looking at the sample XML Schema shown in Listing B.1.

LISTING B.1   Source Code for sample.xsd

```
<?xml version="1.0"?>
<xsd:schema xmlns:xsd="http://www.w3.org/2001/XMLSchema">

<!-- Define an element called "person" that is of type PersonType -->
<xsd:element name="person" type="PersonType">

<!-- Define what PersonType means -->
<xsd:complexType name="PersonType">

<!-- A person has a sequence of elements -->
   <xsd:sequence>
      <xsd:element name="first-name" type="xsd:string"/>
      <xsd:element name="middle-name" type="xsd:string"/>
      <xsd:element name="last-name" type="xsd:string"/>
      <xsd:element name="age" type="xsd:positiveInteger"/>
      <xsd:element name="born" type="xsd:date"/>
      <xsd:element name="children" type="listOfPersonType"/>
   </xsd:sequence>
</xsd:complexType>

<!-- Define listOfPerson as a list of person elements -->
<xsd:simpleType name="listOfPersonType">
   <xsd:list itemType="PersonType"/>
</xsd:simpleType>
```

The XML Schema in Listing B.1 defines a person element that has a type of `PersonType`. Next, it describes `PersonType` as a sequence of different elements, most of which have simple types like string, date, and integer. Finally, it creates a type that represents a list of `PersonType` objects that represent the children of a person.

Listing B.2 shows a sample XML file described by the schema from Listing B.1.

LISTING B.2   Source Code for sample.xml

```
<?xml version="1.0"?>
<person>
    <first-name>Samantha</first-name>
    <middle-name>Lauren</middle-name>
    <last-name>Tippin</last-name>
    <age>9</age>
    <born>1993-08-26</born>
    <children>
        <person>
            <first-name>Edward</first-name>
            <middle-name>Alexander</middle-name>
            <last-name>Wutka</last-name>
            <age>3</age>
            <born>1999-05-11</born>
            <children></children>
        </person>
    </children>
</person>
```

Defining Elements

The `<xsd:element>` element lets you define an element. You simply specify the name of the element and the type. For example, a person's name is usually a string, so a name element can be defined as:

```
<xsd:element name="name" type="xsd:string"/>
```

The type of an element can either be a built-in type like xsd:string or it can be a user-defined type—a simple type or a complex type.

Supported Data Types

XML Schema supports a number of data types. Table B.1 shows some of the most common data types and some sample values.

TABLE B.1 Common Data Types

Data Type	Sample Value(s)
String	This is a string
NormalizedString	This is a normalized string (a string with tabs, newlines, and carriage returns converted to spaces)
Token	This is a token (a string with no tabs, newlines, or carriage returns and no leading or trailing spaces)
Byte	-128, 0, 127
UnsignedByte	0, 128, 255
Integer	-99999, 12345, 98765
PositiveInteger	7, 23, 1986
NegativeInteger	-123, -999
nonNegativeInteger	0, 5, 2000
nonPositiveInteger	0, -5, -2000
Int	-99999, 12345
unsignedInt	99999, 12345
short	-12345, 54321
unsignedShort	12345, 54321
Long	-99999999999, 1234567898765
unsignedLong	9876543212345
decimal	-1.50, 50000.00
float	-5.67, 3.1415927
double	-9898.564, 3.14159265359
Boolean	1, true, 0, false
Date	2002-05-11
Time	12:34:56.765

NOTE

Normally, you put the namespace prefix in front of any elements or type names in XML Schema. If you specify the namespace as xsd (the most common namespace prefix for schemas), the various data types are prefixed with xsd:, like xsd:string, xsd:int, xsd:boolean.

Defining Simple Types

The built-in types are considered simple types, but you can also define your own simple types in a schema. A simple type can be a built-in type with a specific range, a list, a union, or an enumeration.

You can specify a range restriction on an int value by combining the <xsd:minInclusive> and <xsd:maxInclusive> elements with the <xsd:restriction> element, like this:

```
<xsd:simpleType name="FlightNumber">
    <xsd:restriction base="xsd:integer">
        <xsd:minInclusive value="1"/>
        <xsd:maxInclusive value="9999"/>
    </xsd:restriction>
</xsd:simpleType>
```

> **NOTE**
>
> This simpleType element is only a fragment of an XML Schema. A schema must always contain the <?xml?> processing instruction and the <xsd:schema> root element.

You can also define pattern-based simple types using a regular expression pattern:

```
<xsd:simpleType name="SSN">
    <xsd:restriction base="xsd:string">
        <xsd:pattern value="\d{3}-\d{2}-\d{4}"/>
    </xsd:restriction>
</xsd:simpleType>
```

You can define a type as being a list of elements:

```
<xsd:simpleType name="numberList">
    <xsd:list itemType="byte"/>
</xsd:simpleType>
```

Here's an example of a list:

```
<lotto-numbers>5 43 17 9 20 34</lotto-numbers>
```

You can also declare an enumeration—a restricted set of values that are considered valid. One of the most common enumerations in business applications is the complete list of states in the U.S.A.:

```
<xsd:simpleType name="state">
    <xsd:restriction base="xsd:string">
        <xsd:enumeration value="AK"/>
        <xsd:enumeration value="AL"/>
                    .

                    .
    </xsd:restriction>
</xsd:simpleType>
```

Defining Complex Types

Complex types are really the core of XML Schema, because they allow you to define elements within other elements. A typical complex type starts with a sequence and can also include attributes. For example, to define a person's name as a complex type, you might use the definition shown in Listing B.3.

LISTING B.3   Source Code for namedef.xsd

```
<xsd:complexType name="name">
    <xsd:sequence>
        <xsd:element name="prefix">
            <xsd:simpleType>
                <xsd:restriction base="xsd:string">
                    <xsd:enumeration value="Mr."/>
                    <xsd:enumeration value="Mrs."/>
                    <xsd:enumeration value="Ms."/>
                    <xsd:enumeration value="Dr."/>
                </xsd:restriction>
            </xsd:simpleType>
        </xsd:element>
        <xsd:element name="first-name" type="xsd:string"/>
        <xsd:element name="middle-name" type="xsd:string"/>
        <xsd:element name="last-name" type="xsd:string"/>
    </xsd:sequence>
</xsd:complexType>
```

The definition of the prefix element in Listing B.3 shows another interesting XML Schema concept—anonymous types. In previous examples, you saw simple and complex types defined using a name. In Listing B.3, however, the `<xsd:element>` element doesn't specify a type, but instead contains an `<xsd:simpleType>` element that defines the legal values for a prefix.

You can apply this same technique to elements that are complex types. Rather than defining a separate complex type somewhere else in the schema, you can just include the complex type as part of the element. If you need to use the same complex type in different parts of the schema, however, it is better to give it a name. That way, you can reuse the complex type instead of defining it over and over as an anonymous type.

Attributes

To add an attribute to a complex type, use the `<xsd:attribute>` element. You usually list your attributes after the `<xsd:sequence>` declaration, and the syntax is similar to the syntax for `<xsd:element>`. For example, to add a `stockSymbol` attribute to a complex company type, you might do this:

```
<xsd:complexType name="Company">
    <xsd:sequence>
        <xsd:element name="name" type="xsd:string">
        <xsd:element name="CEO" type="PersonType">
        <xsd:element name="address" type="AddressType">
    </xsd:sequence>
    <xsd:attribute name="stockSymbol" type="xsd:string">
</xsd:complexType>
```

You can also add default and fixed values for the attribute just as you did in a DTD. You simply include `default="xxxx"` or `fixed="xxxx"` in the `<xsd:attribute>` element. To specify that an attribute is required or optional, you can include `use="required"` or `use="optional"` in the `<xsd:attribute>` element. For example, to require that the `stockSymbol` attribute always be present, you can change the previous declaration to the following:

```
<xsd:attribute name="stockSymbol" type="xsd:string" use="required">
```

Mixed Content

Sometimes you want to declare that an element has mixed content—text data with tags interspersed inside the text. For example, you can have some sort of form letter with tags to represent the parts that you can replace. For example, your XML could look like this:

```
<letter>
    Dear <name>Mr. Smith</name>,
We received your recent inquiry about our <product>Worm Incubator</product>
and we are forwarding the information to your address at:
<address>
123 Fourth St.
Anytown, GA USA 30123
</address>
    Sincerely,
        WormCo, Inc.
</letter>
```

The complex type definition for `letter` would be:

```
<xsd:element name="letter">
    <xsd:complexType mixed="true">
        <xsd:element name="name" type="xsd:string"/>
```

```
        <xsd:element name="product" type="xsd:string"/>
        <xsd:element name="address" type="AddressType"/>
    </xsd:complexType>
</xsd:element>
```

Notice that the `<xsd:complexType>` tag includes the attribute `mixed="true"`. This allows the complex type to contain a mixture of text and tags.

Using XML Schema in a JWS File

WebLogic Workshop provides some support for XML Schema. You can specify an XML Schema type for a parameter or a return type by specifying the `schema-element` attribute in the `@jws:parameter-xml` or `@jws:return-xml` tags. You can also specify the schema location in the `@jws:schema` tag.

To import a schema called schema.xsd, use the following declaration:

```
@jws:schema file="schema.xsd"
```

You can also select a schema in the WebLogic Workshop by selecting the project properties and entering a value for the schema. Listing B.4 shows an example JWS file that imports a schema.

LISTING B.4   Source Code for `SchemaDemo.jws`

```
/**
 * @jws:schema file="schema.xsd"
 */
public class SchemaDemo
{
    /** @jws:context */
    weblogic.jws.control.JwsContext context;

    /**
     * @jws:operation
     * @jws:parameter-xml schema-element="xsd:string"
     * @jws:return-xml xml-map::
     *     <getPersonResponse xmlns="http://openuri.org/">
     *     <person>
     *         <first-name>{return.firstName}</first-name>
     *         <middle-name>{return.middleName}</middle-name>
     *         <last-name>{return.lastName}</last-name>
     *         <age>{return.age}</age>
     *     </person>
     *     </getPersonResponse>
```

LISTING B.4   Continued

```
    *
    * ::
*/
    public Person getPerson(String personName)
    {
        Person person = new Person();
        if (personName.equalsIgnoreCase("kaitlynn"))
        {
            person.setFirstName("Kaitlynn");
            person.setMiddleName("Dawn");
            person.setLastName("Tippin");
            person.setAge(6);
        }
        else if (personName.equalsIgnoreCase("samantha"))
        {
            person.setFirstName("Samantha");
            person.setMiddleName("Lauren");
            person.setLastName("Tippin");
            person.setAge(9);
        }
        else
        {
            person.setFirstName("??");
            person.setMiddleName("??");
            person.setLastName("??");
            person.setAge(-1);
        }
        return person;
    }
}
```

Listing B.5 shows the schema.xsd file used by SchemaDemo.jws.

LISTING B.5   Source Code for schema.xsd

```
<?xml version="1.0"?>
<xsd:schema xmlns:xsd="http://www.w3.org/2001/XMLSchema">

<!-- Define an element called "person" that is of type PersonType -->
<xsd:element name="person" type="PersonType">
```

LISTING B.5 Continued

```
<!-- Define what PersonType means -->
<xsd:complexType name="PersonType">

<!-- A person has a sequence of elements -->
    <xsd:sequence>
        <xsd:element name="first-name" type="xsd:string"/>
        <xsd:element name="middle-name" type="xsd:string"/>
        <xsd:element name="last-name" type="xsd:string"/>
        <xsd:element name="age" type="xsd:positiveInteger"/>
        <xsd:element name="born" type="xsd:date"/>
        <xsd:element name="children" type="listOfPersonType"/>
    </xsd:sequence>
</xsd:complexType>

<!-- Define listOfPerson as a list of person elements -->
<xsd:simpleType name="listOfPersonType">
    <xsd:list itemType="PersonType"/>
</xsd:simpleType>
```

Related XML Specifications

One of the big advantages of XML is its simplicity. It takes very little time to learn the formatting rules, and anyone with a text editor can create an XML file. The simplicity of XML is slowly being eroded by the number of additional specifications that continue to appear. Just when you think you understand XML, someone throws a bunch of acronyms at you, almost all of them beginning with X, and you feel a little lost. The following overview tells you a little about some of the more popular XML specifications. For more information, visit the World Wide Web Consortium at http://www.w3c.org.

XML Namespaces

One of the early problems with XML was that there was no way to handle duplicate names. A <class> element might mean one thing to a programming company and something different to a university. XML needed a way of grouping elements into separate packages to avoid naming collisions. The solution was a standard called XML Namespaces. A *namespace* is a collection of tag names where the combination of a namespace name and a tag name represents a unique element. That is, a tag called <class> in one namespace is separate from a tag called <class> in another namespace.

An XML namespace is similar to a Java package. You can include a namespace in your XML file similar to the way you import a Java package. If there is any ambiguity between namespaces, you can always specify the namespace within the tag, just as you can always use a fully qualified class name in Java.

You can include a namespace in any XML element, and the namespace is valid for the current element and any elements it contains. For example, the following element declaration includes a namespace using the xmlns attribute:

```
<aircraft:L1011 xmlns:aircraft="http://www.lockheed.com">
    <aircraft:engine manufacturer="Pratt & Whitney"/>
</aircraft:L1011>
```

The general form of a namespace declaration is

```
<namespace-name:tagname xmlns:namespace-name="namespace URI">
```

The actual namespace name you choose for a particular namespace can vary from one XML document to the next. That is, in one case, you might choose the name aircraft for the namespace http://www.lockheed.com and the next time, you could choose lockheed. For example, suppose you want to use a namespace with a URI of http://www.boeing.com that might also use an engine tag. You might do the following:

```
<?xml version="1.0">
<fleet>
    <lockheed:L1011 xmlns="http://www.lockheed.com">
        <lockheed:engine manufacturer="Pratt & Whitney"/>
    </lockheed:L1011>
    <boeing:B777 xmlns="http://www.boeing.com">
        <boeing:engine source="General Electric"/>
    </boeing:B777>
</fleet>
```

The interesting and confusing thing about namespaces is that even though a namespace has a URI, implying that there is a namespace file out there somewhere, the URI is really just a unique identifier for the namespace. There is no namespace file at http://www.lockheed.com. The URI just serves to distinguish one namespace from another.

XSL

The Extensible Stylesheet Language (XSL) is a language for formatting XML documents. The idea is that you take XML data and put it into a printable format using XSL. The XSL formatting objects (XSL-FO) cover many complex areas of publishing and include layout, color, and even sound. Although you might eventually see printer drivers that understand XSL formatting objects, you are more likely to see translators that generate PostScript and PDF files from XSL formatting objects. The idea here is that you separate the data from its presentation. That is, you no longer need to include display information within your XML document. Instead, you store information about the display in a separate XSL document.

One of the confusing aspects of XSL is that there are really two XSL standards—one is the XSL formatting objects (XSL-FO), and the other is called XSL Transformations (XSLT). XSLT defines a mechanism for translating one form of XML document into another (from XML to HTML, For example, if you look at the XSL formatting objects as the printable representation of an XML document, XSLT is the mechanism that transforms your XML document into XSL formatting objects. XSLT is quite useful as a general way to translate XML documents, however. In fact, you find many people using XSLT but few using XSL formatting objects.

XSLT is also frequently used just to translate from one form of XML to another. For example, you can have an application that expects one style of XML document, but you might have several customers sending you data in another XML format. You can use XSLT to reformat the customer data into the style your program expects, which is much better than rewriting your program to understand the different styles.

Although XSLT is powerful, it isn't easy for some developers. An XSLT file looks like something from a functional programming language—it isn't procedural like Java, C++, Visual Basic, and other popular languages. When you get the hang of it, though, it isn't as bad as it looks.

You can find the full XSLT specification at `http://www.w3.org/TR/xslt`.

XPath

In an XSLT document, you often need to refer to XML elements in relation to each other. XPath is basically a query language for XML documents. It lets you refer to XML elements in various ways, such as elements that are direct children of the root node, or elements that are grandchildren of a specific node.

For example, the following XPath query selects all elements named `employee` that are children of a `company` tag:

```
company/employee
```

This query locates all age attributes belonging to a `person` tag:

```
person/@age
```

Seeing XPath in a standalone manner like this looks a little strange. You usually use XPath within the context of another language like XSLT. In fact, XPath is crucial to XSLT—you use it to identify transformations for various elements.

You can find the full XPath specification at `http://www.w3.org/TR/xpath`.

C

Web Service Description Language (WSDL)

IN THIS APPENDIX

- History of WSDL
- WSDL in Workshop
- Obtaining the WSDL Definition for Any Service in Workshop
- Utilizing an External Web Service When You Have Its WSDL URL
- Creating a Service That Complies with a WSDL File
- WSDL Definition
- Communication Processes
- Types
- Messages
- Operations
- Port Type
- Binding
- Port
- Service

The Web Service Description Language provides a way to define the operations and data that travel into and out of your services. The WSDL definition is designed specifically to provide interoperability between various languages and implementations.

History of WSDL

WSDL was originally designed by IBM, Microsoft, and Ariba to provide a standard mechanism for describing Web services. The proposed language was then submitted to the W3C for standardization and has grown to encompass dozens of vendors. The need for WSDL in Web services is akin to the need for distributed systems to define an IDL (Interface Definition Language).

When defined in terms of standards, the Web services stack contains UDDI, WSDL, and SOAP. UDDI provides the means to find a Web service. SOAP provides the means to actually communicate with the service. WSDL is designed to define what you communicate.

In a typical scenario, after you've found a service (such as via a UDDI lookup), what do you do with it? As covered in Chapter 5,"Controls," you can import the WSDL file into Workshop as a control. Workshop is able to do this because it understands how to read a WSDL document just as easily as it knows how to read an EJB or RMI object.

WSDL in Workshop

Fortunately, in 95% of the situations in which Web services are deployed, no human being will ever have to touch the WSDL description. Tools both in Workshop and in other environments do a very good job of both rendering and reading WSDL.

Sometimes it becomes necessary to customize the WSDL for one reason or another. It is for those times that this appendix is available.

Obtaining the WSDL Definition for Any Service in Workshop

The effort involved in laying out a WSDL document by hand is clearly not trivial. You might understandably wish for a way to create the WSDL document simply by introspecting your Java class. Fortunately, most application servers, including Workshop, provide a tool to do just this.

Generate a WSDL for Your Service

To generate the default WSDL file for your service, right-click on the .JWS file in the Project tree. From the context menu, select Generate WSDL from JWS.

View Current WSDL for Service

In Workshop, you can obtain the current WSDL file for your service from the test view. To enter the test view, run or debug your service. From the test view, select the Overview tab. The Overview tab provides you access to a variety of details on the service. The first hyperlink on the Overview tab reads `Complete WSDL`. Clicking on this link will take you to the WSDL definition of your service.

This feature is available regardless of whether or not the WSDL file is visible in the Project tree. This will cause the WSDL file to appear under the JWS file just as a CTRL file would become nested under the JWS, after you created one.

Utilizing an External Web Service When You Have Its WSDL URL

When you want to become a consumer of a Web service, the first step after you find the service is to obtain the URL for its WSDL definition. After you've obtained the URL, you can turn the Web service into a WebLogic Workshop control. To add the new control, from the File menu select Service, Add Control, Add Service Control. From the Design view, you can also use the Add Control drop-down menu and select Add Service Control. Either method will bring up the Add a Service Control dialog box shown in Figure C.1. Enter a name for the new control in the Variable Name for This Control field and select Create a Service Control from a WSDL. You can then enter the URL of the WSDL file directly if you know it, or you can use the UDDI search to find a service that meets your needs.

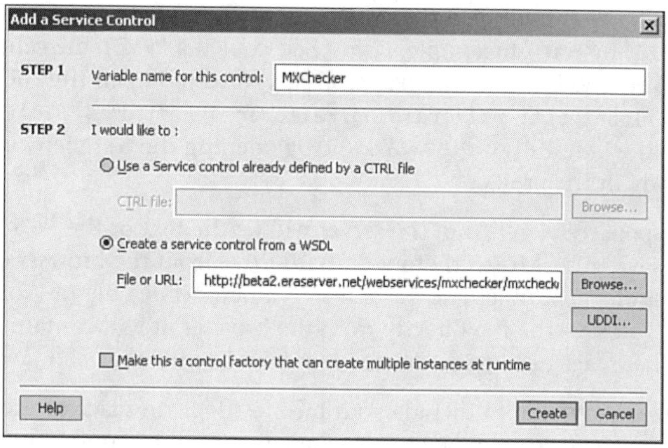

FIGURE C.1   Using a WSDL URL as a control.

Creating a Service That Complies with a WSDL File

Sometimes you want to create a service that complies with a WSDL file defined by somebody else. This would happen if you wanted to create a service that complied with some publicly defined WSDL file. This type of situation is not common today. Although the visionaries of Web services have dreamed of a day when companies could just switch from one service provider to another at will (because they both use the same WSDL definition), this is not yet commonplace. There are some exceptions. For instance, many larger organizations are able to mandate that their providers provide a service according to a specific WSDL. Some organizations are starting to provide proactive messaging, which requires their clients to comply with a WSDL definition. There has also been some headway into areas such as healthcare where public standards are emerging for the transfer of data.

When you find yourself in this situation, it is very useful to be able to automatically create an empty service that complies with the WSDL. When you have gotten this far, you can simply fill in the body of the empty service so that it complies with the stated purpose. This service can be saved as a template for future use.

Building a JWS file that complies with the WSDL is not entirely straightforward. Here are the steps you need to follow:

1. Obtain the WSDL file and copy it to your projects directory. For instance, on a Windows machine, to copy a file into a project called `training`, assuming that you have your projects directory in the default location, you would copy the WSDL file to `C:\bea\weblogic700\samples\workshop\applications\training`.

2. Start the WebLogic server.

3. Open a browser and open the WSDL file with the additional parameter of ?JWSTEST. By way of example, if you had copied a WSDL file called HelloWorld.wsdl to the training project, you would open the URL `http://localhost:7001/Training/HelloWorld.wsdl?JWSTEST`. You can also obtain the base URI of the WSDL file by opening the test view on a service that is already in the project.

4. The response you get from the server will be the text of the JWS file. You can either save this file directly to your hard drive from the browser or copy the text out of the browser and paste it into a new service file in Workshop. Note that if you save the file directly from the browser, it will contain HTML header tags. These tags need to be deleted before you will have valid Java code.

5. Update the JWS file to include your business logic in place of the temporary logic WebLogic created. Note that when a method is required to return a value, WebLogic will insert a bogus return value to try to get the code to be compliant. This code should just be removed and replaced with valid information.

WSDL Definition

Because Workshop can read and write WSDL files so easily, you will not have to read or write WSDL definitions very often. The most likely case when you will have to delve into WSDL will occur when you want to utilize a public service that for some reason or another Workshop is unable to handle. It is for those cases, and those who have an academic interest in the workings of WSDL, that the rest of this appendix is dedicated.

Communication Processes

A WSDL document consists of seven different XML elements, which correspond to different parts of the specification. The elements are

- Types
- Messages
- Operations
- Port Types
- Bindings
- Ports
- Services

Each of these elements serve to describe one segment of the entire Web service.

Types

The most rudimentary element in WSDL is the *type*. The type element is closely related to a type definition in an XSD (XML Schema) document. In fact, a type defined in WSDL and a type defined in XSD format are syntactically identical. For this reason, Schema is the preferred mechanism for description.

You can think of a type as a struct in C/C++. Java has no direct parallel, but it would be the equivalent of a class with variables but no methods. In fact, there are numerous fundamental types that are directly analogous to primitive values in Java.

Types are needed to describe the fundamental elements of a method call. For instance, consider the following Java method:

```
public void myMethod(String parameter){
//do something
}
```

In the most basic sense, to be able to call the method myMethod(), you must be able to define the nature of a String. Fortunately, String *is* predefined as part of XSD. For this reason, the Types construct is something you will be most concerned about when your methods require more complex entries.

Consider the Java code in Listing C.1.

LISTING C.1   Passing Address as a Class

```
public class Address {
  public String name;
  public String address1;
  public String address2;
  public String city;
  public String state;
  public String zip;
}

public class MyClass{
    public void myMethod(Address myAddress){
      //do something
    }
}
```

Using the type system, it is possible to encapsulate the entire structure of the `Address`. In Java, you certainly wouldn't want to pass each of the atomic elements of the `Address` separately, as in the following:

```java
public class MyClass{
    public void myMethod(String name, String address1, String address2,
                         String city, String state, String zip){
        //do something
    }
}
```

You know you want to pass all the elements as a unit, as one encapsulated object, as in Listing C.1. Types allow you to perform the same function in WSDL as seen in Listing C.2.

LISTING C.2   A Type Definition for an Address

```xml
<wsdl:types>
  <xsd:schema
      targetNamespace="http://www.fluidimagination.com/sams/addressType.xsd"
      xmlns:xsd="http://www.w3.org/2001/XMLSchema">
      <xsd:element name="Address">
        <xsd:complexType>
          <xsd:all>
              <xsd:element name="name" type="xsd:string"/>
              <xsd:element name="address1" type="xsd:string"/>
              <xsd:element name="address2" type="xsd:string"/>
              <xsd:element name="city" type="xsd:string"/>
              <xsd:element name="state" type="xsd:string"/>
              <xsd:element name="zip" type="xsd:string"/>
          </xsd:all>
        </xsd:complexType>
      </xsd:element>
  </xsd:schema>
</wsdl:types>
```

The `WSDL:types` element simply contains the Schema definition for the address.

Creating the Address Type for the WSDL Document

All WSDL documents start with a `definition` element as their root, just as XML Schema documents all start with `schema` as their root element.

The type element can contain any type of referenceable namespace, but in practice it's almost always a Schema entry. Listing C.3 shows how the type for the address is defined in WSDL.

LISTING C.3   Address Type in WSDL

```
<?xml version="1.0"?>
<wsdl:definitions name="AddressType"
        targetNamespace="http://www.fluidimagination.com/sams/addressType.wsdl"
        xmlns:tns="http://www.fluidimagination.com/sams/addressType.wsdl"
        xmlns:wsdl="http://schemas.xmlsoap.org/wsdl/">
    <wsdl:types>
      <xsd:schema
          targetNamespace="http://www.fluidimagination.com/sams/addressType.xsd"
          xmlns:xsd="http://www.w3.org/2001/XMLSchema">
          <xsd:element name="Address">
            <xsd:complexType>
              <xsd:all>
                  <xsd:element name="name" type="xsd:string"/>
                  <xsd:element name="address1" type="xsd:string"/>
                  <xsd:element name="address2" type="xsd:string"/>
                  <xsd:element name="city" type="xsd:string"/>
                  <xsd:element name="state" type="xsd:string"/>
                  <xsd:element name="zip" type="xsd:string"/>
              </xsd:all>
            </xsd:complexType>
          </xsd:element>
      </xsd:schema>
    </wsdl:types>
</ws dl:definitions>
```

Notice in this example that the values of the address are defined as elements, and not as attributes. There is, in fact, a reason for this: Types are an abstract definition of the data, and they do not detail the actual wire format of the data; elemental form—not attribute form—is highly recommended for WSDL documents. The elemental form can be translated to non-XML wire formats, whereas the attribute form often cannot.

There are several other standard rules for creating types in WSDL. These rules are also based on the abstract nature of the type system:

- Use element form, not attributes.

- Do not use values that are specific to a specific wire format, such as soap:root or soap:encodingStyle.

- If you are representing an array, at least at the time of this writing, you should use the SOAP array encoding (soap:Array). This would seem to fly in the face of the preceding point, but it stems from the fact that XSD does not currently have complete support for arrays. For instance, the default value of the array entry cannot be specified in the current XML Schema definition. When Schema catches up, the standard will reverse, and at that time arrays should then be represented using the resulting Schema standard that is created.

- If the element's type isn't actually controlled (that is, it could really be any type), use xsd:anyType.

Messages

The next part of a WSDL document is the *message*. Messages have no real direct parallel within Java. However, you can think of a message as a method that can have only one input parameter, one output parameter, and perhaps one parameter for throwing an exception.

Now that you have this type of a system, you want a way to collect those items you'd normally place as an enumeration on a method. Go back to the address example, but this time assume that the method order() actually takes two addresses:

```
public void order(Address shipTo, Address billTo){
  //do something
}
```

At this point you could declare yet another type for each of the two addresses (shipTo and billTo), but the odds are there is nothing different about the two addresses that would cause you to want to go through the process of declaring a new type.

A far more logical process would be to group the two addresses together. Messages are just such a construction.

Using Elemental Form to Create Messages

In WSDL, a message includes a message element, which then contains part elements. The part elements each represent what would be called a parameter to a method in Java. So in the case of the order() method, where you have the shipTo and billTo address elements, each address gets its own part, as shown in Listing C.4.

LISTING C.4   Adding the Address Message

```xml
<?xml version="1.0"?>
<definitions name="addresses"
        targetNamespace="http://www.fluidimagination.com/sams/addressType.wsdl"
        xmlns:tns="http://www.fluidimagination.com/sams/addressType.wsdl"
        xmlns="http://schemas.xmlsoap.org/wsdl/">
    <types>
        <schema
         targetNamespace="http://www.fluidimagination.com/sams/addressType.xsd"
         xmlns="http://www.w3.org/2001/XMLSchema">
            <element name="address">
                <complexType>
                    <all>
                        <element name="name" type="string"/>
                        <element name="address1" type="string"/>
                        <element name="address2" type="string"/>
                        <element name="city" type="string"/>
                        <element name="state" type="string"/>
                        <element name="zip" type="string"/>
                    </all>
                </complexType>
            </element>
        </schema>
    </types>
    <!-- Adding a message that has two addresses -->
    <message name="purchase">
        <part name="billTo" element="tns:address"/>
        <part name="shipTo" element="tns:address"/>
    </message>
</definitions>
```

Pay special attention to the `message` element. Notice that there are two parts, and each part references the `tns:address` element defined in the type section.

Using Types to Create Messages

Referencing the `address` element in the `part` works fine in many cases. However, there are other situations in which it is more appropriate to reference the type directly. To do this, you must ensure that the `part` tag has a `type` attribute rather than an `element` attribute. Consider the situation in Listing C.5, which continues the ISBN and UPC example discussed earlier in the chapter.

LISTING C.5   Creating a Part with a Specified Type

```
<?xml version="1.0"?>
<definitions name="AddressType"
        targetNamespace=
➥"http://www.fluidimagination.com/sams/addressType.wsdl"
       xmlns:tns=http://www.fluidimagination.com/sams/addressType.wsdl
       xmlns="http://schemas.xmlsoap.org/wsdl/">
    <types>
        <xsd:schema
         targetNamespace="http://www.fluidimagination.com/sams/addressType.xsd"
                xmlns:xsd="http://www.w3.org/2001/XMLSchema">
            <xsd:complexType name="scannerType">
                <xsd:all>
                    <xsd:element name="upc" type="upcType"/>
                    <xsd:element name="isbn" type="isbnType"/>
                </xsd:all>
            </xsd:complexType>
            <xsd:simpleType name="upcType">
                <xsd:restriction base="xsd:string">
                    <xsd:pattern value="[0-9]{12}"/>
                </xsd:restriction>
            </xsd:simpleType>
            <xsd:simpleType name="isbnType">
                <xsd:restriction base="xsd:string">
                    <xsd:pattern value="([0-9]- ){13}"/>
                </xsd:restriction>
            </xsd:simpleType>
        </xsd:schema>
    </types>
    <!-- Adding message which has two addresses -->
    <message name="purchase">
        <part name="productCode" type="tns:scannerType"/>
    </message>
</definitions>
```

Notice that in this example the productCode part refers to the type and not the
element. This is similar to declaring a new element in a schema.

NOTE

In Listing C.5 you see an example of creating a restricted entry. The restriction means that a value entered into the element is valid only if it complies with the restriction. In the case of the upcType, values are legitimate only if they are 12 characters long and consist of the numbers 0–9. In the case of isbnType, 13 characters (0–9, a space, or a hyphen) will work. In truth, a more complex regular expression can be created for ISBN numbers that more accurately reflects the requirement to have exactly three spaces or three hyphens. The expression here is intended to be only a sample.

Operations

The next WSDL element, operation, is perhaps the easiest of all the WSDL elements to understand. An operation is, as its name clearly suggests, a parallel to a Java method. There are several key differences, of course. One of them is that an operation has three and only three messages:

- Input message

- Output message

- Fault message

This isn't a great stretch from Java methods. After all, a Java method has only one return object, and it is not uncommon for a method to throw only one type of exception. The main difference here lies in the fact that an operation has just one input message, rather than a list of input parameters.

Types of Operations

Operations generally fall into four forms, based on the nature of the communication: one-way, request/response, notification, and solicit/response.

One-way operations are characterized by a message from the client to the service, as shown in Figure C.2.

FIGURE C.2   One-way operation.

Request/response operations are characterized by a message from the client and a response from the service, as shown in Figure C.3.

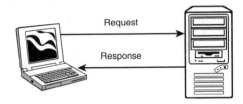

FIGURE C.3   Request/response operation.

Notification operations are the opposite of one-way; they are characterized by a message from the service to the client, as shown in Figure C.4.

FIGURE C.4   Notification operation.

Solicit/response operations are the opposite of request/response. With solicit/response, the original message is from the service and it's the client that responds, as shown in Figure C.5.

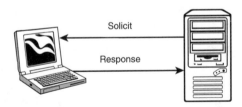

FIGURE C.5   Solicit/response operation.

When talking to a Workshop service, all operations are either request/response or solicit/notify. This is because WebLogic ensures that there is transactional integrity to all messages, meaning that messages are guaranteed to be delivered, and if there is a fault in the middle of the process, the transaction is rolled back. Even if a method returns void, there is a response method that acknowledges that the method was processed, or received (the latter being the case if the method is buffered).

The response in the case of a void method can be used by the client to record that the message was received by WebLogic. After WebLogic sends this response, WebLogic will ensure that the message is fully processed. Therefore a client can rely on the transactional integrity of any message with Workshop. Since the one-way and notify operations cannot be relied upon for their transactional integrity, they are not used by Workshop.

Creating a One-Way Operation

Operations in general consist of an operation element, and the operation element can contain one or more of the messages: input, output, and fault. The fault message is akin to Java's exception mechanism. The other two (input and output) are the messages that determine the nature of the operation. In the case of the one-way operation, the operation has only an input message. The simple operation for sending a purchase would be

```
<operation name="submitPurchase">
   <input message="purchase"/>
</operation>
```

Note that the name parameter refers back to the message created in Listing C.4 (and Listing C.5).

Creating a Request/Response Operation

Request/response operations are declared exactly like one-way operations, plus they add an output message. If you want to send back a confirmation message when the purchase is completed, the operation might look like this:

```
<operation name="submitPurchase">
   <input message="purchase"/>
   <output message="confirmation"/>
</operation>
```

Note that with request/response and solicit/response operations, you can also have fault messages. You might use a fault message if, for example, the purchase was supposed to be shipped to a location for which you don't have service. To do this, you just need to add one or more fault messages, as in the following:

```
<operation name="submitPurchase">
   <input message="purchase"/>
   <output message="confirmation"/>
   <fault message="faultMessage"/>
</operation>
```

Creating a Notification Operation

A notification operation is the logical opposite of a one-way operation. A one-way operation is sent from the client to the service; a notification operation originates from the service and goes out to the client. Take, for instance, the situation where you want to actively notify the client of the shipping state of a purchase. You might have an operation such as this:

```
<operation name="deliveryStatus">
   <output message="trackingInformation"/>
</operation>
```

Notice that the notification operation does not have an input operation; it has just an output.

> **NOTE**
>
> Notification and one-way operations are not allowed to have fault messages.

Creating a Solicit/Response Operation

The last operational form is the solicit/response. The solicit/response operation is used when a service wants to request information from the client. The simple example for this is when you want to request further information about the client's status. If you were building a high-bandwidth/low-bandwidth site, for instance, you might define an operation that looks like this:

```
<operation name="clientQuery">
    <output message="bandwidthRequest"/>
    <input message="bandwidthInfo"/>
    <fault message="faultMessage"/>
</operation>
```

Although you have seen operations appear as standalone elements so far, in reality they are defined within the body of a port type.

Port Type

A *port type* is defined in W3C terms this way: "A port type is a named set of abstract operations and the abstract messages involved." What this really means is that it is the equivalent of an interface. A port type is used to define a group of operations, along with their messages.

As with all of the elements you have seen so far, the port type is not directly realizable. Instead, the port type only provides abstract definitions and requires some of the elements we will cover later to actually be realized. On the other hand, as a consumer of a service, much like the consumer of an interface, the port type provides all the information you will need when you are actually talking to the service.

Creating a Port Type with a One-Way Operation

A port type is really just a <portType> element enclosing one or more operations. The following example shows a port type for the submitPurchase operation:

```
<portType name="submitPurchaseType">
    <operation name="submitPurchase">
        <input message="purchase"/>
    </operation>
</portType>
```

Binding

Up to this point in the appendix, you have been dealing with elements that, in UML terms, would be called unrealizable. In other words, you can't actually realize the port type by itself. The port type is like an interface. After you actually have an instance of a port type object, you have all the information you need to use it, but you can't take the port type and instantiate it directly. This is the same situation that prevents you from instantiating a new interface; you can only instantiate an object that implements the interface. So you can't write the following:

```
public interface SomeInterface(){
    public submitPurchase(Address billTo, Address sendTo);
}
public class SomeClass{
    public void myMethod(){
        //This is illegal
        SomeInterface si = new SomeInterface();
    }
}
```

To realize a port, you must provide some concrete information about how to talk to the port—in particular, the methods the port will use for transport. So, for instance, when you define a port type for the submitPurchase operation, you don't deal with any of the wire format issues. So up to this point, the port type could be carried over SOAP, SMTP, standard HTML, or a variety of other forms. The binding provides the implementation details for the port type.

Binding myMethod to SOAP over HTTP

To utilize the SOAP binding schema, it's necessary to first expand the list of schemas you include in the definition header. In particular, you must now include the xmlns for the WSDL SOAP schema at http://www.schemas.xmlsoap.org/wsdl/soap/.

With that said, it's time to look at a simple binding:

```
<wsdl:binding name="purchaseBinding" type="tns:purchaseType">
    <soap:binding style="document"
        transport="http://schemas.xmlsoap.org/soap/http"/>
    <wsdl:operation name="tns:purchaseOperation">
        <wsdl:input>
            <soap:body use="literal"/>
        </wsdl:input>
    </wsdl:operation>
</wsdl:binding>
```

Binding myMethod to Multiple Transports

Just because you have created a binding to HTTP/SOAP does not mean that the port type cannot also be used for a SOAP message sent over SMTP. To accomplish that, you simply bind the port type to SMTP in addition to HTTP, as shown in Listing C.6.

LISTING C.6   Multiple Bindings

```
<?xml version="1.0" encoding="UTF-8"?>
<wsdl:definitions name="PurchaseExample"
    targetNamespace="http://www.fluidimagination.com/sams/PurchaseExample.wsdl"
    xmlns:tns="http://www.fluidimagination.com/sams/PurchaseExample.wsdl"
    xmlns:soap="http://www.schemas.xmlsoap.org/wsdl/soap/"
    xmlns:wsdl="http://schemas.xmlsoap.org/wsdl/">

    <wsdl:types>
        <xsd:schema
                targetNamespace=
➥"http://www.fluidimagination.com/sams/productType.xsd"
                xmlns:xsd="http://www.w3.org/2001/XMLSchema">
            <xsd:complexType name="scannerType">
                <xsd:all>
                    <xsd:element name="upc" type="upcType"/>
                    <xsd:element name="isbn" type="isbnType"/>
                </xsd:all>
            </xsd:complexType>
            <xsd:simpleType name="upcType">
```

LISTING C.6 Continued

```
                    <xsd:restriction base="xsd:string">
                        <xsd:pattern value="[0-9]{12}"/>
                    </xsd:restriction>
                </xsd:simpleType>
                <xsd:simpleType name="isbnType">
                    <xsd:restriction base="xsd:string">
                        <xsd:pattern value="([0-9]- ){10}"/>
                    </xsd:restriction>
                </xsd:simpleType>
            </xsd:schema>
        </wsdl:types>
        <!-- Adding a message that has two addresses -->
        <wsdl:message name="purchaseMessage">
            <wsdl:part name="productCode" element="tns:scannerType"/>
        </wsdl:message>
        <!--create a port type with one operation -->
        <wsdl:portType name="purchaseType">
            <wsdl:operation name="purchaseOperation">
                <wsdl:input name="tns:purchaseMessage"/>
            </wsdl:operation>
        </wsdl:portType>
        <!--Bind the message to SOAP using HTTP -->
        <wsdl:binding name="purchaseBinding" type="tns:purchaseType">
            <soap:binding style="document"
                    transport="http://schemas.xmlsoap.org/soap/http"/>
            <wsdl:operation name="tns:purchaseOperation">
                <wsdl:input>
                    <soap:body use="literal"/>
                </wsdl:input>
            </wsdl:operation>
        </wsdl:binding>
        <!--Bind the message to SOAP over  SMTP -->
        <wsdl:binding name="purchaseBindingSMTP" type="tns:purchaseType">
            <soap:binding style="document"
                    transport="http://schemas.xmlsoap.org/soap/smtp"/>
            <wsdl:operation name="tns:purchaseOperation">
                <wsdl:input>
                    <soap:body use="literal"/>
                </wsdl:input>
            </wsdl:operation>
        </wsdl:binding>
</wsdl:definitions>
```

It should be clearer now why each element is handled separately. If you allow the port type to be bound to several protocols, you can reuse the work needed in the production of the port across multiple bindings.

It's also worth noting that for most developers, the nature of the bindings will be nearly transparent except when you are scripting the WSDL, because almost all the architectures out there allow you to switch out the binding almost transparently.

Port

Now that you have defined the method of the transport, you can finally start to tie the whole thing to a specific IP address. The binding identified that you were using SOAP over HTTP or SOAP over SMTP, but did not yet define what the network address was of the machine that was hosting the service. The port element adds that information.

Defining a Port

A port consists primarily of a name, a binding, and the wire-specific address information. The port name must be unique in the entire WSDL document and represents the name by which the port will be known. The binding name is, of course, the name of the binding you created in the earlier section. Finally, the specific wire format you are using provides the address information via extension. The next example shows the purchaseBinding defined in Listing C.6 bound to the address of the Apache SOAP server at www.fluidimagination.com:

```
<port binding="tns:purchaseBinding" name="Purchase_ServicePort">
    <soap:address
       location="http://www.fluidimagination.com:8080/soap/servlet/rpcrouter"/>
</port>
```

Service

The service element ties all the previous elements together into a single offering. In general, the service element can be thought of as an entire Java class. The service element is the element that your customers see first when they obtain your WSDL document.

The service element is designed to bring all the related ports together into one solid group. If the complete list is provided, a consumer can go through and determine all the port types a particular service supports. The service allows a client to determine whether a particular service supports all the operations that the client needs.

There is one rule about combining ports within the service: The ports within the service cannot communicate between each other. In other words, they can't be chained so that one port's output is the input to another port.

Declaring the Service

A service consists of just a `service` element, its name, and the ports included in the service. Listing C.7 shows the previous `Purchase_ServicePort` port as part of the `Purchase_Service` service.

LISTING C.7   The Complete WSDL

```
<?xml version="1.0" encoding="UTF-8"?>
<wsdl:definitions name="PurchaseExample"
➥targetNamespace="http://www.fluidimagination.com/sams/PurchaseExample.wsdl"
         xmlns:tns="http://www.fluidimagination.com/sams/PurchaseExample.wsdl"
         xmlns:soap="http://www.schemas.xmlsoap.org/wsdl/soap/"
         xmlns:wsdl="http://schemas.xmlsoap.org/wsdl/">

    <wsdl:types>
        <xsd:schema
          targetNamespace="http://www.fluidimagination.com/sams/productType.xsd"
          xmlns:xsd="http://www.w3.org/2001/XMLSchema">
            <xsd:complexType name="scannerType">
                <xsd:all>
                    <xsd:element name="upc" type="upcType"/>
                    <xsd:element name="isbn" type="isbnType"/>
                </xsd:all>
            </xsd:complexType>
            <xsd:simpleType name="upcType">
                <xsd:restriction base="xsd:string">
                    <xsd:pattern value="[0-9]{12}"/>
                </xsd:restriction>
            </xsd:simpleType>
            <xsd:simpleType name="isbnType">
                <xsd:restriction base="xsd:string">
                    <xsd:pattern value="([0-9]- ){10}"/>
                </xsd:restriction>
            </xsd:simpleType>
        </xsd:schema>
    </wsdl:types>
    <!-- Adding a message that has two addresses -->
    <wsdl:message name="purchaseMessage">
        <wsdl:part name="productCode" element="tns:scannerType"/>
    </wsdl:message>
    <!--create a port type with one operation -->
    <wsdl:portType name="purchaseType">
        <wsdl:operation name="purchaseOperation">
```

LISTING C.7   Continued

```
                <wsdl:input name="tns:purchaseMessage"/>
        </wsdl:operation>
    </wsdl:portType>
    <!--Bind the message to SOAP over  HTTP -->
    <wsdl:binding name="purchaseBinding" type="tns:purchaseType">
        <soap:binding style="document"
             transport="http://schemas.xmlsoap.org/soap/http"/>
        <wsdl:operation name="tns:purchaseOperation">
            <wsdl:input>
                 <soap:body use="literal"/>
            </wsdl:input>
        </wsdl:operation>
    </wsdl:binding>
    <!--Bind the message to SOAP over SMTP -->
    <wsdl:binding name="purchaseBinding" type="tns:purchaseType">
        <soap:binding style="document"
             transport="http://schemas.xmlsoap.org/soap/smtp"/>
        <wsdl:operation name="tns:purchaseOperation">
            <wsdl:input>
                 <soap:body use="literal"/>
            </wsdl:input>
        </wsdl:operation>
    </wsdl:binding>

    <service name="Purchase_Service">
        <documentation>Purchase service,
                     offering purchase of ISBN or UPC based matterials
                     to the world!</documentation>
        <port binding="tns:purchaseBinding" name="Purchase_ServicePort">
            <soap:address
        location="http://www.fluidimagination.com:8080/soap/servlet/rpcrouter"/>
        </port>
    </service>

</wsdl:definitions>
```

Notice that in the service you also see the use of the <documentation> element. In truth, it is a good idea to include documentation elements throughout your WSDL, as it is good practice to document all your elements. For the sake of conserving a few trees, we've left these elements out of the rest of this chapter, but the documentation element is shown here so that you don't forget about it.

Combining Port Types Within a Service

Within the same service, you can place several of the same port type elements that each use a different binding (service), or a different port (address). This is precisely what happens in Workshop if you set multiple Protocol values to true. (You can set the protocols by selecting a message in the Design view and setting the protocol values on the Properties panel.)

When multiple protocols are supported by a single port, each port must have semantically equivalent behavior. The idea here is to allow consumers to choose the best type of communication for their situation, but for them to have identical results regardless of the protocol they select. For instance, you might want to publish your service where the most ideal performance would come from a binding to JMS, but you also want to make the service available to users behind a firewall that need to use an HTTP proxy. You accomplish this by providing two different ports: one for the JMS and another for HTTP.

D

SOAP

IN THIS APPENDIX

- SOAP Message Exchange
- Web Services and SOAP
- SOAP Message Format
- SOAP Data Encoding
- SOAP over HTTP
- SOAP Headers

The Simple Object Access Protocol (SOAP) is a method for exchanging XML messages in a distributed environment. SOAP allows you to send messages and receive replies or error messages. You can think of SOAP as a remote procedure call mechanism for XML.

Although SOAP defines a basic message format, it does not define the actual message semantics. That is, apart from the basic message framework, SOAP doesn't specify the format for the actual data passed back and forth. SOAP itself is protocol-independent, but the SOAP specification does specify how to send SOAP requests over HTTP (the most common form of SOAP). WebLogic Workshop also allows you to send SOAP messages over the Java Message Service (JMS).

You normally don't need to worry about the SOAP protocol when you use WebLogic Workshop. It handles all of the SOAP encoding and decoding for you. It is useful, however, to understand what SOAP is and how it works, especially if you need to use SOAP to interact with non-WebLogic SOAP applications.

The SOAP specification is available online at
http://www.w3.org/TR/soap12-part0/. The specification is actually in three parts—soap12-part0, soap12-part1, and soap12-part2.

SOAP Message Exchange

SOAP involves the exchange of one or more messages between a sender and a receiver. In a typical scenario, the sender and receiver interact using a request-reply pattern, where the sender sends a request to the receiver, and the receiver processes the request and then sends a reply back to the sender. Figure D.1 illustrates this kind of scenario.

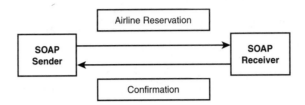

FIGURE D.1   SOAP typically involves request-reply messages between a sender and a receiver.

A SOAP message contains information indicating what kind of message it is. The receiver uses this information to determine how to process the message. For example, a SOAP message might indicate that it is an order placement, so the receiver might need to add the order to a database. Another SOAP message to the same receiver might be an order cancellation or an order status inquiry. Again, the receiver examines the message type and processes it accordingly.

SOAP allows the sender and receiver to use a Remote Procedure Call (RPC) pattern, where the sender invokes a particular method or procedure on the receiver side, passing appropriate parameters and expecting a specific response. This kind of inter-action isn't really any different from the request-reply pattern you have already seen. It is just a different way to look at the messages.

The SOAP specification also calls for the possibility of multinode SOAP environ-ments, which is quite a bit more complicated than most of the SOAP implementa-tions you see today. In a multinode environment, a message passes through many "actors" before reaching the receiver. These actors can modify the contents of the message along the way. For example, one actor might encrypt or decrypt the contents of a message. Another actor might examine the data contents and fill in missing parts with default values. Yet another actor might act as a load balancer, routing the message to one of a number of message processors to spread the work out over several servers. Figure D.2 shows a possible multinode SOAP environment.

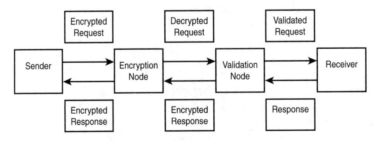

FIGURE D.2   In a multinode SOAP environment, actors can process parts of a message.

Web Services and SOAP

SOAP is really the core of Web services because you typically invoke Web service methods via SOAP (WebLogic Workshop provides other ways to invoke methods, such as via JMS or HTTP). Web services use a typical RPC mechanism to implement their services, exposing any number of methods to SOAP clients.

Web services add some additional features that address some of the necessities that SOAP doesn't include. For example, although SOAP allows you to invoke remote methods, it doesn't define a way to find out what methods a receiver supports or what parameters each method expects. The Web Service Description Language (WSDL) makes up for this shortcoming. SOAP doesn't provide a way to locate Web services, so Web services can use Universal Description, Discovery and Integration (UDDI) to locate services and service providers. In fact, Web services can even use UDDI to locate WSDL files, which then provide information about specific Web services and SOAP receivers.

Web services often need to keep track of client information across multiple method invocations. This requires the sender and receiver to establish some kind of session. Typically, a receiver sends a reply containing a unique session identifier. The sender then sends this session identifier along with any future requests, letting the receiver know what session the request belongs to. WebLogic Workshop refers to these sessions as "conversations" and provides a mechanism to start, continue, and finish a conversation.

Although SOAP doesn't specifically provide a session mechanism, it provides a special "header" area that can contain information like session identifiers. By providing a special area for these session identifiers, the actual body of the SOAP request just contains the data specific to the Web service.

SOAP Message Format

A SOAP message is actually an XML document, containing a single root XML element enclosing the contents of the message. In SOAP, this single root element is called `Envelope` and contains a `Body` element and an optional `Header` element. Although SOAP specifies the `Body` and `Header` elements, including allowable attributes, it does not say anything about what tags can be included within these elements.

SOAP messages typically use the SOAP XML namespace, currently `http://www.w3.org/2001/12/soap-envelope`. A simple SOAP request message with no `Header` looks like this:

```
<?xml version="1.0"?>
<soap:Envelope xmlns:soap="http://www.w3.org/2001/12/soap-envelope">
   <soap:Body>
```

```
        <sampleParam>This is a simple parameter</sampleParam>
    </soap:Body>
</soap:Envelope>
```

Although this example uses the namespace value soap to represent the SOAP namespace, you can use other values. For example, the SOAP specification uses env, so that all the tags are of the form <env:Envelope> and <env:Body>. This is true for any XML document.

A reply message looks just like a request, unless there is an error. Here is an example of a reply:

```
<?xml version="1.0"?>
<soap:Envelope xmlns:soap="http://www.w3.org/2001/12/soap-envelope">
    <soap:Body>
        <sampleReply>This is a simple reply</sampleReply>
    </soap:Body>
</soap:Envelope>
```

In the case of an error, SOAP defines several tags for relaying the cause of the error. First, the Body element contains a single Fault element. The Fault element should contain a faultcode element indicating the basic cause of the error, and a faultstring element providing a human-readable description of the error.

If the error occurs as a result of a processing error on the receiver side, the faultcode element indicates that it is a Receiver error (that is, soap:Receiver if the namespace is soap). If the error occurs as a result of improper message formatting or an invalid request, the faultcode element indicates that it is a Sender error (soap:Sender when the namespace is soap).

For example, the following error response indicates that the sender sent an invalid request:

```
<?xml version="1.0"?>
<soap:Envelope xmlns:soap="http://www.w3.org/2001/12/soap-envelope">
    <soap:Body>
        <soap:Fault>
            <faultcode>soap:Sender</faultcode>
            <faultstring>Invalid Request Format</faultstring>
        </soap:Fault>
    </soap:Body>
</soap:Envelope>
```

This error response indicates that the receiver encountered an error while processing the request:

```
<?xml version="1.0"?>
<soap:Envelope xmlns:soap="http://www.w3.org/2001/12/soap-envelope">
   <soap:Body>
      <soap:Fault>
         <faultcode>soap:Receiver</faultcode>
         <faultstring>Unable to access Personnel database</faultstring>
      </soap:Fault>
   </soap:Body>
</soap:Envelope>
```

A `Fault` element can also include a `detail` element including application-specific information about the error. For example:

```
<?xml version="1.0"?>
<soap:Envelope xmlns:soap="http://www.w3.org/2001/12/soap-envelope">
   <soap:Body>
      <soap:Fault>
         <faultcode>soap:Receiver</faultcode>
         <faultstring>Internal error processing request</faultstring>
         <detail>
            <module>com.mycompany.BusinessProcess.OrderEntry</module>
            <exception>java.lang.NullPointerException</exception>
         </detail>
      </soap:Fault>
   </soap:Body>
</soap:Envelope>
```

SOAP Data Encoding

Although XML is very flexible when it comes to data representation, SOAP must impose some additional restrictions in order to support RPC-type requests. SOAP splits data values into two different types—simple values and compound values. A *simple value* is a single item without any additional parts. An example of a simple value would be a particular number or a string. A *compound value* is made up of multiple parts, which can be either simple values or other compound values. A compound example might be an address, which contains simple values for the street, city, state, and zip code. A compound object that contains other compound objects might be a person, which might contain simple values like first and last name, but also a compound address value.

SOAP further classifies compound values into two categories—arrays and structs. An *array* is a compound value that contains multiple instances of the same value. For example, the set of employees at a company might be an array of employee values. A *struct* is a compound value in which each value has a particular name. An address is an example of a struct—the named fields are "street," "city," "state," and "zip."

SOAP also uses the idea of data "types." A simple type indicates the kind of values that a simple value can have. For example, "integer" is a simple type and indicates that a value can contain whole numbers. A "string" is another simple type indicating that a value can contain a sequence of characters. A compound type indicates that a value is a compound value. The compound type indicates whether a compound value is an array or a struct, and furthermore, what types of values belong to the compound type. For example, the type for a compound "address" would indicate that an address must contain strings named "street," "city," "state," and "zip."

If you read Appendix B, "XML," some of this might sound familiar because it is similar to XML Schema—the XML standard for specifying data types and data structures. In fact, it is identical, because SOAP uses XML Schema to define data types and structures.

SOAP over HTTP

The SOAP message format is independent of the mechanism you use to transport the message. This allows you to use SOAP over a variety of different networking and messaging protocols. The most common protocol used for SOAP messaging is HTTP (the standard Web protocol).

HTTP is ideal for B2B communications (Business to Business) because most businesses are able to send and receive HTTP requests easily. These days, companies typically have complex and restrictive network firewalls that prevent many requests from getting through. These firewalls have made it difficult to use other communication systems like RMI and CORBA for B2B applications. Because most companies need to allow their users or applications to access the Web, they are already able to send HTTP requests, and because most of these companies operate Web sites, they are already able to receive HTTP requests.

There are several different kinds of HTTP request—the two most common being GET and POST. An HTTP GET is the request a browser typically makes to retrieve a Web page or an image. A POST request is frequently what the browser uses to send HTML form data to a server (HTTP GET can also be used to submit a form, but in these cases, the form data appears in the URL and is restricted to 4K in length).

For HTTP SOAP messaging, the SOAP standard only mentions HTTP POST for exchanging messages. Although it is technically possible to use GET, there is no SOAP standard for using GET. The only two things you need to know about SOAP and HTTP is that you normally embed the name of the remote function you are invoking (that is, the name of the receiver) in the POST URL, and the content-type for the data you are posting should be application/soap.

In previous versions of SOAP, the content-type was text/xml. As of SOAP version 1.2, however, application/soap is now the official standard. Also, in older versions of SOAP, you had to specify the name of the remote function using a special HTTP header value. Although that is still possible, the SOAP standard doesn't require it.

Here is an example of an HTTP 1.1 SOAP request:

```
POST /soap-requests/OrderEntry HTTP/1.1
Host: user123.mycompany.com
Content-Type: application/soap
Content-Length: 329


<?xml version="1.0">
<soap:Envelope xmlns:soap="http://www.w3.org/2001/12/soap-envelope">
    <soap:Body>
        <order>
            <customer id="123456"/>
            <items>
                <part id="P101">1</part>
                <part id="P307">10</part>
            </items>
        </order>
    </soap:Body>
</soap:Envelope>
```

When an HTTP SOAP request is successful, HTTP returns a status code in the 200–299 range indicating a successful request. Here is a sample response:

```
HTTP/1.1 200 OK
Content-Type: application/soap
Content-Length: 208


<?xml version="1.0">
<soap:Envelope xmlns:soap="http://www.w3.org/2001/12/soap-envelope">
    <soap:Body>
        <order>
            <id>01572-C12345</id>
            <status>Processing</status>
        </order>
    </soap:Body>
</soap:Envelope>
```

In the case of an error, HTTP requires the response to use a status code of 500 (Internal Server Error). For example:

```
HTTP/1.1 500 Internal Server Error
Content-Type: application/soap
Content-Length: 237


<?xml version="1.0"?>
<soap:Envelope xmlns:soap="http://www.w3.org/2001/12/soap-envelope">
   <soap:Body>
      <soap:Fault>
         <faultcode>soap:Sender</faultcode>
         <faultstring>Invalid Request Format</faultstring>
      </soap:Fault>
   </soap:Body>
</soap:Envelope>
```

SOAP Headers

So far, you haven't seen any SOAP examples that use the Header section of a SOAP envelope. The Header section is not a critical part of the request—it exists to define environmental information. In other words, it provides additional information that might not be passed to the routine actually handling the request.

One use of a header might be to provide additional handling information to the SOAP server itself. If you have a series of SOAP actors (additional nodes that preprocess the data), each actor can examine the header for any special processing information. In general, you should assume that you don't actually have access to the header information from your Web service.

WebLogic Workshop can store conversation and callback information in the header. For example, a Header section might look like this:

```
<soap:Header>
   <StartHeader>
      <conversationID>AB7D76576E291390</conversationID>
      <callbackLocation>http://localhost/webapp/Original.jws>
   </StartHeader>
</soap:Header>
```

Currently, there is no requirement that the Header section be present, and even if it is, there is no specific standard for what fields can or must be present in the Header. As SOAP becomes more widespread, a more detailed specification for the Header section may emerge.

Index

Symbols

@ symbol (attributes), 141

\ (backslash), 234

, (comma), 136

{ } (curly braces), 98, 129, 132, 141, 191

   if-else statement, 241

   Java templates, 231

:: (ending statements), 96

( ) (parentheses)

   DTD tags, 259

   operator, 142

   parameters, 43

+ (plus sign), 259

(pound sign), 197

? (question mark)

   list items, 259

   operator, 237

; (semicolon), Java code, 42

' (single quotation mark), 233-234

]]> tag, 257

-- (two consecutive dashes), 257

.. (two dots), 141

* (asterisk), 259

*/ (block comments), 45

/> (forward slash, greater than symbol) end tag, 21

/ (JavaDoc comment), 45

/* (block comments), 45

/** (JavaDoc comment), 45

// (line comments), 45

<? XML tag, 255

?> XML tag, 255

> special character, 257

< special character, 257

< > XML (Extensible Markup Language) tags, 255

< (less than symbol), XML start tag, 21

<!-- --> comment tags, 257

<![CDATA tag, 257

A

!A (Java operator), 236

~A (Java operator), 236

++A (Java operator), 236

--A (Java operator), 236

A-- (Java operator), 236

A++ (Java operator), 236

A != B (Java operator), 236

A && B (Java operator), 236

A || B (Java operator), 236

A < B (Java operator), 236

A <= B (Java operator), 236

A == B (Java operator), 236

A > B (Java operator), 236

A >= B (Java operator), 236

A instance of B (Java operator), 236

A%=B (Java operator), 237

A%B (Java operator), 235

A&=B (Java operator), 237

A&B (Java operator), 236

A*/B (Java operator), 235

A*=B (Java operator), 236

A*B (Java operator), 235

A/=B (Java operator), 237

A^=B (Java operator), 237

A^B (Java operator), 236

A|=B (Java operator), 237

A|B (Java operator), 236

A+=B (Java operator), 236

A+B (Java operator), 235

A<<=B (Java operator), 237

A<<B (Java operator), 235

A-=B (Java operator), 236

A>>=B (Java operator), 237

A>>>=B (Java operator), 237

A>>>B (Java operator), 236

A>>B (Java operator), 235

A-B (Java operator), 235

access modifiers, class fields and methods, 239

accessor methods (get and set), 167

Account.java file, source code, 146-148, 172-173

Account.jsp file, 185-186

AccountClientEJB proxy, 185

AccountEJB bean, 171-178

AccountExample.jws file, code, 176-181

AccountFilterScript.jsx file, source code, 148-150

AccountHome.java file, source code, 173-176

Accounting.jws file, source code, 145-146

accounts, despositing or finding, 178

Active Server Pages (ASP), Web services, 8

activities, comparing asynchronous and synchronous, 57-59

actors, SOAP (Simple Object Access Protocol) messages, 296

Add a Service Control dialog box, 274

Add Control command (Service menu), 93, 153, 157

Add Control menu commands

    Add Service Control, 274

    Add Timer Control, 76

Add Database Control dialog box, 93

Add EJB Control dialog box, 170

Add JMS Control dialog box, 160-161

Add Method (Add Operation combo box), 38

Add Operation combo box, Add Method, 38

Add Service Control

command (Add Control menu), 274

dialog box, 88

Add Timer Control command (Add Control menu), 76

add(element) function, 142

addData method, 219

addr variable, 135

address type element, WSDL (Web Service Description Language) documents, 278-280

addresses

messages, adding (code), 280-281

order( ) method, 280

passing as classes (code), 277

type definition, code, 278

Admin.jws (source code), 105-107

aliases, creating for tables, 97

appendChild(child) function, 142

application/soap (SOAP standard), 301

applications. See also conversant applications; HelloWorld

business, layers, 165-167

database controls, 102-112

Web services, 8

architectures, CORBA (Common Object Request Broker Architecture) Web services, 11-12

arrays, SOAP (Simple Object Access Protocol), 300

arrows, bidirectional messages (HelloWorld), 39-40

ASP (Active Server Pages), Web services, 8

assignment operators, shorthand (Java), 236-237

asterisk (*), 259

asychronous communication, simplifying development environments, 60

asychronous conversations, 63-64

asynchronous and synchronous activities, comparing, 57-59

asynchronous patterns, 60-62

asynchronous responses to clients, 62

<!ATTLIST> tag, 258-260

attribute(attributeName) function, 142

attributes

@ symbol, 141

connection-factory-jndi-name (@jws:jms tag), 160, 193

home-jndi-name (JavaDoc), 181

@jws:jms tag, 160, 192-193

part tag, 281

receive-correlation-property (@jws:jms tag), 160, 193

receive-jndi-name (@jws:jms tag), 160, 193

receive-selector (@jws:jms tag), 160, 193

send-correlation-property (@jws:jms tag), 160, 193

send-jndi-name (@jws:jms tag), 160, 193

type (@jws:jms tag), 160, 193

variable-type, 135

XML (Extensible Markup Language), 256, 265-266

<xm:multiple>, 136-137

Attributes( ) function, 142

B

\b (Java special character), 234

B2B communications (Business to Business), 300

backslash (\), 234

Bean-Managed Persistence (BMP), 168

beans. *See* EJBs

beginning. *See* starting

bidirectional messages (HelloWorld Web service), 39-40

bin directory (JDK Java Development Kit), 230

binding

myMethod, 288-290

port types, 287-289

block comments (*/) or (/*), 45

blocking responses, asynchronous patterns, 62

blocks

finally, 246-247

try-catch, 245-246

BMP (Bean-Managed Persistence), 168

Body element, 297-298

books, *Special Edition Using Java 2 Platform*, 83

Boolean

data type, 263

values, 233

boolean getCoalesceEvents( ) method, 84

boolean (primitive data type), 232

braces, 98

curly ({ }), 129, 132, 141, 191

if-else statement, 241

Java templates, 231

Indent After Opening Brace, 34

break statement, 244-245

breakpoints, setting, 115-117

broadcasting, current dates, 84-86

Browser Path value, 36

browsers

Project, 17-18

Web, Browser Path value, 36

buffered JavaDoc comments, 64

buffered messages, 63-64

buffering callbacks, 68

Build command (Debug menu) or icon, 41

building

files in HelloWorld Web service, 41-42

JWS files, 275-276

XML (Extensible Markup Language) maps, 127-131

business applications, business logic layer, 165-167

Business to Business (B2B) communications, 300

buttons

getGreeting, 64, 78

Hello, 20

Byte data type, 263

byte primitive data type, 232

BytesMessage class, 153

C

Calendar object, 82

Call Stack window, debugging code, 123

callbackID, 61

callbacks

buffering, 68

CTRL (Control) files, 92

handlers, variableName_methodName, 92

HelloConversationAsync Web service, 64

manual edits, 65-66

methods, 65-67, 155

parameters, changing, 65

calling

callback method, 66-67

EJB control methods, 171

myMethod( ) method, 277

case sensitivity (Java), 230

cast operator, 238

CGI (Common Gateway Interface) Web services, 8

cgSampleDataSource data source, 202

char (primitive data type), 232

characters

single, ' (single quotation mark), 233

special, 233-234, 257

tab (\t), 34

values, 233

childIndex( ) function, 142

Children function, 143

classes

beans, using as, 168

BytesMessage, 153

constructors, 240-241

Customer, 205-207

declaring as public, 239

definition, syntax, 239

fields, access modifiers, 239

functions, 229

"Hello World!," printing, 231

initializer methods, 240

Java

packages, 248-251

programs, 229-232

templates, 231

java.io package, 250

java.lang package, 250

java.net package, 251

java.sql package, 251

java.util package, 251

MapMessage, 153

members, 229

Message, 153

methods, 229, 239-240

names and filenames, matching, 230

ObjectMessage, 153

objects, 238-241

Order, 207-208

OrderItem, 208-210

package fields or methods, 239

Person, JavaBean version (code), 167

private fields or methods, 239

Product, 203-204

protected fields or methods, 239

public fields or methods, 239

returning in result sets, 99-100

StreamMessage, 153

TextMessage, 153

upper- and lowercase letters, 239

variables, 51-52

clauses, FROM (creating table aliases), 97

Clear All Breakpoints command (Debug menu) or icon, 117

client-side of Web services, 183-185

clients, 60-62, 169-170

CMP (Container-Managed Persistence), 168

coalesce-events, 81-84

code

AccountExample.jws file, 179-181

AccountFilterScript.jsx file, 148-150

Accounting.jws file, 145-146

Account.java file, 146-148, 172-176

Account.jsp file, 185

Account.jws file, 176-181

addresses, 277-281

Admin.jws, 105-107

class definitions, 239

CTRL (Control) files, 90

Customer.java file, 107-108, 205-207

CustomJMSControlControl.ctrl file, 160-163

DBAdmin.jws file, 217-219

DBControl.ctrl file, 202-203, 210-216

debugging, 120-123

errors, 113-114

Extractor.jsx file, 144

Hello method, 39

HelloAggregate, 89

HelloConversationAsync Web service, 66-67

HelloConversation.jws file, 54-55

HelloDelayed service, 84-86

HelloWorld, 44-48

HelloWorld.java, 229-230

HelloWorld.jws file, 46

if-else statement, 241

Java, 42, 134-135

methods, declaring, 240

namedef.xsd file, 265

Order.java file, 207-208

OrderEntry.jws file, 219-222

OrderItem.java file, 208-209

Orders.jws, 109-111

OrderStatus.java, 108

OrderStatusCtrl.ctrl, 102-105

OrderTracking.jws file, 222-226

parts, creating with specified types, 281-282

Person class, JavaBean version, 167

Person.java file, 133-134

Person.xmlmap file, 138

port types, binding, 288-289

Product.java file, 203-204

QueueReceiver.jws file, 156

QueueSender.jws file, 154-155

sample.xml file, 262

sample.xsd file, 261

schema.xsd file, 268-269

SchemaDemo.jws file, 267-268

statements, ending with ::, 96

step into (option), 117-118

step out (option), 119

step over (option), 119

stepping through, 117

timeout values, changing, 69

timer controls, 79-82

TopicExample.jws file, 157

TopicReceiver.jws file, 159

WDSL, PurchaseService service, 291-292

Web services, 114-117

XML (Extensible Markup Language), initializing, 140-141

code completion (editor), 34

colors, changing, 34-35

combo boxes, 38, 51

comma (,), 136

commands

    Add Control menu

        Add Service Control, 274

        Add Timer Control, 76

    Context menu, Generate WSDL from JWS, 274

    Debug menu

        Build, 41

        Clear All Breakpoints, 117

        Continue, 120

        Start, 20, 42

        Start and Debug, 114

        Step Into, 117

        Step Out, 119

        Step Over, 119

        Stop, 43

        Toggle Breakpoint, 115

File menu

    New Project, 37

    Open Project, 17

    Service, 274

Javac, 230

paths, setting, 230

Service menu, Add Control, 93, 153, 157

Tools menu

    Preferences, 31

    Start WebLogic Server, 19

comments

    <!-- -->, 257

    block (*/) or (/*), 45

    buffered JavaDoc, 64

    HelloWorld Web service, 44-48

    illegal, 257

    JavaDoc, /* and /, 45

    line (//), 45

    XML (Extensible Markup Language) documents, 257

Common Gateway Interface (CGI) Web services, 8

Common Object Request Broker Architecture (CORBA) Web services, 11-12

communication

    asychronous, simplifying development environments, 60

    processes, WSDL (Web Service Description Language) documents, 276

    two-way, 68

companies, Web services, 8-9

comparing

    asynchronous and synchronous activities, 57-59

    objects, 236

    strings, 236

    Web services, RMI, CORBA, DCOM, 11-12

compiling

    HelloWorld Web service, 41

    programs with javac command, 230

complex types, XML (Extensible Markup Language) Schema (defining), 265

compliance, Web services with WSDL (Web Service Description Language) files, 275-276

compound data, 299-300

Config Directory, 34

configuration data, structuring with XML (Extensible Markup Language), 253

configuring

    JMS (Java Message Service) controls, 192-193

    system paths, 34-36

    timer controls, 193-194

conn.close( ) statement, 247

connection factories, 152-153, 160, 193

connection-factory-jndi-name attribute (@jws:jms tag), 160, 193

connection pools, creating, 94

connections, 94-95, 152-153, 192

Console tab (Test view), 29

consoles, WebLogic server, 94-95

constants, named (XML special characters), 257

constructors, 240-241

Container-Managed Persistence (CMP), 168

containers, returning row result sets, 101

contents (mixed), XML (Extensible Markup Language) Schema, 266-267

Context menu commands, Generate WSDL from JWS, 274

Continue command (Debug menu) or icon, 120

continue statement, 244-245

Continue this conversation link, 55

Control files (CTRL), 87-92

control tags, @jws:control or @jws:timer, 79

ControlException, 91

controls. *See also* database controls
    CTRL (Control) files, callbacks, 92
    EJB (Enterprise JavaBeans), 171-178
    flow control (Java), 241-245
    HelloDelayed service, 78-79
    HelloWorld service (CTRL files), 86-91
    HelloWorldControl (HelloAggregate), 88
    JMS (Java Message Service), 153-158, 192-193
    JMSControl, 153-154
    @jws JavaDoc tags, 192-194
    TimerControl,
        weblogic.jws.control.TimerControl, 79
    timers, 75-86, 193-194
    variableName, 92
    Web services, adding, 274
    WSDL URLs (uniform resource locators), 274
conversant applications
    asynchronous patterns, 60-62
    callbacks, buffering, 68
    conversations, developing, 49
    HelloConversation Web service, 55-63
    HelloConversationAsync Web service, 63-68
    idle time, setting, 70
    idle timeout values, defining, 69
    maximum context age values, setting, 70
    timeout parameters or values, 69
conversational phase combo box, accessing, 51
conversationID, 61
conversations
    asynchronous, 60-64
    boundaries, 189-190
    callbacks, buffering, 68
    class variables, declaring, 51
    Continue this conversation link, 55
    continuing, 53

    ending, 53-55, 70
    HelloConversation Web service, 55-63
    HelloConversationAsync Web service, 63-68
    idle time, setting, 70
    idle timeout values, defining, 69
    JMS (Java Messaging System), 60
    @jws:conversation-lifetime tag, 194
    lifecycle, 49
    lifetime, defining, 69
    maximum context age values, setting, 70
    onFinish( ) method, 71
    phases, 53-54
    S (conversation started), 50
    SessionIDs, 56-57
    setName method, editing, 51-52
    starting, 50
    stateful interactions, 49
    timeout parameters or values, 69
    two-stages, 50
    two-way communications, 68
    Workshop JavaDoc variables, 53
conversions (Java), 238
copy function, 143
copying CTRL (Control) files, 92
CORBA (Common Object Request Broker
    Architecture) Web services, 11-12
create method, creating beans, 176-177
Create New File dialog box, 37-38
CREATE TABLE statements, 203
Create Timer Control dialog, 76
createAccount Web service method, 178
createDatabase method, 219
creditreport folder, 23
CreditReport.jws file, 23

CTRL (Control)

    files, 87-92

    icon, 87

    methods, 89-91

Ctrl+B keyboard shortcut, 41

Ctrl+F5 keyboard shortcut, 20, 42-43

Ctrl+Shift+F9 keyboard shortcut, 117

curly braces ({ }), 98, 129, 132, 141, 191

    if-else statement, 241

    Java templates, 231

current dates, broadcasting, 84-86

current timeout, obtaining, 83

Customer class, 205-207

customer registration services, online ordering systems, 201

Customer.java file, code, 107-108, 205-207

customers. *See* online ordering systems

customizing XML (Extensible Markup Language) map contents, 127

CustomJMSControlControl.ctrl file, source code, 160-163

D

dashes, -- (two consecutive), 257

data

    configuration, structuring with XML (Extensible Markup Language), 253

    encoding, SOAP (Simple Object Access Protocol), 299-300

    exchanges, Web services, 9

    exposing as fields, 167

    sources, 93-95, 202

    types, 232, 262-263, 300

    values, compound or simple, 299

    XML (Extensible Markup Language), 143-144, 257-258

data layer (business applications), 165-167

database controls

    Admin.jws (source code), 105-107

    application samples, 102-112

    cgSampleDataSource data source, 202

    connection pools, creating, 94

    creating, 93

    Customer.java (source code), 107-108

    data source, 93-95

    database connections, defining, 94-95

    EJBs (Enterprise JavaBeans), 112

    Orders.jws (source code), 109-111

    OrderStatus.java (source code), 108

    OrderStatusCtrl.ctrl (source code), 102-105

    result sets, 98-101

    SQL (Structured Query Languge) strings, 95-98

    statements, 96, 101-102

    variables, 98

databases

    business applications, 165

    connections, 94-95, 192

    online ordering systems, 201-219

    relationships to Web services, 93

    SQL (Structured Query Languge), java.sql package, 251

    tables, creating, 202

Date

    data type, 263

    objects, 82

dates, 83-86, 251

DBAdmin Web service, 219

DBAdmin.jws file, code, 217-219

DBControl.ctrl file, code, 202-203, 210-216

DCOM (Web services, RMI, CORBA), comparing, 11-12

debates (political), comparing asynchronous and synchronous activities, 58-59

Debug menu commands

Clear All Breakpoints, 117

Continue, 120

Start, 20

Start and Debug, 114

Step Into, 117

Step Out, 119

Step Over, 119

Toggle Breakpoint, 115

debug sessions, starting, 114

debuggers, 15-16

debugging, 113-122

Debut menu commands

Build, 41

Start, 42

Stop, 43

decimal data type, 263

declarations, parameter-xml, 136

declaring

class variables for conversations, 51

classes as public, 239

Java variables, 232-235

map variables, 135

methods, syntax, 240

services, 291-292

string variables, 234

defaults

constructors, 240

of timers, 82-83

defining

complex types, 265

conversation lifetime, 69

database connections, 94-95

elements, 262

filewide enhancements with @jws JavaDoc tags, 194-197

idle timeout values, 69

onTimeout method, 77

ports, 290

property names, 167

responses, 41

simple types, 263-264

timer controls in code, 79-82

definitions

class, syntax, 239

data source, 93

JavaBean, 167

type for addresses (code), 278

Web services, 7

WSDL (Web Service Description Language), 274-276

delayedTimer_onTimeout method, 77

DELETE statement, 97-99

deleting breakpoints, 117

deposit method, 178

Description pane, 26

descriptions, HelloWorld Web service, 46-48

descriptive languages. *See* WSDL

Design

pane, 24-25

panel, adding controls to CTRL (Control) files, 88

Design view, 24-27, 39, 171

Design View Sorting, 32

designing online ordering systems, 199-201

despositing accounts, 178

development environments, simplifying, 60

diagrams, comparing asynchronous and synchronous activities, 58-59

dialog boxes. *See individual dialog box names*

directories

Config Directory, 34

JDK (Java Development Kit), bin or jr/bin, 230

JNDI (Java Naming and Directory Interface), 169

WEB-INF\lib, jar files, 170

display properties, changing, 31-32

Display tab (Tools Preferences dialog box), 31

displaying

EJB control methods, 171

JavaDoc, 48

panes, 24

<!DOCTYPE> tag, 260

Document Object Model (DOM), JavaScript, 138

Document Type Definitions (DTDs), 258-260

documentation (Java), downloading, 251

documents

WSDL (Web Service Description Language), 274-293

XML (Extensible Markup Language), 255-260

DOM (Document Object Model), JavaScript, 138

dots, two (..), 141

double data type, 263

double primitive data type, 232

double-precision floating-point numbers, 233

downloading

Eclipse (Java IDE), 230

ECMAScript specification, 138

Forte (Java IDE), 230

Java, 184, 230, 251

JDK (Java Development Kit), 230

proxy jar files, 184

dragging and dropping CTRL (Control) files from Project trees, 88

Draw Lines Between Functions value, 32

DTDs (Document Type Definitions), 258-260

E

Eclipse (Java IDE), downloading, 230

ECMAScript (European Computer Manufacturers Association version of JavaScript), 114, 138-140, 145-150

Edit Maps and Interface dialog box, 127-131

editing

callbacks, manually, 65-66

setName method, 51-52

editor

properties, changing, 33

settings, 32-34

EJBs (Enterprise JavaBeans)

Account.java file, source code, 172-173

AccountEJB, 171-178

AccountExample.jws file, code, 176-181

AccountHome.java file, source code, 173-176

beans, 168

BMP (Bean-Managed Persistence), 168

business applications, layers, 165-167

client jar files, 169-170

CMP (Container-Managed Persistence), 168

controls, 171-178

create method, 176-177

database controls, 112

entity, 168-172

events, 168

get method, 167

interfaces

   home, 169, 192

   remote, 169

JavaDoc options, 181

JNDI (Java Naming and Directory Interface), 169

message driven, 169

method, 167, 176

property, 167

remote methods, accessing, 178

RMI (Remote Method Invocation), 169

session, 168-169

set method, 167

using as classes, 168

<!ELEMENT> tag, 258

elements

   Body, 297-298

   Envelope, 297

   Fault, 298

   faultcode, 298

   Header, 297

   <portType>, 287

   simpleType, 264

   WSDL (Web Service Description Language), 287-293

   XML (Extensible Markup Language), 277-287

encoding data, SOAP (Simple Object Access Protocol), 299-300

ending

   conversations, 53-56, 70-71

   statements with ::, 96

enhancements, filewide (defining with @jws JavaDoc tags), 194-197

Enterprise JavaBeans. *See* EJBs

entity beans (EJBs), 168-172

entries

   order entry services, creating, 219-222

   restricted, creating, 282-283

Envelope element, 297

envelopes (SOAP), Header section, 302

environments

   development, simplifying, 60

   IDE (Integrated Development Environment), 22, 113, 230

   multinode, SOAP (Simple Object Access Protocol), 296

   Workshop, 17-18, 22, 30-31

equals method, 236

errors

   code, 113-114

   HTTP requests, 302

   messages (Java), 42

   SOAP (Simple Object Access Protocol) messages, 298-299

European Computer Manufacturers Association (ECMAScript), 114, 138-140, 145-150

evaluations, short-circuit (Java), 237

events, 81-84, 168

exceptions

   ControlException, 91

   CTRL (Control) methods, 91

   Java, 245-247

   NullPointerException, 247

   RuntimeException, 91, 247

   throwing, 176, 247

   weblogic.jws.control.ControlException, 91

exchanging data, Web services, 9

exchanging messages, SOAP (Simple Object Access Protocol), 295-296

executing statements in database controls, 101-102

exposing data as fields, 167

Extensible Markup Language. *See* XML

Extensible Stylesheet Language (XSL), 270-271

extensions of files

    .jar, 184

    .java, 230

    .jsx, 143

    .jws, 44

    .xmlmap, 137

external files, storing maps, 137-138

Extractor.jsx file, source code, 144

F

\f (Java special character), 234

factories, connection, JMS (Java Message Service), 152-153

Fault element, 298

fault messages, 286

faultcode element, 298

FedEx (Federal Express), Web site to track packages, 9

fields

    class member variables, 51

    of classes, 239

    data, exposing as, 167

    Name (WebLogic server), 34

    in objects, accessing, 239

File menu commands

    New Project, 37

    Open Project, 17

    Service, 274

filenames and class names, matching, 230

files

    Account.java, source code, 146-148, 172-173

    Account.jsp, 185-186

    AccountExample.jws, code, 176-181

    AccountFilterScript.jsx, source code, 148-150

    AccountHome.java, source code, 173-176

    Accounting.jws, source code, 145-146

    Admin.jws (source code), 105-107

    building in HelloWorld Web service, 41-42

    client jar, 169-170

    creating for projects, 37

    CreditReport, 23

    CTRL (Control), 87-92

    Customer.java, code, 107-108, 205-207

    CustomJMSControlControl.ctrl, source code, 160-163

    DBAdmin.jws, code, 217-219

    DBControl.ctrl, code, 202-203, 210-216

    external, storing maps, 137-138

    Extractor.jsx, source code, 144

    HelloConversation.jws, code, 54-55

    HelloWorld.jws, code, 46

    inline, 194-195

    jar, 170, 186

    .jar extension, 184

    .java extension, 230

    java.io package, 250

    .jsx extension, 143

    JWS, 44, 267-269, 275-276

    .jws file extension, 44

    log, searching for code errors, 113

    managing, 22-23

    namedef.xsd, source code, 265

    Order.java, code, 207-208

    OrderEntry.jws, code, 219-222

    OrderItem.java, code, 208-209

    Orders.jws, source code, 109-111

    OrderStatus.java, source code, 108

OrderStatusCtrl.ctrl, source code, 102-105

OrderTracking.jws, code, 222-226

Person.java, source code, 133-134

Person.xmlmap, source code, 138

Product.java, code, 203-204

proxy jar, 184, 187

QueueReceiver.jws, source code, 156

QueueSender.jws, source code, 154-155

sample.xml, source code, 262

sample.xsd, source code, 261

schema.xsd, 267-269

SchemaDemo.jws, source code, 267-268

TopicExample.jws, source code, 157

TopicReceiver.jws, source code, 159

WSDL (Web Service Description Language), 187, 197, 274-276

XML (Extensible Markup Language), processing instructions, 255

.xmlmap extension, 137

filewide enhancements, defining with @jws JavaDoc tags, 194-197

filters, stream (java.io package), 250

finally blocks, 246-247

find methods, 178

findByPrimaryKey method, 178-179

finding accounts, 178

finish method, 53

finishing. *See* **ending**

firing event, time of, 84

firing timers, immediately or repeatedly, 81

float data type, 263

float primitive data type, 232

floating-point numbers, 233

flow control (Java), 241-245

folders, creditreport, 23

fonts, Window Font Size, 31

for loop, 243

form-get type (@jws:protocol tag), 195

form-post type (@jws:protocol tag), 195

formats

JMS (Java Message Service), headers or messages, 193

message, SOAP (Simple Object Access Protocol), 297-299

XML (Extensible Markup Language) Schema, 261-267

XSL-FO (XSL formatting objects), 270

forms

Overview, 29

test, 28, 43

Test XML, 30

Forte (Java IDE), downloading, 230

forward slash and greater than symbol (/>), 21

frameworks, testing in Workshop, 20

FROM clause, tables (creating aliases), 97

functionName parameter, 143

functions

add(element), 142

appendChild(child), 142

attribute(attributeName), 142

Attributes( ), 142

childIndex( ), 142

Children, 143

copy, 143

Draw Lines Between Functions value, 32

importClass, 143

in classes, 229

innerXML(newXML), 143

length( ), 143

parent( ), 143

prependChild(child), 143

Remove, 143

removeChild(child), 143

tagName, 143

toArray, 143

toString, 143

XML (Extensible Markup Language) manipulation, 142-143

xpath(xpathExpression), 143

G

Generate WSDL from JWS command (Context menu), 274

get method, defining property names, 167

GET requests, HTTP (Hypertext Transfer Protocol), 300

getBalance method, 178

getCustomer method, 222

getGreeting

button, 64, 78

message, 78

method, 53, 66, 77

getNextProductId method, 210

getRepeatsEvery( ) method, 83

getResults method, 137

getTimeout( ) method, 83

getTimeoutAt( ) method, 83

goodBye method, 54

Google Web site, 9

graphical views of services, 24

greetings, not receiving, 78

H

handlers, callback, 92

HashMaps, returning in result sets, 100

Header

element, 297

section (SOAP envelopes), 302

headers, 193, 302

Hello

button, 20

keyword, 39

method, 39, 46-47, 89-90

"Hello World!," printing, 231

HelloAggregate, 88-90

helloByHand( ) method, creating, 45-46

HelloConversation Web service, 51-62

HelloConversation.jws file, code, 54-55

HelloConversationAsync Web service, 63-68

HelloDelayed service, 75-79, 84-86

HelloWorld, 17

class, "Hello World!" (printing), 231

conversations, 50-55

running, 20

service, 21, 86-92

starting, 20

testing, 19-21

Web service, 37-48

HelloWorld.java source code, 229-230

HelloWorld.jws file, code, 46

HelloWorldControl, HelloAggregate, 88

helloWorldControl variable, 90

hexadecimal numbers, 233

hiding panes, 24

histories, WSDL (Web Service Description Language), 273

home interfaces, 169, 173-176, 192

home-jndi-name attribute (JavaDoc), 181

HTML (Hypertext Markup Language), form-get or form-post types, 195

HTTP (Hypertext Transfer Protocol)

B2B communications (Business to Business), 300

form-get type, 195

form-post type, 195

GET requests, 300

myMethod, binding to SOAP (Simple Object Access Protocol), 288

port types, binding (code), 288-289

POST requests, 300

requests, 300-301

responses, 301-302

SOAP (Simple Object Access Protocol), 300-302

Web services, 11

http-soap type (@jws:protocol tag), 196

http-xml type (@jws:protocol tag), 196

HTTPS, Web services, 11

hyperlinks, 55-56, 68

hypertext, PHP (Hypertext Pre-Processor) Web services, 8

Hypertext Transfer Protocol. See HTTP

I

icons. See individual icon names

IDE (Integrated Development Environment), 22, 113, 230

Indentation section, 33-34

idle time, setting, 70

idle timeout values, defining, 69

IDs, 56-57, 61

if-else statement, 241-242

illegal comments, 257

importClass function, 143

importing schema.xsd or schemas, 267

Indent After Opening Brace, 34

Indent Width, 33

Indentation section (editor), 33-34

information, passing to HelloWorld Web service, 43-44

initializer methods (constructors), 240-241

initializing

strings, 234

XML (Extensible Markup Language), code, 140-141

inline files (@jws:define tag), 194-195

innerXML(newXML) function, 143

input maps, 128-134

INSERT statement, 97-99

Int data type, 263

int primitive data type, 232

Integer data type, 263, 300

integers, returning, 99

Integrated Development Environment (IDE), 22, 113, 230

interactions, stateful (conversations), 49

interfaces

CGI (Common Gateway Interface), 8

Edit Maps and Interface dialog box, 127-131

EJBs (Enterprise JavaBeans), 169, 192

home, 169, 173-176

Java, 247-248

JNDI (Java Naming and Directory Interface), 169

remote, 169

Internet, java.net package, 251

J

.jar file extension, 184

jar files, 169-170, 183-187

Java. *See also* **EJBs; JMS; operators**

addresses, passing as classes (code), 277

\b (special character), 234

boolean (primitive data type), 232

byte (primitive data type), 232

case sensitivity, 230

char (primitive data type), 232

classes, 231, 239

code, ; (semicolon), 42

conversions, 238

data types, 232

documentation, downloading, 251

double (primitive data type), 232

error messages, 42

exceptions, 245-247

\f (special character), 234

filenames and class names, matching, 230

float (primitive data type), 232

flow control, 241-245

HelloWorld class, printing "Hello World!," 231

HelloWorld.java source code, 229-230

IDE (Integrated Development Environment), downloading, 230

int (primitive data type), 232

interfaces, 247-248

java.io package, 250

java.lang package, 250

java.net package, 251

java.sql package, 251

java.util package, 251

JDK (Java Development Kit), downloading, 230

JNDI (Java Naming and Directory Interface), 153-157, 169

JPDA (Java Platform Debugging Architecture), 113

language specification, downloading, 251

long (primitive data type), 232

\n (special character), 234

objects, 232

classes, 238-241

data, exposing as fields, 167

mapping, 133-135

RMI (Remote Method Invocation), 169

operators, 235-237

packages, 248-250

paths, setting, 230

pointers, 234

primitive data types, 232

programs, 229-232

proxy, 183-186

\r (special character), 234

servlets, Web services, 8

short (primitive data type), 232

short-circuit evaluations, 237

shorthand assignment operators, 236-237

special characters, 233-234

strings, 234-235

\t (special character), 234

templates, curly braces ({ }), 231

variables, 232-235

Web services, 183-185

XML (Extensible Markup Language), mapping into, 145-150

.java file extension, 230

Java Message Service. *See* **JMS**

Java Naming and Directory Interface (JNDI), 153-157, 169

Java Platform Debugging Architecture (JPDA), 113

java.io package, 250

java.lang package, 250

java.net package, 251

java.sql package, 251

java.util package, 251

JavaBean, 167

javac command, 230

JavaDoc

   comments

      /* and /, 45

      buffered, 64

      HelloWorld Web service, 44-45

   displaying, 48

   EJBs (Enterprise JavaBeans), 181

   home-jndi-name attribute, 181

   JMS (Java Message Service), 160

   @jws JavaDoc tags, 44, 189-197

   @jws:ejb tag, 181

   Workshop variables, 53

JavaScript, DOM (Document Object Model), 138

JavaServer Pages (JSP), 8, 185-186

JDK (Java Development Kit), downloading, 230

JMS (Java Message Service), 60, 196

   callback methods, 155

   connection factories, 152-153

   controls, 153-159, 192-193

   header formats, 193

   JavaDoc, options, 160

   JMSControl, 153-154

   JNDI (Java Naming and Directory Interface), 153-154, 157

   @jws:jms tag, attributes, 160, 192-193

   messages, 153-154, 163, 193

   messaging, 151-152

   Object messages, 154

   point-to-point messaging, 151-152

   publish-subscribe messaging, 151

   QueueConnectionFactory, 152

   sendJMSMessage method, 154

   sendMessage method, 154

   sendObjectMessage method, 154

   sendTextMessage method, 154

   sessions, 153

   Text messages, 154

   TopicConnectionFactory, 152

   topics, creating, 157-158

   transacted connections, 153

   weblogic.jws.jms.QueueConnectionFactory, 153

   XAQueueConnectionFactory, 152

   XATopicConnectionFactory, 152

   XML (Extensible Markup Language)

      Map messages, 154

      messages, sending, 160-163

jms-soap type (@jws:protocol tag), 196

jms-xml type (@jws:protocol tag), 196

JMSControl, 153-154

JMX sessions, threads, 153

JNDI (Java Naming and Directory Interface), 153-157, 169

joining tables in SQL (Structured Query Languge) strings, 97-98

JPDA (Java Platform Debugging Architecture), 113

jr/bin directory, JDK (Java Development Kit), 230

JSP (JavaServer Pages), 8, 185-186

.jsx file extension, 143

.jws file extension, 44

JWS files, 44, 267-269, 275-276

@jws JavaDoc tags, 44, 189-197

@jws:connection tag, 192

@jws:control tag, 79, 90

@jws:conversation tag, 189-190

@jws:conversation-lifetime tag, 194

@jws:define tag, 194-195

@jws:ejb tag, 181, 192-193

@jws:jms tag, 160, 192-193

@jws:jms-header tag, 193

@jws:jms-message tag, 193

@jws:jms-property tag, 193

@jws:operation tag, 46, 190

@jws:parameter-xml tag, 190-191

@jws:protocol tag, 195-196

@jws:return-xml tag, 191

@jws:schema tag, 196

@jws:sql tag, 191

@jws:target-namespace tag, 192

@jws:timer tag, 79, 193-194

@jws:wsdl tag, 197

@jws:xmlns tag, 197

K

keyboard shortcuts

Ctrl+B, 41

Ctrl+F5, 20, 42-43

Ctrl+Shift+F9, 117

Shift+F11, 119

keywords

Hello, 39

public, 39

throws, 247

L

languages. *See also* WSDL; XML

specification (Java), downloading, 251

SQL (Structured Query Language), 95-98, 191, 251

XSL (Extensible Stylesheet Language), 270-271

layers of business applications, 165-167

length( ) function, 143

less than symbol (<), XML start tag, 21

lifecycles of conversations, 49, 69

line comments (//), 45

lines, values (Draw Lines Between Functions or Show Line Numbers), 32

links (hyperlinks), 55-56, 68

listings. *See* code

lists

? (question mark), 259

refreshing, HelloConversationAsync Web service, 68

literals. *See* values

Locals window, displaying variables, 121-122

locations of Web services, changing, 186-187

log files, searching for code errors, 113

log messages, debugging, 114

logic, business logic layer, 165-167

Long data type, 263

long primitive data type, 232

long values, 233

loops, 242-243

M

manually editing callbacks, 65-66

MapMessage class, 153

How can we make this index more useful? Email us at indexes@samspublishing.com

mapping

Java objects, 133-135

XML (Extensible Markup Language) into Java, 145-150

maps

creating, 127

Edit Maps and Interface dialog box, 127-131

HashMaps, returning in result sets, 100

input, 128-131

Java object (code), 134-135

output, 129-131

root elements, 129

storing in external files, 137-138

variables, declaring, 135

XML (Extensible Markup Language), 127-150

markup languages. *See* **XML**

matching filenames and class names, 230

max-age value, 69

max-idle-time value, 69

maximum context age values, setting, 70

members of classes, 229

Message class, 153

message-driven beans (EJBs), 169

messages. *See also* **JMS**

actors, 296

addresses, adding (code), 280-281

bidirectional (HelloWorld Web service), 39-40

buffered, 63-64

conversations, 49-56

creating, 280-282

errors, 298-299

exchanging, SOAP (Simple Object Access Protocol), 295-296

fault, notification or one-way operations, 286

formats, SOAP (Simple Object Access Protocol), 297-299

getGreeting, 78

greetings, not receiving, 78

Java errors, 42

@jws:target-namespace tag, 192

log, debugging, 114

Object, 154

operations, 283

point-to-point messaging, 151-152

publish-subscribe messaging, 151

queue, 154-156

receiving, 78

request-reply, exchanging, 295

sendGreeting, 78

SOAP (Simple Object Access Protocol), 295

Text, 154

topic, 157-159

void responses, 40

XML (Extensible Markup Language), 154, 160-163

methods

accounts, finding and depositing, 178

Add Method (Add Operation combo box), 38

addData, 219

adding in HelloWorld code, 44-46

bean, 167

boolean getCoalesceEvents( ), 84

Call Stack window, 123

callback, 65-67, 155

in classes, 229, 239

create (creating beans), 176-177

createAccount Web service, 178

createDatabase, 219

CTRL (Control), 89-91

declaring, syntax, 240

deposit, 178

delayedTimer_onTimeout, 77

of EJB controls, calling or displaying, 171

equals, 236

exceptions, throwing, 176, 247

find, 178

findByPrimaryKey, 178-179

finish, 53

get, defining property names, 167

getBalance, 178

getCutomer, 222

getGreeting, 53, 66, 77

getNextProductId, 210

getRepeatsEvery( ), 83

getResults, 137

getTimeout( ), 83

getTimeoutAt( ), 83

goodBye, 54

Hello, 39, 46-47, 89-90

helloByHand( ), creating, 45-46

HelloWorld Web service, 38-39

initializers (constructors), 240-241

Java programs, 229

JMS (Java Message Service) message types, 154

@jws JavaDoc tags, 189-192

@jws:operation tag, 190

myMethod( ), calling, 277

onFinish( ), conversations, 71

onTimeout, defining, 77

operation, creating, 45

order( ), addresses, 280

Ordering service, 201

OrderTracking service, 201

package, 239

placeOrder, 222

private, 239

protected, 239

public, 239

receiveMessages, 156

remote, accessing, 178

restart( ), 84

selectors (Source view), 27-28

sendJMSMessage method, 154

sendMessage method, 154

sendObjectMessage method, 154

sendTextMessage method, 154

set, defining property names, 167

setCoalesceEvents(boolean), 84

setName, 50-52

setTimeoutAt(Date), 82

signatures, 39-40

start( ), 77

stop, 78-79

variables, 52, 121-122

WebLogic Workshop, 14

withdraw, 178

mixed content, XML (Extensible Markup Language) Schema, 266-267

modifiers, access (class fields and methods), 239

multinode environments, SOAP (Simple Object Access Protocol), 296

multithreaded clients, asynchronous patterns, 62

myMethod, 277, 288-290

<MyRootTag> tag, 255

N

\n (Java special character), 234

Name field (WebLogic server), 34

namedef.xsd file, source code, 265

names

of constants (XML special characters), 257

filenames and class, matching, 230

Java classes, upper- and lowercase letters, 239

JNDI (Java Naming and Directory Interface), 169

of properties, defining, 167

variableName, 92

namespaces

@jws:target-namespace tag, 192

prefixes, 263

SOAP XML, Web site, 297

XML (Extensible Markup Language), 197, 269-270

NegativeInteger data type, 263

New Project command (File menu), 37

nodes, multinode environments, 296

nonNegativeInteger data type, 263

nonPositiveInteger data type, 263

NormalizedString data type, 263

notification operations, 284-286

null value, 235

NullPointerException, 247

numbers, 32, 233, 251

numerical representation (XML special characters), 257

O

Object messages, 154

ObjectMessage class, 153

objects

Calendar, 82

classes, 238-241

comparing, 236

Date, 82

fields, accessing, 239

Java, 232

data, exposing as fields, 167

mapping, 133-135

RMI (Remote Method Invocation), 169

references, 234-235

XSL-FO (XSL formatting objects), 270

octal numbers, 233

one-way operations, WSDL (Web Service Description Language) documents, 283-286

onFinish( ) method, conversations, 71

online ordering systems

customer registration services, 201

Customer.java file, code, 205-207

databases, 201-219

DBAdmin.jws file, code, 217-219

DBControl.ctrl file, code, 202-203, 210-216

designing, 199-201

order entry services, 200, 219-222

order tracking services, 200, 222-226

Order.java file, code, 207-208

OrderEntry.jws file, code, 219-222

OrderItem.java file, code, 208-209

OrderTracking.jws file, code, 222-226

packages, tracking, 9

Product.java file, code, 203-204

onTimeout method, defining, 77

Open Project command (File menu), 17

operation element, WSDL (Web Service Description Language) documents, 283-286

operation method, creating, 45

operation tags (@jws:), 46

operations

messages, 283

notifications, 284-286

one-way, 283-287

request/response, 284-285

solicit/response, 284-286

Start operations link, 56

operators. *See also individual operator names*

( ), 142

?, 237

Java, 235-237

Order class, 207-208

order entry services, creating, 219-222

order( ) method, addresses, 280

order tracking services, 222-226

Order.java file, code, 207-208

OrderEntry.jws file, code, 219-222

Ordering service methods, 201

OrderItem class, 208-210

OrderItem.java file, code, 208-209

orders. *See* online ordering systems

Orders.jws (source code), 109-111

OrderStatus.java (source code), 108

OrderStatusCtrl.ctrl (source code), 102-105

OrderTracking service methods, 201

OrderTracking.jws file, code, 222-226

output maps, 129-135

output window, 20-22

Output XML Map icon, 127-128

Overview forms or tab (Test view), 29

P

packages

CTRL (Control) files, accessing, 91

fields, 239

Java, 248-250

java.io, 250

java.lang, 250

java.net, 251

java.sql, 251

java.util, 251

methods, 239

tracking online, 9

pages

ASP (Active Server Pages), Web services, 8

JSP (JavaServer Pages), 8, 185-186

test (WebLogic Workshop), 14-15

panels, Design, adding controls to CTRL (Control) files, 88

panes

Description, 26

Design, 24-25

hiding, 24

Properties, 25-26

showing, 24

Structure, 23-24

Structure Pane Sorting, 32

Tasks, 26-27

Parameter XML tab (Edit Maps and Interface dialog box), 128-129

parameter-xml declaration, 136

parameters

of callbacks, changing, 65

extracting from XML data, 143-144

functionName, 143

parentheses ( ), 43

scriptFileName, 143

timeout (conversations), 69-70

parent( ) function, 143

parentheses ( ), 142

DTD tags, 259

parameters, 43

part tag, attributes, 281

parts, creating with specified types (code), 281-282

passing

addresses as classes (code), 277

information to HelloWorld Web service, 43-44

Path tab (Tools Preferences dialog box), 34

paths

setting, 230

system, 34-36

patterns, asynchronous, 60-62

persistence, BMP (Bean-Managed Persistence) or CMP (Container-Managed Persistence), 168

Person class, JavaBean version (code), 167

Person.java file, source code, 133-134

Person.xmlmap file, source code, 138

PHP (Pre-Processor Hypertext) Web services, 8

placeOrder method, 222

platforms, Web services (not supporting asynchronous patterns), 61

plus sign (+), 259

point-to-point messaging, 151-152

pointers (Java), 234

political debates, comparing asynchronous and synchronous activities, 58-59

pools, connection (creating), 94

ports

defining, 290

port element, WSDL (Web Service Description Language) documents, 290

Port setting, 34

protocols, 293

types, 287-293

<portType> element, 287

PositiveInteger data type, 263

POST requests, HTTP (Hypertext Transfer Protocol), 300

pound sign (#), 197

Preferences command (Tools menu), 31

prefixes, namespaces, 263

prependChild(child) function, 143

presentation layer (business applications), 165-167

primitive data types (Java), 232

printing "Hello World!," 231

private fields or methods, 239

processing instructions, XML (Extensible Markup Language) files, 255

processors, PHP (Pre-Processor Hypertext) Web services, 8

Product class, 203-204

Product.java file, code, 203-204

programs

compiling with javac command, 230

HelloWorld.java, 230

Java

classes, 229-232

methods, 229

Project

browser, 17-18

trees, 22-23, 88

projects

CTRL (Control) files, 91

EJB controls, adding, 170

files, creating, 37

Samples, opening, 17-18

properties

bean, 167

display, changing, 31-32

editor, changing, 33

JMS (Java Message Service) messages, 193

names, defining, 167

Properties pane, 25-26

protected fields or methods, 239

Protocol values, 293

protocols. *See also* **HTTP; SOAP**

ports, 293

Protocol values, 293

SMTP (Simple Mail Transfer Protocol), port types, binding (code), 288-289

transport, asychronous patterns, 60-61

UDDI (Universal Description, Discovery, and Integration), 13-15, 297

Web Service, 12 195-196

WebLogic Workshop, 14

XML (Extensible Markup Language), 12

proxies

AccountClientEJB, Account.jsp file (code), 185

jar files, 184, 187

Java, 183-186

public classes, declaring, 239

public fields, 239

public keyword, 39

public methods, 239

publish-subscribe messaging, 151

PurchaseService service, code, 291-292

Q

queries, SQL (Structured Query Language), 95-98, 191, 251

question mark (?), list items, 259

queue messages

receiving, 155-156

sending, 154-155

QueueConnectionFactory, 152

QueueReceiver.jws file, source code, 156

QueueSender.jws file, source code, 154-155

QueueSession, 153

quotation marks, single ('), 233-234

R

\r (Java special character), 234

realizable, unrealizable port types, 287

receive-correlation-property attribute (@jws:jms tag), 160, 193

receive-jndi-name attribute (@jws:jms tag), 160, 193

receive-selector attribute (@jws:jms tag), 160, 193

receiveMessages method, 156

receiving

JMS (Java Message Service) messages, 153

messages, 78

queue messages, 155-156

topic messages, 159

references of objects, 234-235

Refresh link, 68

refreshing lists (HelloConversationAsync Web service), 68

relationships, Web services and databases, 93

remote debugging, 114

remote interfaces, 169

Remote Method Invocation (RMI), 11-12, 169

remote methods, accessing, 178

Remove function, 143

removeChild(child) function, 143

removing breakpoints, 117

repeats-every value, 76, 81-83

request-reply messages, 295

request/response operations, 284-285

requests, HTTP (Hypertext Transfer Protocol), 300-301

resources, *Special Edition Using Java 2 Platform*, 83

responses

asynchronous to clients, 62

blocking, 62

defining, 41

HTTP (Hypertext Transfer Protocol) requests, 301-302

service, 20

synchronous, 62

void, 40

restart( ) method, 84

restarting timers, 84

restricted entries, creating, 282-283

result sets in database controls, 98-101

return statement, 245

Return XML tab (Edit Maps and Interface dialog box), 128, 131

returning

classes in result sets, 99-100

HashMaps in result sets, 100

integers in statements, 99

row result sets, 99-101

values in SELECT statements, 98

variables in result sets, 98-99

RMI (Remote Method Invocation), 11-12, 169

row result sets, returning, 99-101

running

HelloWorld, 20

HelloWorld Web service, 42-44

Java proxy outside of WebLogic server, 186

RuntimeException, 91, 247

S

S (conversation started), 50

sample.xml file, source code, 262

sample.xsd file, source code, 261

Samples project, opening, 17-18

Sams Publishing Web site, SQL (Structured Query Language), 95

SchemaDemo.jws file, source code, 267-268

schema.xsd file

importing, 267

source code, 268-269

schemas

importing or selecting, 267

WSDL SOAP schema Web site, 288

XML Schema, 196, 261-269, 300

scriptFileName parameter, 143

scripts

ECMAScript (European Computer Manufacturers Association version of JavaScript), 114, 138-150

XMLScript (XML maps), 138-150

SELECT statement, 96-98

selecting

schemas, 267

values for SQL (Structured Query Languge) strings, 96

selectors, variable and method (Source view), 27-28

semicolon (;), Java code, 42

send-correlation-property attribute (@jws:jms tag), 160, 193

send-jndi-name attribute (@jws:jms tag), 160, 193

sendGreeting message, 78

sending messages

JMS (Java Message Service), 153

queue, 154-155

topic, 157-158

XML (Extensible Markup Language), 160-163

sendJMSMessage method, 154

sendMessage method, 154

sendObjectMessage method, 154

sendTextMessage method, 154

sensitivity, case (Java), 230

Server Stopped, 19

servers

HelloWorld service (CTRL files), 86-92

Web, Web services, 8

WebLogic

console, 94-95

development, configuring system paths, 34

Java proxy, 184-186

Name field, 34

proxy jar files, downloading, 184

starting, 19-20, 42

Service

command (File menu), 274

menu commands, Add Control, 93, 153, 157

services. *See also* JMS; Web services

declaring, 291-292

graphical views, 24

HelloDelayed service, 75-79, 84-86

HelloWorld, 21, 86-92

HelloWorld Web service, 37-48

order entry, creating, 219-222

order tracking, creating, 222-226

port types, combining, 293

PurchaseService, code, 291-292

responses, 20-21

service element, 290-293

structural views, 24-25

servlets, Java (Web services), 8

session beans (EJBs), 168-169

SessionIDs, conversations, 56-57

sessions, 114, 153

set method, defining property names, 167

setCoalesceEvents(boolean) method, 84

setName method, 50-52

setTimeoutAt(Date) method, 82

Shift+F11 keyboard shortcut, 119

shipping companies (Web services), 9

short data type, 263

short primitive data type, 232

short-circuit evaluations (Java), 237

shortcuts. *See* keyboard shortcuts

shorthand assignment operators (Java), 236-237

Show Line Numbers value, 32

Show Whitespace value, 32

showing. *See* displaying

signatures

callback methods, changing, 65

of methods, 39-40

simple data values, 299

Simple Mail Transfer Protocol (SMTP), port types, binding (code), 288-289

Simple Object Access Protocol. *See* SOAP

simple types, XML (Extensible Markup Language) Schema (defining), 263-264

simpleType element, 264

single characters, ' (single quotation mark), 233-234

slashes, back (\), 234

SMTP (Simple Mail Transfer Protocol), port types, binding (code), 288-289

SOAP (Simple Object Access Protocol)

application/soap standard, 301

arrays, 300

B2B communications (Business to Business), 300

Body element, 297-298

compound data type, 300

data encoding, 299-300

data types, 300

data values, compound or simple, 299

Envelope element, 297

envelopes (Header section), 302

Fault element, 298

faultcode element, 298

Header element, 297

headers, 302

HTTP (Hypertext Transfer Protocol), 300-302

http-soap type (@jws:protocol tag), 196

integer data type, 300

Java proxy, 183

jms-soap type (@jws:protocol tag), 196

messages, 295-299

multinode environments, 296

myMethod, binding, 288

request-reply messages, 295

specification (Web site), 295

string data type, 300

structs, 300

Web services, 297

WSDL (Web Service Description Language) schema Web site, 288

XML (Extensible Markup Language), 253, 297, 300

solicit/response operations, 284-286

sorting, Design View Sorting or Structure Pane Sorting, 32

source code. *See* code

Source view, variable and method selectors, 27-28

Source View tab, 27

sources of data, 93, 202

special characters, 233-234, 257

Special Edition Using Java 2 Platform, 83

specifications

ECMAScript, downloading, 138

Java language, downloading, 251

SOAP (Simple Object Access Protocol) Web site, 295

XML (Extensible Markup Language), 254, 269-272

XPath Web site, 272

XSLT (XSL Transformations) Web site, 271

spring icon (buffered messages), 63-64

SQL (Structured Query Language), 95-98, 191, 251

stack traces, code errors, 114

stages, two-stage conversations, 50-55

standards, application/soap (SOAP), 301

Start

command (Debug menu), 20, 42

icon, 42

operations link, 56

Start and Debug command (Debug menu) or icon, 114

Start WebLogic Server command (Tools menu), 19

start( ) method, 77

starting

conversations, 50

debug sessions, 114

HelloConversation Web service conversations, 56

HelloWorld, 20

timer control in HelloDelayed service, 77

WebLogic server, 19-20, 42

stateful interactions, conversations, 49

statements

    break, 244-245

    conn.close( ), 247

    continue, 244-245

    CREATE TABLE, 203

    in database controls, executing, 101-102

    DELETE, 97-99

    ending with ::, 96

    if-else, 241-242

    INSERT, 97-99

    return, 245

    SELECT, 96-98

    SQL (Structured Query Language), 191

    switch, 243-244

    UPDATE, 97-99

Step Into

    command (Debug menu), 117

    icon, 117-118

Step Out, command (Debug menu) or icon, 119

Step Over

    command (Debug menu), 119

    icon, 119-120

stepping through code, 117

Stop command (Debug menu) or icon, 43

stop method, 78-79

stopping

    HelloWorld Web service, 43

    timers, 78-79

storing maps in external files, 137-138

stream filters (java.io package), 250

StreamMessage class, 153

String data type, 263

strings

    comparing, 236

    data type, SOAP (Simple Object Access Protocol), 300

    initializing, 234

    Java, 234-235

    SQL (Structured Query Language), 95-98

    values, 235

    variables, declaring, 234

structs, SOAP (Simple Object Access Protocol), 300

structural views of services, 24-25

Structure pane, 23-24

Structure Pane Sorting, 32

Structured Query Language (SQL), 95-98, 191, 251

structuring configuration data with XML (Extensible Markup Language), 253

stylesheets, XSL (Extensible Stylesheet Language), 270-271

switch statement, 243-244

synchronous and asynchronous activities, comparing, 57-59

synchronous responses, 62

syntax. *See* code

system paths, 34-36

T

\t (tab character), 34, 234

Tab Size, 33

tables

    aliases, creating, 97

    for databases, creating, 202-203

    joining in SQL (Structured Query Languge) strings, 97-98

tagName function, 143

How can we make this index more useful? Email us at indexes@samspublishing.com

tags. *See also individual names of tags listed under XML*

DTDs (Document Type Definitions), 258-260

end, /, 21

@jws JavaDoc, 44, 181, 189-197

@jws:connection, 192

@jws:control, 79, 90

@jws:conversation, 189-190

@jws:conversation-lifetime, 194

@jws:define, 194-195

@jws:ejb, 181, 192-193

@jws:jms, 160, 192-193

@jws:jms-header, 193

@jws:jms-message, 193

@jws:jms-property, 193

@jws:operation, 46, 190

@jws:parameter-xml, 190-191

@jws:protocol, 195-196

@jws:return-xml, 191

@jws:schema, 196

@jws:sql, 191

@jws:target-namespace, 192

@jws:timer, 79, 193-194

@jws:wsdl, 197

@jws:xmlns, 197

part, attributes, 281

start, < (less than symbol), 21

<xm:use>, 143

Tasks pane, 26-27

templates (Java), 231

Test view, 20, 28-30

Test XML

forms, 30

tab (Test view), 29

testing

Hello method, 89-90

HelloAggregate Hello method, 89-90

HelloConversation Web service, 55-56

HelloConversationAsync Web service, 67

HelloDelayed service, 78-79

HelloWorld, 19-21

HelloWorld Web service, 41-43

tests

forms, 28, 43

frameworks, 20

pages, 14-15

Text messages, 154

TextMessage class, 153

this value (class variables), 52

threads, JMS (Java Message Service) sessions, 153

throwing exceptions, 176, 247

throws keyword, 247

time, 70, 80-84

Time data type, 263

timeout-in value, 76

timeout parameters (conversations), 69-70

timeout time, changing, 82-83

timeout values, changing in code, 69

timer controls, 75-86

TimerControl, 79

timers, 76-81, 193-194

toArray function, 143

Toggle Breakpoint

command (Debug menu), 115

icon, 116

toggling coalesce-events, 84

Token data type, 263

Tools menu commands

Preferences, 31

Start WebLogic Server, 19

Tools Preferences dialog box, 31, 34

topic messages, 157-159

TopicConnectionFactory, 152

TopicExample.jws file, source code, 157

TopicReceiver.jws file, source code, 159

topics, creating, 157-158

TopicSession, 153

toString function, 143

traces, stack (code errors), 114

tracking

    order tracking services, 222-226

    packages online, 9

transacted connections, 153

transports

    protocols, asychronous patterns, 60-61

    myMethod, binding, 288-290

trees, Project, 22-23, 88

try-catch blocks, 245-246

two consecutive dashes (--), 257

two dots (..), 141

two-stage conversations, 50-55

two-way communications, 68

Type attribute (@jws:jms tag), 160

types

    data, 232, 262-263, 300

    definitions for addresses (code), 278

    form-get, 195

    form-post, 195

    http-soap, 196

    http-xml, 196

    JMS (Java Message Service) messages, methods, 154

    jms-soap, 196

    jms-xml, 196

    messages, creating, 281-282

    parts, creating (code), 281-282

    port, 287-293

    type attribute, 193

    WSDL (Web Service Description Language) address type element, 277-280

    XML (Extensible Markup Language) Schema (complex or simple), 263-264

U

UDDI (Universal Description, Discovery, and Integration), 13-15, 297

uniform resource locators (URLs), 187, 274

United Parcel Service (UPS), Web site to track packages, 9

unrealizable port types, 287

UnsignedByte data type, 263

unsignedInt data type, 263

unsignedLong data type, 263

unsignedShort data type, 263

UPDATE statement, 97-99

updating values in SQL (Structured Query Langue) strings, 97

upper- and lowercase letters (Java classes), 239

UPS (United Parcel Service), Web site to track packages, 9

URLs (uniform resource locators), 187, 274

Use Tabs, 34

V

values

    AccountEJB bean, accessing, 176-177

    Boolean, 233

    character, 233

How can we make this index more useful? Email us at indexes@samspublishing.com

data, compound or simple, 299

double-precision floating-point numbers, 233

Draw Lines Between Functions, 32

floating-point numbers, 233

hexadecimal numbers, 233

idle timeout, defining, 69

Java variables, declaring, 233-234

long, 233

max-age, 69

max-idle-time, 69

maximum context age, setting, 70

null, 235

octal numbers, 233

Protocol, 293

repeats-every, 76, 81

returning in SELECT statements, 98

Show Line Numbers, 32

single characters, ' (single quotation mark),
    233

SQL (Structured Query Languge) strings,
    96-97

strings, 235

this (class variables), 52

timeout, changing in code, 69

timeout-in, 76

of variables, viewing, 121

variable-type attribute, 135

variableName, 92

variableName_methodName (callback handler),
    92

variables

    addr, 135

    classes, 51-52

    code, debugging, 120-122

    database controls, 98

    displaying in Locals window, 121-122

helloWorldControl, 90

Java, 232-235

of maps, declaring, 135

method, 52

returning in result sets, 98-99

selectors (Source view), 27-28

strings, 234-235

values, viewing, 121

watches, adding in Watch window, 122

weblogic.jws.control.TimerControl, 79

Workshop JavaDoc, 53

xm:bind, 135

View menu, hiding or showing panes, 24

viewing

    variable values, 121

    WSDL (Web Service Description Language)
        files, 274

views

    Design, 24-26, 38-39, 171

    Design View Sorting, 32

    graphical of services, 24

    Source, 27-28

    Test, 20, 28-30

void responses, 40

W

W3C (World Wide Web Consortium) Web site,
    269-272

watches, adding to variables, 122

Web browsers, Browser Path value, 36

Web servers, Web services, 8

Web Service, protocols, 195-196

Web Service Description Language. *See* WSDL

Web services. *See also* **online ordering systems**

accessing from Java, 183

advantages, 10-11

applications, 8

ASP (Active Server Pages), 8

CGI (Common Gateway Interface), 8

client side, 183-184

companies, 8

controls, adding, 274

CORBA (Common Object Request Broker Architecture), 11

data exchanges, 9

databases, relationships to, 93

DBAdmin, 219

debugging, 114-123

definition, 7

disadvantages, 11

examples, 7

Google Web site, 9

HelloConversation Web service, 51-62

HelloConversationAsync Web service, 63-68

HelloWorld, 37-48

HTTP (Hypertext Transfer Protocol), 11

HTTPS, 11

Java

proxy, 183-185

servlets, 8

JSP (JavaServer Pages), 8

locations, changing, 186-187

PHP (Hypertext Pre-Processor), 8

platforms, not supporting asynchronous patterns, 61

protocols, 12

RMI, CORBA, DCOM (comparing), 11-12

shipping companies, 9

SOAP (Simple Object Access Protocol), 297

UDDI (Universal Description, Discovery and Integration), 297

Web servers, 8

Web sites, 9

WebLogic Workshop, 14-16

WSDL (Web Service Description Language), 274-276

XML (Extensible Markup Language), 21

Web sites

Eclipse (Java IDE), downloading, 230

ECMAScript specification, downloading, 138

FedEx (Federal Express), tracking packages, 9

Forte (Java IDE), downloading, 230

Google, 9

Java, downloading documentation, 230, 251

JDK (Java Development Kit), downloading, 230

Sams Publishing, SQL (Structured Query Language), 95

SOAP (Simple Object Access Protocol) specification, 295

XML (Extensible Markup Language) namespace, 297

UDDI (Universal Description, Discovery, and Integration), 13

UPS (United Parcel Service), tracking packages, 9

W3C (World Wide Web Consortium), 269-272

Web services, 9

WSDL SOAP schema, 288

XML (Extensible Markup Language) specification, 254

WEB-INF\lib directory, jar files, 170

WebLogic Workshop

advantages of using, 14-16

debuggers, 15-16

development server, configuring system paths, 34

methods, 14

protocols, 14

starting, 19

test pages, 14-15

WebLogic server, 19-20, 34, 42, 94, 184-186

weblogic.jws.control.ControlException, 91

weblogic.jws.control.TimerControl variable, 79

weblogic.jws.jms.QueueConnectionFactory, 153

while loop, 242

whitespace, Show Whitespace value, 32

widths, Indent Width, 33

Window Font Size, 31

windows

Call Stack, debugging code, 123

Locals, displaying variables, 121-122

output, 20-22

Watch, variables (adding watches), 122

withdraw method, 178

words (Java classes), upper- and lowercase letters, 239

World Wide Web Consortium (W3C) Web site, 269-272

WSDL (Web Service Description Language)

definitions, 274-276

documents, 274-293

elements, 287-293

files, 187, 197, 274-296

history, 273

JWS files, building, 275-276

messages, creating, 280-282

operations, messages, 283

port types, 287-290

PurchaseService service, code, 291-292

restricted entries, creating, 282-283

SOAP (Simple Object Access Protocol) schema Web site, 288

types, address (code), 279

Web services, 274-276

X-Z

XAQueueConnectionFactory, 152

XATopicConnectionFactory, 152

<xm:attribute> element, 133

xm:bind variable, 135

XML(Extensible Markup Language). *See also* **SOAP**

-- (two consecutive dashes), 257

< > tag, 255

]] tag, 257

< special character, 257

<!-- --> comment tags, 257

<![CDATA[tag, 257

> special character, 257

<? XML tag, 255

>? XML tag, 255

<!ATTLIST> tag, 258-260

Boolean data type, 263

Byte data type, 263

comments, illegal, 257

configuration data, structuring, 253

Date data type, 263

decimal data type, 263

<!DOCTYPE> tag, 260

documents, 255-260, 276-29

double data type, 263

effectiveness of, 254

elements, 277-287

<!ELEMENT> tag, 258

end tag (/>), 21

files, processing instructions, 255

float data type, 263

functions to manipulate, 142-143

http-xml type, 196

initializing (code), 140-141

Int data type, 263

Integer data type, 263

jms-xml type, 196

@jws:parameter-xml tag, 190-191

@jws:return-xml tag, 191

Long data type, 263

Map messages, 154

mapping into Java, 145-150

maps, 127-150

messages, sending, 160-163

<MyRootTag> tag, 255

namedef.xsd file, source code, 265

namespaces, 197, 263, 269-270, 297

NegativeInteger data type, 263

nonNegativeInteger data type, 263

nonPositiveInteger data type, 263

NormalizedString data type, 263

PositiveInteger data type, 263

protocol (Web services), 12

sample.xml file, source code, 262

sample.xsd file, source code, 261

Schema, 196, 261-269, 300

schema.xsd file, source code, 268-269

SchemaDemo.jws file, source code, 267-268

short data type, 263

simpleType element, 264

special characters, 257

specifications, 254, 269-272

start tag (<), 21

String data type, 263

tags, 21-22, 254-255. *See also individual tag names within XML*

Test XML tab, 29

Time data type, 263

Token data type, 263

UnsignedByte data type, 263

unsignedInt data type, 263

unsignedLong data type, 263

unsignedShort data type, 263

Web services, 21

XPath, 271-272

XSL (Extensible Stylesheet Language), 270-271

XSLT (XSL Transformations), 271

<xm:java-import> element, 137

.xmlmap file extension, 137

<xm:multiple> attribute, 136-137

XMLScript (XML maps), 138-150

<xm:use> tag, 143

<xm:value> element, 132

<xm:xml-map> element, 137

XPath, 271-272

xpath(xpathExpression) function, 143

XSL (Extensible Stylesheet Language), 270-271

XSL-FO (XSL formatting objects), 270

XSLT (XSL Transformations), specification (Web site), 271

Hey, you've got enough worries.

Don't let IT training be one of them.

Get on the fast track to IT training at InformIT,
your total Information Technology training network.

 | **www.informit.com** | **SAMS**

■ Hundreds of timely articles on dozens of topics ■ Discounts on IT books from all our publishing partners, including Sams Publishing ■ Free, unabridged books from the InformIT Free Library ■ "Expert Q&A"—our live, online chat with IT experts ■ Faster, easier certification and training from our Web- or classroom-based training programs ■ Current IT news ■ Software downloads ■ Career-enhancing resources

InformIT is a registered trademark of Pearson. Copyright ©2001 by Pearson.
Copyright ©2001 by Sams Publishing.

RELATED TITLES

Sams Teach Yourself Java 2 in 21 Days, Third Edition

by Laura Lemay and Rogers Cadenhead

0-672-32370-2
$39.99 US/$62.99 CAN

Sams Teach Yourself J2EE in 21 Days

by Martin Bond, Dan Haywood, Debbie Law, Andy Longshaw, and Peter Roxburgh

0-672-32384-2
$49.99 US/$77.99 CAN
CD-ROM included

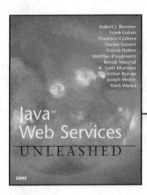

Java Web Services Unleashed

by Robert Brunner, et al.

0-672-32363-X
$49.99 US/$77.99 CAN

Sams Teach Yourself JavaServer Pages in 21 Days

by Steven Holzner

0-672-32449-0
$39.99 US/$62.99 CAN
Coming September, 2002

Sams Teach Yourself BEA WebLogic Server 7.0 in 21 Days

by Mandar Chitnis, Lakshmi Ananthamurthy, and Pravin Tiwari

0-672-32433-4
$39.99 US/$62.99 CAN
Coming October, 2002

Building Web Services with Java

by Steve Graham, Simeon Simeonov, et al.

0-672-32181-5
$49.99 US/$77.99 CAN

SAMS   www.samspublishing.com

KICK START

< QUICK >
< CONCISE >
< PRACTICAL >

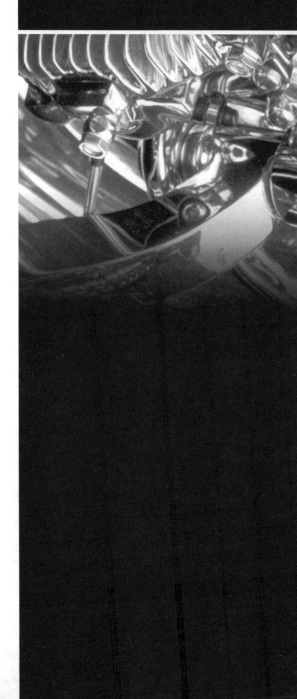

JSTL: JSP Standard Tag Library Kick Start

by Jeff Heaton

0-672-32450-4
$34.99 US/$54.99 CAN
Coming September 2002

EJB 2.0 Kick Start

by Peter Thaggard

0-672-32178-5
$34.99 US/$54.99 CAN
Coming October 2002

JAX: Java APIs for XML Kick Start

by Aoyon Chowdhury and Parag Chaudhary

0-672-32434-2
$34.99 US/$54.99 CAN
Coming October 2002

Tomcat Kick Start

by Martin Bond and Debbie Law

0-672-32439-3
$34.99 US/$54.99 CAN
Coming November 2002

PHP 5 Kick Start

by Luke Welling and Laura Thomson

0-672-32292-7
$34.99 US/$54.99 CAN
Coming November 2002

Struts Kick Start

by James Turner and Kevin Bedell

0-672-32472-5
$34.99 US/$54.99 CAN
Coming January 2003

What's on the CD-ROM

The companion CD-ROM contains all of the source code for the examples developed in the book and evaluation versions of BEA's WebLogic product line.

Windows Installation Instructions

1. Insert the disc into your CD-ROM drive.

2. From the Windows desktop, double-click the My Computer icon.

3. Double-click the icon representing your CD-ROM drive.

4. Double-click on start.exe. Follow the on-screen prompts to access the CD-ROM information.

NOTE

If you have the AutoPlay feature enabled, start.exe will be launched automatically whenever you insert the disc into your CD-ROM drive.

By opening this package, you are also agreeing to be bound by the following agreement:

You may not copy or redistribute the entire CD-ROM as a whole. Copying and redistribution of individual software programs on the CD-ROM is governed by terms set by individual copyright holders.

The installer and code from the author(s) are copyrighted by the publisher and the author(s). Individual programs and other items on the CD-ROM are copyrighted or are under an Open Source license by their various authors or other copyright holders.

This software is sold as-is without warranty of any kind, either expressed or implied, including but not limited to the implied warranties of merchantability and fitness for a particular purpose. Neither the publisher nor its dealers or distributors assumes any liability for any alleged or actual damages arising from the use of this program. (Some states do not allow for the exclusion of implied warranties, so the exclusion may not apply to you.)

NOTE

This CD-ROM uses long and mixed-case filenames requiring the use of a protected-mode CD-ROM Driver.